Hands-On Server-Side Web Development with Swift

Build dynamic web apps by leveraging two popular Swift web frameworks: Vapor 3.0 and Kitura 2.5

Angus Yeung

BIRMINGHAM - MUMBAI

Hands-On Server-Side Web Development with Swift

Commissioning Editor: Kunal Chaudhari
Acquisition Editor: Karan Gupta
Content Development Editor: Francis Carneiro
Technical Editor: Akhil Nair
Copy Editor: Safis Editing
Project Coordinator: Pragati Shukla
Proofreader: Safis Editing
Indexer: Mariammal Chettiyar
Graphics: Alishon Mendonsa
Production Coordinator: Nilesh Mohite

First published: November 2018

Production reference: 1301118

Published by Packt Publishing Ltd.
Livery Place
35 Livery Street
Birmingham
B3 2PB, UK.

ISBN 978-1-78934-117-1

www.packtpub.com

`mapt.io`

Mapt is an online digital library that gives you full access to over 5,000 books and videos, as well as industry leading tools to help you plan your personal development and advance your career. For more information, please visit our website.

Why subscribe?

- Spend less time learning and more time coding with practical ebooks and videos from over 4,000 industry professionals

- Improve your learning with Skill Plans built especially for you

- Get a free ebook or video every month

- Mapt is fully searchable

- Copy and paste, print, and bookmark content

Packt.com

Did you know that Packt offers ebook versions of every book published, with PDF and ePub files available? You can upgrade to the ebook version at `www.packt.com` and as a print book customer, you are entitled to a discount on the ebook copy. Get in touch with us at `customercare@packtpub.com` for more details.

At `www.packt.com`, you can also read a collection of free technical articles, sign up for a range of free newsletters, and receive exclusive discounts and offers on Packt books and ebooks.

Contributors

About the author

Angus Yeung works for Intel, and is responsible for the architectural design of backend cloud services for virtual reality sports broadcasting. He is also a computer science lecturer at San Jose State University. Prior to Intel, he held CTO and engineering director positions at several companies, including a start-up he founded in 2002.

Angus' technical interests include mobile computing, distributed computing, computer vision, and artificial intelligence. He holds an BS, MS, and PHD in Electrical Engineering from Univ. of Rochester, and an MBA from UC Berkeley. Angus owns 18 pending and granted patents. Angus lives with his lovely wife and three handsome boys in Palo Alto, California.

> *Many thanks to my publishers, Isha and Francis. Without their encouragement and persistence I wouldn't have even started my journey of writing this book. My thanks also go to Francis and his team for tediously reviewing this book and dutifully running the code in each chapter. Finally, thanks to my wife, Leslie, and my sons, Neil, Ryan, and Kyle, for their endless patience and support.*

About the reviewer

Tibor Bödecs is an enthusiastic software developer with more than a decade of experience in the IT industry. In his past, Tibor was the technology leader at one of the biggest mobile development-focused companies in Hungary. He is a self-taught programmer with a true passion for Swift from the very beginning. He has a good ability to work with different languages, technologies, and extensive experience in product management. Nowadays he is a freelancer developer focusing mostly on web, mobile, and server-side Swift projects. Tibor has a personal blog where he regularly writes about the Swift programming language.

Packt is searching for authors like you

If you're interested in becoming an author for Packt, please visit `authors.packtpub.com` and apply today. We have worked with thousands of developers and tech professionals, just like you, to help them share their insight with the global tech community. You can make a general application, apply for a specific hot topic that we are recruiting an author for, or submit your own idea.

Table of Contents

Preface

Swift is a strongly and statically typed programming language that has been used extensively for client-side development in iOS, macOS, tvOS, and watchOS. The open source developer community has brought Swift to the Linux platforms, making Swift a cross-platform programming language. This book will get you started with Vapor and Kitura by teaching you about development workflows, unit tests, and the build and release process. You'll then dive into the details of designing web applications with template engines, the Bootstrap framework, databases, and user authentication. Finally, you'll move on to building APIs for web services, full-stack development with iOS applications, and deploying web services as containerized application.

Who this book is for

This book is for anyone interested in building professional web applications and web services using Swift and two popular Swift web frameworks: Vapor 3.0 and Kitura 2.5.

What this book covers

Chapter 1, *Introducing Server-Side Swift*, explains why you should extend Swift for server-side development on Linux and take advantage of using Swift for both server- and client-side development. You will survey an array of popular web frameworks in Swift and learn about the merits of each of them. If you are interested in starting the journey of developing web apps and services using Swift, you will find the chapter's recommendations for references, online resources, forums for discussion and technical questions, and the list of developer community support very helpful.

Chapter 2, *Getting Started with Vapor and Kitura*, aims at getting you started with both Vapor, a server-side framework with very strong developer community support, and Kitura, a server-side framework with backing from IBM. You'll be introduced to Vapor Toolbox, a **command line interface** (**CLI**) that allows you to rapidly develop Vapor apps from boilerplate Vapor projects. You'll follow step-by-step guidance to install Vapor Toolbox on macOS or Linux, and then check your system's readiness by using Vapor CLI tools to verify system compatibility with required development environment. Similarly, you'll be introduced to Kitura development workflows and follow step-by-step instructions to install Kitura tools and libraries on your system.

`Chapter 3`, *Building Your First Web App*, takes you directly to server-side Swift coding with detailed instructions on creating a new web app project from a template provided in a web framework. You'll be guided on how to create, build, run, and test a "Hello World!" web app using Vapor 3.0. After that, you'll learn how to expand the features of the web app by adding more new routes to handle additional requests from clients. You will continue your journey to create a similar "Hello World!" web app with the Kitura web framework. After going through the exercises of building a simple web app with both Vapor and Kitura, you'll be able to note the similarities between the two web frameworks and appreciate the different approaches taken by them.

`Chapter 4`, *Debugging and Testing*, introduces the basics of the agile development process and recommends some of best practices in developing, debugging, and testing server-side Swift code. When it comes to web development frameworks, both Vapor and Kitura offer very good logging and debugging support. You are going to learn how to use the logging and unit test features to help in debugging and error-proofing your code.

`Chapter 5`, *Setting Up Routes and Controllers*, dives into the details of handling custom requests with routes and controllers. A route is an object used to represent a custom request embedded in a URL and a controller is the component that contains the business logic to handle the request routed to it. You'll learn how to add custom routes for requests, create controllers to handle the routes, and construct responses for the requests. You'll manipulate custom parameter types and process a group of routes in a collection. Finally, you'll learn how to take advantage of the `Codable` class in Swift to encode and decode complex **JavaScript Object Notation (JSON)** objects in easy ways.

`Chapter 6`, *Working with Template Engines*, introduces you to two template engines: Leaf for Vapor and Stencil for Kitura. Templating languages allow you to work with content automatically generated by a script. For dynamic content, you'll learn how template engines help in accelerating the development of dynamic web pages. Dynamic content creation is useful when presenting results of data that is generated at runtime and not known beforehand. For static content, you'll learn how template engines help ensure a consistent structure with features such as headers, footers, color schemes, and backgrounds. You'll also be introduced to the nuts and bolts of Leaf and Stencil templating languages and learn how to use variables in template scripts to communicate information between Swift classes and script functions.

`Chapter 7`, *Bootstrapping Your Design*, introduces you to the Bootstrap framework, which is a collection of CSS and JavaScript libraries, and explains how the Bootstrap framework allows you to build responsive website easily. You'll follow step-by-step instructions to insert Bootstrap components into your templates and learn how to beautify different UI elements in your template with Bootstrap. Toward the end of the chapter, you'll learn how to include Bootstrap in your project when you are ready to deploy your web apps.

Chapter 8, *Employing Storage Frameworks*, has you take advantage of the **Object Relational Mapping** (**ORM**) abstraction between the web application and the database to streamline your workflow when working with a database. One of the major advantages of using an ORM tool is that you don't have to deal with a database directly, avoiding the painful process of writing different querying commands for each type of database. Swift web frameworks support a number of database engines, and sometimes you can use multiple databases in the same session. In this chapter, you'll learn how to work with the Fluent abstraction framework in Vapor and the Kuery database abstraction layer in Kitura. You'll interact with your model with **Create**, **Retrieve**, **Update**, and **Delete** (**CRUD**) operations using these abstraction layers.

Chapter 9, *Adding Authentication*, introduces you to the key features in user-access management: user authentication, cookies, and sessions management. You'll learn how to set up a user model and password-protected content. With the authentication API, you're going to grant and remove access for different users. You'll then learn how to manipulate cookies and manage user login sessions, and implement logic to authenticate user to get access to protected content.

Chapter 10, *Understanding Technologies for Web Services*, reviews the underlying technologies that empower web apps and web services. You'll learn the server/client model based on HTTP/HTTPS in more details. For the architecture and design of web services, it'd better to divide the design into a three-tiered architecture consisting of a frontend API gateway, some business logic in the middle, and then backend database services. You'll learn how a typical frontend API gateway is designed, how to encapsulate a middle component with business logic into a standalone microservice, and how to design and work with a backend storage framework.

Chapter 11, *Designing for API Gateway*, teaches you how to build a RESTful API, introduce you to the basic rules for API design, teach you how to create endpoints for requests that a client sends to a server, and explain how to define response status codes. You'll then learn how the design of a RESTful API can be extended, specifically through the building of API Gateway, which is the single entry point for all clients and routes client requests to different MVC components or microservices.

Chapter 12, *Deploying to the Cloud*, tells you how to deploy your web services to the cloud. You'll be introduced to popular hosted cloud solutions: Vapor Cloud (AWS) and IBM Cloud (Bluemix). Vapor Cloud is the official hosting service for Vapor and there is built-in support in Vapor CLI to let you deploy and manage your Vapor instance easily without installing additional libraries and tools. Similarly, IBM Cloud is a natural choice of hosted solution for Kitura web services, since both IBM Cloud (Bluemix) and Kitura are IBM cloud solutions.

Chapter 13, *Developing an iPhone Client*, puts everything you'll have learned so far about server-side Swift together and uses an iOS app to show how a client "journal" app can leverage your PostgreSQL database, and other cloud services that you can build with a Swift web framework. You'll first get started with building a journal iOS app, adding logic and UI components to the app design. You'll create a model for journal data and add the support of CRUD operations for a PostgreSQL database. At the end of this chapter, you'll have a functional journal app that works seamlessly with your web services.

Chapter 14, *Developing Microservices*, teaches you how to build independent microservices and add them to a Swift web framework. Container technology, such as Docker, is used to deploy and run a Swift package artifact as a microservice. You'll learn how to deploy a Docker container and use container orchestration tool such as Kubernetes to manage and scale the deployment of containerized applications in a cluster.

Appendix A, *Vapor Boilerplate Project*, gives you a clear understanding of the boilerplate code in Vapor: you'll review Vapor-generated files, examine the file structure in a typical Vapor project, check out the project's configuration in manifest file, and go through the sequence of initialization steps before and after application instantiation. It also explains to you the sample routes, controllers and data model included in the boilerplate project.

Appendix B, *Kitura Boilerplate Project*, provides you with a better idea with the boilerplate project generated using kitura init. You'll review Kitura-generated files, file structure in a Kitura project, and configuration in the project's manifest file. The work flow in the boilerplate project will be carefully examined. At the end, you'll also check out the metrics-monitoring and diagnostic services already included in the boilerplate code.

To get the most out of this book

Some working knowledge of the Swift programming language would be required. You could be a beginner in terms of Swift programming, a seasoned iOS or macOS developer, or a software developer who wants to work on practical Swift applications while learning the language itself. By the end of the book, you will be able to successfully create your own web applications and web services by leveraging the powerful ecosystem of Swift.

Download the example code files

You can download the example code files for this book from your account at www.packt.com. If you purchased this book elsewhere, you can visit www.packt.com/support and register to have the files emailed directly to you.

You can download the code files by following these steps:

1. Log in or register at `www.packt.com`.
2. Select the **SUPPORT** tab.
3. Click on **Code Downloads & Errata**.
4. Enter the name of the book in the **Search** box and follow the onscreen instructions.

Once the file is downloaded, please make sure that you unzip or extract the folder using the latest version of:

- WinRAR/7-Zip for Windows
- Zipeg/iZip/UnRarX for Mac
- 7-Zip/PeaZip for Linux

The code bundle for the book is also hosted on GitHub at `https://github.com/PacktPublishing/Hands-On-Server-Side-Web-Development-with-Swift`. In case there's an update to the code, it will be updated on the existing GitHub repository.

We also have other code bundles from our rich catalog of books and videos available at `https://github.com/PacktPublishing/`. Check them out!

Conventions used

There are a number of text conventions used throughout this book.

`CodeInText`: Indicates code words in text, database table names, folder names, filenames, file extensions, pathnames, dummy URLs, user input, and Twitter handles. Here is an example: "The `decode()` function returns a future for `HTTPStatus`".

A block of code is set as follows:

```
router.post("new") { req -> Future<HTTPStatus> in
    return req.content.decode(Entry.self).map { entry in
        print("Appended a new entry: \(entry)")
        return HTTPStatus.ok
    }
}
```

When we wish to draw your attention to a particular part of a code block, the relevant lines or items are set in bold:

```
import Foundation

struct Entry: Codable {
    var id: String
    var title: String?
    var content: String?
    init(id: String, title: String? = nil, content: String? = nil) {
        self.id = id
        self.title = title
        self.content = content
    }
}
```

Any command-line input or output is written as follows:

```
$ vapor build
$ vapor run
```

Bold: Indicates a new term, an important word, or words that you see onscreen. For example, words in menus or dialog boxes appear in the text like this. Here is an example: "Navigate down the list and click on the **Swift Web App with Kitura** icon".

Warnings or important notes appear like this.

Tips and tricks appear like this.

Get in touch

Feedback from our readers is always welcome.

General feedback: If you have questions about any aspect of this book, mention the book title in the subject of your message and email us at customercare@packtpub.com.

Errata: Although we have taken every care to ensure the accuracy of our content, mistakes do happen. If you have found a mistake in this book, we would be grateful if you would report this to us. Please visit www.packt.com/submit-errata, selecting your book, clicking on the Errata Submission Form link, and entering the details.

Piracy: If you come across any illegal copies of our works in any form on the Internet, we would be grateful if you would provide us with the location address or website name. Please contact us at copyright@packt.com with a link to the material.

If you are interested in becoming an author: If there is a topic that you have expertise in and you are interested in either writing or contributing to a book, please visit authors.packtpub.com.

Reviews

Please leave a review. Once you have read and used this book, why not leave a review on the site that you purchased it from? Potential readers can then see and use your unbiased opinion to make purchase decisions, we at Packt can understand what you think about our products, and our authors can see your feedback on their book. Thank you!

For more information about Packt, please visit packt.com.

Introducing Server-Side Swift

Swift is a strongly and statically typed programming language that has been used extensively for client-side development in iOS, macOS, tvOS, and watchOS. The open source developer community has brought Swift to the Linux platforms, making Swift a cross-platform programming language. In this chapter, we will explain why the open source developer community has extended Swift for server-side development, and how they have streamlined the workflow for both server and client-side development using the same programming language.

There are several server-side Swift frameworks, and most of them are developed and maintained by the Swift developer community. We will take a closer look at the three top server-side Swift frameworks: Vapor, Kitura, and Perfect. Each of these frameworks has a different set of features and benefits. We hope that you feel comfortable with choosing the right Swift server-side framework for your next server-side project.

In this chapter, we will cover the following topics:

- Introducing Swift
- Surveying Swift server-side frameworks
- Choosing the right framework

Introducing Swift

Swift is a high-performance modern programming language that was first announced at the Apple World Wide Developers Conference (WWDC) in September 2014. Thanks to Apple's strong support and endorsement from the developer community, Swift has become one of the fastest growing new languages in computer science history. Swift 2.0 was released in September 2015, followed by Swift 3.0 a year later, and Swift 4.0 in September 2017. There have been two additional releases: Swift 4.1 in March 2018 and Swift 4.2 in September 2018.

As a modern language, Swift offers a clean syntax and many modern programming language constructs. Even though Swift is inspired by many other popular programming languages, Swift is an independent language completed with all the core features of a modern language. We will find the familiar low-level constructs in Swift, such as data structure, classes, functions, enums, as well as many useful modern features, such as protocols, optionals, closures, and generics.

Type safety is enforced from the ground up in Swift. The emphasis of type safety shifts the detection of many nasty errors from runtime to compile time. As a result of dramatically reduced runtime errors, Swift developers enjoy relatively increased productivity and an ease of programming.

Swift keeps many of the constructs found in modern programming languages, but also eliminates some features that are frequently seen in other languages. One example is that Swift uses modules instead of headers, eliminating code duplication often seen in using headers. Moreover, Swift does not support exceptions and an automatic garbage collector. In Swift, memory safety is ensured by default. Instead of a garbage collector, Swift uses a thread-safe **Automatic Reference Counting** (**ARC**) for an object's life cycle management.

As a compiled language, Swift is very fast at execution. The source code of Swift is first checked for type safety, then compiled into a machine-independent intermediate code in a **Low Level Virtual Machine** (**LLVM**) for optimization, and eventually used to generate machine code that is native to the system. Swift's execution performance often matches that of modern native programming languages and exceeds that of interpreted programming languages.

Open sourcing Swift and components

The official version of open source Swift was first launched in December 2015. Since being opened up to wider community support and development, open source Swift continues to grow in both popularity and maturity in terms of the contribution of open source community and the addition of new features. The contributors to open source Swift include Apple, IBM, PayPal, and other industry and academic institutions.

The effort of the open source developer community is coordinated through the Swift programming language evolution (`https://github.com/apple/swift-evolution`) process. The process governs the evolution of Swift by defining the process for accepting new proposals, stating the goals for upcoming Swift releases, reviewing and tracking the status of proposals, and specifying the decision-making procedure for accepting or rejecting a proposal. The evolution process ensures that Swift can evolve into a robust language while imposing constraints to maintain **application binary interface** (**ABI**) stability. With ABI stability, the binary compatibility between applications and libraries is ensured with different Swift versions.

Open source Swift includes more than the specification of the Swift programming language. On the official website of open source Swift, `https://swift.org/`, there is information on the fundamental components for the language, including the Swift compiler, standard library, package manager, core libraries, test framework, and REPL/debugger.

The source code repositories for the fundamental Swift components are hosted on GitHub at `https://github.com/apple/swift`. The following diagram shows the main components in open source Swift:

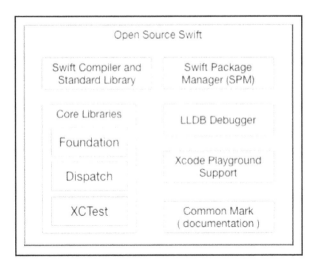

The license for the open source Swift projects is Apache 2.0 with a runtime library exception (`https://github.com/apple/swift/blob/master/LICENSE.txt`) .The **runtime library exception** clause in such a license allows you to compile the code into the binary product and distribute it.

Swift compiler

The Swift compiler translates Swift source code into efficient machine code in an executable way. When parsing the source code, the Swift compiler will perform full type-checking and generate an intermediate language called the **Swift Intermediate Language (SIL)** for further code analysis and optimization. The intermediate code will then be reduced to **Low Level Virtual Machine Intermediate Representation (LLVM IR)** (`http://llvm.org/`) for the LLVM to turn that into machine code:

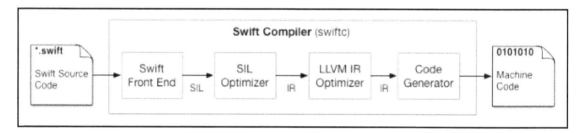

Swift standard library

The **standard library** provides basic language and type system support. The core of the standard library includes the definitions of fundamental data types, collections, protocols, algorithm, and low-level primitives. There is also the language support runtime, which is layered between the compiler and the core of the standard library. This runtime handles the dynamic features of Swift, such as typecasting, generics, reflection, and memory management.

Swift foundation framework

The **foundation framework** comprises features outside of the language and runtime that are common to all applications. The base layer of functionality provided in the foundation framework includes data storage and persistence, string handling, data formatting, date and time support, sorting and filtering, and networking. The design principle for the foundation framework is to keep the features in small sets of utility class, consistent across in convention, and with internationalization and localization support. As such, the foundation framework is highly portable for cross-platform support. There are two foundation frameworks: Objective-C and the open source Swift foundation.

Dispatch framework

The *libdispatch* is the wrapper for **Grand Central Dispatch (GCD)**, the concurrency library used across all Swift platforms to provide support for concurrent code execution in multicore processors. GCD uses a dispatch queue to achieve the goal of executing tasks in parallel. Each queue is a block of code (task) that can be executed synchronously or asynchronously on the main thread or worker thread. Tasks submitted to dispatch queues are executed efficiently on a pool of threads managed by the system. Submitted tasks are executed serially by default, but several tasks can be configured to run concurrently when submitted to the dispatch queue.

XCTest testing framework

The `XCTest` library is a common framework for writing unit tests in Swift. Usually, we just have to write the unit tests once and they can be executed across different platforms without rewriting. Each test is organized into an `XCTestCase` subclass with many different test methods. Each method shall be started with a prefix "test". We can run the tests from a Terminal on Linux or macOS. For Linux, an extra Linux main file with an array containing all available tests is needed. For macOS, XCode CLI tools to execute the tests are required. The XCTest framework is also well integrated into the workflow in XCode. We can use **the scheme editor** to specify which targets, classes, and methods to include a test, and use **the XCode test navigator** to run tests and view the results.

Swift Package Manager

We use the **Swift Package Manager (SPM)** to manage the distribution of Swift projects. The Swift package manager integrates the package dependencies into the Swift build system, automating the downloading, compiling, and linking the other packages that are required in a Swift project. In a typical Swift project, the source code is organized into *packages*. We use the Swift package manager to set up target executable modules in a project and specify each executable's dependent modules. An executable is a Swift program that can be run by the host's platform. For example, we build one executable module for product release and another executable module for testing.

LLDB debugger

In open source Swift, the **LLDB debugger** is both a full-featured debugger for Swift and a **read-eval-print-loop** (**REPL**) tool for the language. The LLDB debugger is tightly coupled to the Swift compiler itself, in order for it to inspect Swift types accurately and evaluate expressions correctly. REPL takes advantage of the robust debugging features such as breakpoint settings, interactive context during failures, evaluating expressions, reporting, and formatting results at breakpoints.

CommonMark documentation

CommonMark is the built-in Markdown syntax for documenting source code in open source Swift. Markdown is a plain text format for writing structured documents using very straightforward formatting conventions. Open source Swift adopts CommonMark as the implementation of a strongly defined, unambiguous, and highly compatible specification of Markdown.

Bringing Swift to the server-side

Swift has been used extensively for client-side development in iOS, macOS, tvOS, and watchOS. Since the open source developer community brought Swift to the Linux platforms and made Swift a cross-platform programming language, it makes sense for developers to use Swift for server-side development as well.

Client developers that are already skillful with the Swift language and are accustomed to the tools and libraries used in Swift projects, will find the transition to server-side development straightforward. They can enjoy the same benefits offered by Swift in server-side projects: type-safety, ease of programming, and compiled performance. By using Swift in both client- and server-side development, developers are expected to be more productive and more skillful.

Of course, the client developers are required to learn some new server-side skills. The workflow on the client side is very different from that of server-side development. On the client side, developers often work to enhance user interfaces, build data models and develop application logic that works with remote cloud services. For server-side development, they need to be able to implement and test network requests, add logic to handle the requests, and route the requests to other backend modules to handle them.

As developers gain expertise in writing both server and client code, they will share code between the server and a client's modules, and optimize the code for both client and server-side development.

SwiftNIO

It is worth mentioning **SwiftNIO** here, together with other Swift technologies. Apple's SwiftNIO is an open source server-side kernel that provides low-level networking support to the high-level event-driven network application framework. Even though SwiftNIO is not part of open source Swift, this server-side kernel is the fundamental building block for Swift server-side frameworks such as Vapor 3.0. Support for SwiftNIO was also added to Kitura 2.5 in August 2018.

SwiftNIO targets high-performance protocol servers and clients with Netty-like event loops and asynchronous non-blocking calls. The rationale for SwiftNIO is that using the thread-per-connection model of concurrency for low-utilization connections in any server is highly inefficient. SwiftNIO uses the non-blocking I/O model, so we do not need to wait for data to be sent from the network or received from it. The kernel will notify us when an I/O operation is complete.

Under the hood of SwiftNIO, the event processing for managing the execution of work items is conceptualized into EventLoop, which is similar to a dispatch queue in Swift. There are usually a few event loops per CPU core. Event loops run for the entire lifetime of the application, dispatching events to all the objects they own in a SwiftNIO application. Event loops are grouped into an `EventLoopGroup`. When an `EventLoopGroup` receives tasks, it will distribute work around the event loops while ensuring thread safety in doing so.

We usually ask `EventLoop` to schedule work but the work itself will be done by `ChannelHandlers` in a `Channel`. Each file descriptor (socket, file, or pipe) in SwiftNIO is associated with a `Channel`, which performs operations on top of it. The `Channel` uses `ChannelHandler` to process each work item. `ChannelHandler` can handle either inbound or outbound data traffic or both. A sequence of `ChannelHandler` objects forms a `ChannelPipeline` so the data in a channel can be transformed as it passes through each `ChannelHandler` object in the pipeline.

There are several implementations of `Channels` in SwiftNIO, which are listed as follows:

- **ServerSocketChannel**: A channel for sockets that accepts connections like a server
- **SocketChannel**: A channel for TCP connections
- **DatagramChannel**: A channel for UDP sockets
- **EmbeddedChannel**: A channel for testing purposes

In a summary, SwiftNIO implements basic I/O primitives and protocols at low levels of abstraction. It is narrowly focused on providing a powerful building block for high-level networked applications.

Surveying Swift server-side frameworks

There are many Swift web frameworks that aim to bring the benefits of Swift to server-side development. We will take a quick survey of several top Swift server-side frameworks now.

Vapor

Vapor is one of the most popular frameworks, and it enjoys the support of a very active developer community. The support from a developer community means that there are a lot of releases, bug fixes, and help that can be expected. In fact, the development of Vapor has been closely following the Swift evolution development. With the launch of SwiftNIO from Apple, as well as Swift 4.1, the Vapor developer community quickly launched Vapor 3.0 (`https://github.com/vapor/vapor/releases/tag/3.0.0`), which adopts asynchronous and non-blocking event-driven networking stacks, alongside futures and promises throughout the framework, fully aligning with the latest technology in the Swift ecosystem.

Overall, Vapor caters for both beginner and veteran server-side Swift developers with simple and concise syntax, strong community support, and the appeal of pure Swift implementation.

Kitura

Kitura, a Swift server-side framework from IBM that is Apache 2.0 licensed, is the result of the enterprise partnership between IBM and Apple, announced in 2014. It goes without saying that the framework has a strong backing from IBM. Kitura is well integrated into IBM's cloud product offerings, including Watson and IBM Cloud. It offers native connectors for some Watson API services, and it is easy to deploy a Kitura project to Bluemix hosting platforms using Kitura CLI. On IBM's website, there are also plenty of educational resources and support for Kitura.

The Kitura framework was migrated to support Swift 4.0 in the Kitura 2.0 that was released in October 2017. In Kitura 2.5, released in August 2018, the framework also added the support of SwiftNIO (enabled using `env KITURA_NIO=1 swift build`). The development of Kitura follows closely with the evolution of Swift itself.

For many Swift server-side developers, Kitura is an ideal framework choice for tapping into IBM's extensive cloud technology ecosystem and developing with enterprise applications in mind.

Perfect

Perfect (`https://github.com/PerfectlySoft/Perfect`) stands out as a mature and powerful Swift server-side framework. The first version of Perfect was released to the public even before Apple made Swift open source in 2015. It offers a complete array of features that a software developer may need for developing a lightweight and maintainable web application. Perfect uses a high-performance asynchronous networking engine called Perfect-Net (`https://github.com/PerfectlySoft/Perfect-Net`), supports secure sockets layer encryption, and adds the option for WebSockets and iOS push notifications that are commonly required by internet servers. Perfect even provides a macOS desktop application, Perfect Assistant, to help server-side developers with the deployment of their Perfect projects to AWS and Google Cloud.

We see Perfect as a good choice for Swift server-side developers who are looking for a mature and well-balanced framework for developing a scalable and solid web application.

Choosing the right framework

When it comes to choosing the right Swift server-side framework to work with, we shall compare the different frameworks in terms of the several factors that follow:

- How fast is the framework's execution performance?
- How complete are the features that the framework offers?
- What kind of ecosystem does the framework adopt?
- What kind of community support is there for the framework?

Performance

Since Swift is a compiled language, server-side frameworks written in pure Swift are not necessarily slower than frameworks written in other native programming languages. However, different Swift server-side frameworks may adopt different low-level software stacks or handle events differently.

A collection of benchmarks for popular web frameworks, including both Swift and non-Swift implementations, are documented here: `https://medium.com/@codevapor/vapor-3-0-0-released-8356fa619a5d`. As we can see, Swift frameworks perform better than most of the web frameworks that are written in interpreted languages such as JavaScript and Python. The benchmarks were based on processing plain text and demonstrated how fast Swift can process HTTP headers. All three Swift server-side frameworks, Vapor, Perfect, and Kitura, are comparable in their performance of plain text processing.

If you are interested in evaluating different aspects of a web framework, for example, the performance for handling routing and parsing path parameters, you can use the Benchmark tool (`https://github.com/vapor/benchmarks`) to generate specific benchmarks for comparison.

Feature sets

Performance is not the only factor we should consider. A production release of web application includes a complete set of robust features. Swift server-side frameworks often offer many useful functions that are common to most applications. Some common feature sets for Swift frameworks are listed as follows:

- **CLI tool**: Offers tools for generating boilerplates, building, and deploying an application
- **Templating engine**: Supports templating language for web content
- **Networking I/O**: Facilitates the handling of requests over the network
- **Database ORM**: Simplifies the querying for the back-end database
- **Logging framework**: Helps catch useful information during runtime
- **Test framework**: Creates unit tests for testing the web application
- **Authentication**: Provides authentication features, such as user login or social login
- **Security framework**: Adds encryption to communication and messaging pipelines, and sockets
- **Monitoring and diagnostics**: Offers real-time monitoring and diagnostics
- **User session management**: Manages a user's session after login
- **Cloud deployment**: Helps deploy a server application in an automated way
- **Swift support**: Updates to the latest Swift version quickly

When choosing the right server-side framework, we will need to check whether any of the features mentioned have already been integrated in the framework, or if integration of third-party libraries that implement such features are easy and straightforward.

Ecosystem

Ecosystem here can be interpreted as the choices of libraries or tools that a Swift server-side adopts and integrates into the framework. We may have preferences for some technologies, and at the same time, we may have reasons for avoiding other technologies as trade-offs in the design of our application. Sometimes, the effort will be daunting if we want to integrate a third-party library into the chosen framework that does not have the library included already. The best time-saving tip is to choose the framework that has the most preferred libraries so we can minimize the effort to do integration ourselves.

The main components and choices of third-party libraries in Vapor and Kitura are listed in the following table:

Feature	Vapor	Kitura
OS support	macOS, Linux	macOS, Linux
CLI	`Vapor Toolbox CLI`, `Vapor Console API`	`Kitura CLI`, `Project Generator`
Templating engine	`Leaf`	`Stencil`, `Mustache`, `Markdown`
Networking I/O	`SwiftNIO`	`Kitura-NIO` (use `SwiftNIO` and `NIOOpenSSL`), `BlueSocket`, `Kitura-net`
ORM	`Fluent: SQLite`, `MySQL`, `PostgreSQL`, `Redis`	`Swift-Kuery-ORM`, `Swift-Kuery:`, `PostgreSQL`, `SQLite`, `Redis`
Logging	`Logging API`, `PrintLogger`, `SwiftyBeaver Logging`	`LoggerAPI`, `HeliumLogger`
Route-type validation	`Vapor Validation`	n/a
Authentication	`Turnstile`	`Kitura-Credentials: HTTP`, `Facebook`, `Google`, `GitHub`
Security	`Vapor-Crypto` / `SwiftNIO SSL`	`BlueSSLService`
User session	`SessionMiddleware`	`Kitura-Session`
Monitoring & diagnostics	n/a	`SwiftMetrics`, `Health`
Container	`Docker`	`Docker`
Orchestration	n/a	`Kubernetes` / `Helm`
Cloud deployment	`Vapor Cloud`	`IBM Cloud`

In the rest of this book, we will visit most of the previously mentioned technologies again when we learn how to build web applications and services with Vapor and Kitura.

Community support

Developer community support is sometimes a deciding factor in the choice of a Swift server-side framework. Strong developer community support means that a framework's feature set is more complete, and there will be enough support when we encounter hurdles in working with the framework.

Vapor

Vapor enjoys healthy developer community support. Vapor users are well-known for their support and eagerness to help newcomers to Vapor community. There is a lot of activity in social channels. The Vapor community has recently moved their forums from Slack to Discord (`http://discord.gg/BnXmVGA`). There are also plenty of online learning resources, sample codes, tutorials, books, and community-contributed library plugins available to Vapor users. A word of caution, though: many of the tutorial and learning material for Vapor 2.0 or earlier, are outdated. Due to the substantial changes in Vapor 3.0, especially the migration to asynchronous non-blocking stacks based on SwiftNIO, many of the tutorials need to be revised and updated for Vapor 3.0.

Kitura

Kitura may have smaller community involvement currently, but IBM's engineers have been active and helpful on GitHub and online forums for new learners of server-side Swift. Kitura has a more complete cloud computing stack. It is easy for users to find the documentation and learning materials for not only the Swift server-side framework but also for other cloud technologies that are often used together with the Swift framework.

Perfect

Perfect stands out as having extensive tutorials, documentation, and training materials available on its website (`https://perfect.org/tutorials.html`) for Swift server-side developers. The Perfect framework is more mature, and its learning materials are well-organized. Currently, the Perfect user community has 69 repositories in the Perfect examples (`https://github.com/PerfectExamples`) repository on GitHub. New Perfect users can use the Slack (`http://www.perfect.ly/`) channels to interact with other developers and to get help from others.

Summary

In this chapter, we have covered open source Swift and its components and learned about the advantages of using Swift in server-side development. We have also reviewed three top server-side Swift frameworks: Vapor, Kitura, and Perfect, and explained how to choose a suitable Swift web framework for your own project. The background material in this chapter helps prepare you for hands-on server-side development. In the next chapter, you will roll your sleeves up and install both Vapor and Kitura frameworks on your system.

Getting Started with Vapor and Kitura

2

This chapter aims at getting you started with both **Vapor** and **Kitura**. You'll be introduced to **Vapor Toolbox**, a **command-line interface** (**CLI**), which allows you to rapidly develop Vapor apps from several boilerplate Vapor projects. You'll follow a step-by-step guideline to install Vapor Toolbox on macOS or Linux, and then check your system's readiness by using Vapor CLI tools to verify system compatibility with the required development environment. Similarly, you'll get introduced to the Kitura development environment and follow step-by-step instructions to install Kitura tools and libraries on your system.

In this chapter, we'll cover the following topics:

- Installing Vapor and Kitura on macOS
- Installing Vapor and Kitura on Ubuntu
- Exploring Vapor Toolbox and the Kitura CLI

Installing Vapor and Kitura on Mac

Even though you can start server-side Swift development on either macOS or Linux, you'll find it more convenient to develop server-side Swift projects on macOS with Apple's free Integrated Development Environment (IDE) tool, Xcode. Xcode has integrated many powerful editing and debugging features to streamline the workflow for code development with Swift; for example, syntax highlight, auto completion, refactoring, and code coverage for unit tests.

Follow the steps in the following sections to prepare your Mac for server-side Swift development with both Vapor 3.0 and Kitura 2.5. Skip the installation steps for macOS and go directly to the next section if you want to use the Linux environment instead.

Preparing your Mac for server-side Swift development

If you choose macOS as the platform for server-side Swift development, you're recommended to use Xcode 10.0 or greater for this book. The Xcode IDE is available only on macOS and not available on Linux.

Installing the Xcode IDE on your Mac

Download Xcode 10.1 or greater from Apple's Mac App Store:

After downloading, you must launch Xcode to continue the installation process. This may take a while.

Once Xcode is installed successfully on your macOS, you can verify the version of installed Swift by running the following command on the Terminal:

```
# Step 1a: Check Swift installation after have Xcode installed
$ swift --version
```

You should expect to see output similar to the following:

```
Apple Swift version 4.2.1 (swiftlang-1000.11.42 clang-1000.11.45.1)
Target: x86_64-apple-darwin17.7.0
```

The code samples in this book require Swift 4.2.1 or greater installed on your macOS.

Installing Xcode Command Line Tools

It is also useful for you to install Xcode Command Line Tools on your Mac. The **Command Line Tools Package** is a self-contained package from the Xcode installation. It allows you to do command-line development in macOS. You must download it separately from your Apple Developer Account.

Point your web browser to `https://developer.apple.com/download/more/`. Enter `Command Line Tools` in the search box. A list of Command Line Tools downloads will be shown:

Choose the latest Command Line Tools download for your macOS version. For example, you should download **Command Line Tools (macOS 10.13) for Xcode 10.1** if you're using macOS High Sierra (version 10.13).

Installing Homebrew

Homebrew is a free open source software package manager for macOS. Run the following in the Terminal if you don't already have Homebrew installed:

```
# Step 1b: Install Homebrew package manager
$ /usr/bin/ruby -e "$(curl -fsSL
https://raw.githubusercontent.com/Homebrew/install/master/install)"
```

You'll need Homebrew to install the Vapor CLI tools or many useful libraries on your Mac. If you encounter any problem installing Homebrew, you may want to visit Homebrew's official website, `https://brew.sh/`. With the Homebrew software package manager, you're ready to finish the rest of the installation process on your Mac.

Installing Vapor Toolbox on Mac

Vapor Toolbox is a CLI tool for you to develop Vapor apps and make your life easier in deploying them to Vapor Cloud, an optional hosting service created by Vapor.

Checking your system's compatibility with Vapor

To prepare for the installation, you can run the following command in the Terminal to check for Vapor compatibility:

```
# Step 2a: Check system compatibility with Vapor
$ eval "$(curl -sL check.vapor.sh)"
```

The output is as follows:

```
Xcode 10.1 is compatible with Vapor 2.
Xcode 10.1 is compatible with Vapor 3.
Swift 4.2.1 is compatible with Vapor 2.
Swift 4.2.1 is compatible with Vapor 3.
```

Installing Vapor Toolbox using Homebrew

If the previous step shows that your Xcode and Swift versions are compatible with Vapor 3.0, you're ready to continue the installation. Use Homebrew to install Vapor Toolbox:

```
# Step 2b: Install Vapor Toolbox
$ brew install vapor/tap/vapor
```

Homebrew `tap` is a tool to tap into another repository. The previous one-liner install command gives Homebrew installation access to all of Vapor's macOS packages.

Verifying Vapor installation

You're now done with Vapor 3.0 installation on Mac. Double check the installation by running the following Vapor Toolbox command in the Terminal:

```
# Step 2c: Check Vapor installation
$ vapor --help
```

If your installation of Vapor Toolbox is completed properly, the `help` command should list the available commands and flags.

Installing the Kitura CLI on Mac

Similar to Vapor Toolbox, you can install the Kitura CLI to simplify the process of creating Kitura applications.

With Homebrew on your Mac, go ahead and install the Kitura CLI:

```
# Step 3a: Install Kitura on macOS
$ brew install ibm-swift/kitura/kitura
```

The output is as follows:

```
==> Installing dependencies for ibm-swift/kitura/kitura: node
==> Installing ibm-swift/kitura/kitura dependency: node
==> Downloading https://homebrew.bintray.com/bottles/node-11.2.0.high_sierra.bottle.tar.gz
################################################################ 100.0%
==> Pouring node-11.2.0.high_sierra.bottle.tar.gz
==> Caveats
Bash completion has been installed to:
/usr/local/etc/bash_completion.d
==> Summary
 /usr/local/Cellar/node/11.2.0: 3,936 files, 47MB
==> Installing ibm-swift/kitura/kitura
==> Downloading https://registry.npmjs.org/kitura-cli/-/kitura-cli-0.0.12.tgz
################################################################ 100.0%
==> npm install -ddd --global --build-from-source --
cache=/Users/fyeung1/Library/Caches/Homebrew/npm_cache --
prefix=/usr/local/Cellar/kitura/0.0.12/libexec /pri
 /usr/local/Cellar/kitura/0.0.12: 676 files, 4.1MB, built in 9 seconds
==> Caveats
==> node
```

Bash completion has been installed to:
/usr/local/etc/bash_completion.d

Installing Vapor and Kitura on Ubuntu

This section is for installing Vapor and Kitura on Ubuntu. Skip this section if you intend to develop on your Mac only.

Working with the Ubuntu APT

You're going to work with the **Advanced Packaging Tool** (**APT**) library to perform installation of Vapor and Kitura. APT is a package manager for Debian-based Linux operating systems such as Ubuntu. The package manager keeps a list of packages that it can install in repository or cache and sorts out the dependencies required for the software packages. Run the following at Command Prompt:

```
$ sudo apt-get install <package>
```

The `apt-get` install command checks for the repository for the package specified as `<package>`. If the package is available in the list, it will proceed to download and install the software and all of the required dependencies. The `sudo` command in the previous code temporarily grants you elevated privileges as root or superuser in the installation step.

Installing the Swift Toolchain on Linux

The **Swift 4 Toolchain** is hosted on `www.Swift.org` and it contains the Swift compiler CLI, libraries, debugger, and package manager for Ubuntu platforms. Go to `swift.org` and download the latest stable Swift release for your Ubuntu version: `https://swift.org/download/`.

Go ahead and extract the `.tar.gz` file of `Swift 4 toolchain`. You'll need to update your `PATH` environment variable in order to include the Toolchain:

```
# Step 1a: Update PATH environment after installing Swift 4 toolchain
$ export PATH=<path to the extracted tool chain>/usr/bin:$PATH
```

Check that the expected version of Swift by entering the following Swift command:

```
# Step 1b: Check the installed version of Swift
$ swift --version
```

Next, go on installing Vapor and Kitura on your Ubuntu.

Installing Vapor on Ubuntu

Installing Vapor on Ubuntu is straightforward. Vapor supports the same versions of Ubuntu that Swift does: Ubuntu 14.04, 16.04, and 16.10.

Option 1 – using script to clone Vapor packages

On Ubuntu, you can use Vapor's APT repository to get access to all of Vapor's packages.

If you don't have `curl` on your system, use this command to install `curl` first:

```
# Step 2a: Prepare the curl tool on Ubuntu
$ sudo apt-get install curl
```

Now, you can use this script to add Vapor's APT repository to the source list:

```
# Step 2b: Use script to add Vapor APT repo
$ eval "$(curl -sL https://apt.vapor.sh)"
```

If you have any problem with the script approach here, you can jump to option 2 in the next section to clone Vapor packages manually on Ubuntu. Otherwise, you're all set to continue the installation of Vapor on your Ubuntu.

Option 2 – cloning Vapor packages manually

Optionally, you can add Vapor's APT repository manually if you have a problem using the script approach in the previous section:

```
# Step 2a: Add Vapor APT repo manually (optional)
$ wget -q https://repo.vapor.codes/apt/keyring.gpg -O- | sudo apt-key add -
echo "deb https://repo.vapor.codes/apt $(lsb_release -sc) main" | sudo tee
/etc/apt/sources.list.d/vapor.list
$ sudo apt-get update
```

Installing Vapor on Ubuntu

You can install the Vapor packages after you have added the APT repository:

```
# Step 3a: Install Vapor on Ubuntu
$ sudo apt-get install vapor
```

That's it. You now have Vapor properly installed on your Ubuntu. Try the following commands to double-check that the Vapor CLI works as expected:

```
# Step 3b: Check Swift and Vapor installation
$ vapor --help
```

Installing Kitura on Ubuntu

Kitura is fully tested on Ubuntu 14.04 LTS and Ubuntu 16.04 LTS. After you've downloaded and installed the Swift 4 Toolchain, install the following packages using the `apt-get install` command on Ubuntu.

Installing required Linux system packages

```
# Step 3a: Install required packages for Kitura
$ sudo apt-get update
$ sudo apt-get install clang libicu-dev libcurl4-openssl-dev libssl1.0-dev
```

These are the prerequisites for your Kitura installation. Kitura requires OpenSSL v1.0.x so it won't work with a newer version such as OpenSSL v1.1.x in some of the latest Linux system.

In order to install the Kitura CLI itself, you need to install **Node.js** and its package manager, npm, first. **Node Package Manager** (**npm**) is a CLI for managing modules in a Node.js project.

Install Node.js and npm using the apt package manager on Ubuntu:

```
# Step 3b: Install the NPM package
$ sudo apt install nodejs npm
```

With the npm package manager properly installed on your machine, proceed to install the Kitura CLI via npm:

```
# Step 3c: Install the Kitura package
$ npm install -g kitura-cli
```

The previous command will do a global installation of the Kitura CLI.

Run the following command to test the Kitura CLI tool you've just installed:

```
# Step 3d: Test the installed Kitura
$ kitura --help
```

Exploring Vapor Toolbox and the Kitura CLI

Vapor Toolbox and the Kitura CLI are provided to make your life easy with extensive command-line tools and to accelerate your server-side Swift project development effort with many useful boilerplate projects. Since Vapor and Kitura projects are built with Swift Toolchains, you also have access to an array of tools in **Swift Package Manager** (**SPM**), the standard software package manager for managing the distribution of Swift projects.

SPM includes the following handy commands:

Useful CLI Commands	Usage
`swift build`	Compiles the package in the current directory
`swift run`	Runs the executable in this package (for only one executable in the package)
`swift run`	Runs the executable in this package
`swift package resolve`	Resolves the dependencies and download missing packages
`swift package xcode-generateproj`	Creates an Xcode project and reset build scheme (Mac only)
`swift package init --type=executable`	Starts a new standard Swift application
`swift package init --type=library`	Starts a new standard Swift library
`swift package describe`	Parses `Package.swift` and lists all modules
`swift package show-dependencies`	Shows the dependency tree

For example, the `swift package describe` command is used to parse the content of `Package.swift` and it may be useful to verify whether the file can be parsed correctly.

Using Vapor Toolbox Commands

The Vapor CLI command, `vapor --help`, comes in handy if you want to check out all available Vapor commands.

The output of this Vapor command looks like this:

```
Usage: vapor command
Join our Slack if you have questions, need help,
or want to contribute: http://vapor.team
Commands:
new Creates a new Vapor application from a template.
  Use --template=repo/template for github templates
  Use --template=full-url-here.git for non github templates
```

```
Use --web to create a new web app
Use --auth to create a new authenticated API app
Use --api (default) to create a new API
build Compiles the application.
run Runs the compiled application.
fetch Fetches the application's dependencies.
update Updates your dependencies.
clean Cleans temporary files--usually fixes
a plethora of bizarre build errors.
test Runs the application's tests.
xcode Generates an Xcode project for development.
Additionally links commonly used libraries.
version Displays Vapor CLI version
cloud Commands for interacting with Vapor Cloud.
heroku Commands to help deploy to Heroku.
provider Commands to help manage providers.
Use `vapor command --help` for more information on a command.
```

The following table lists all of the useful Terminal commands for managing your Vapor projects:

Useful CLI Commands	Usage
vapor --help	Lists all available commands and flags supported in the Vapor CLI
vapor [command] --help	Prints the usage for the given command
vapor version	Checks the current Vapor CLI version
vapor new [name]	Creates a new Vapor project with the supplied name
vapor new [name] --template=api	Creates a new project from the API template (default)
vapor new [name] --template=web	Creates a new project from the web template
vapor new [name] --template=auth	Creates a new project for the authenticated app
vapor new [name] --template=[repo/template]	Creates a new project from a GitHub template
vapor build	Builds the project in the current path
vapor run	Runs the compiled app in the current path
vapor test	Runs the unit tests contained in this project
vapor xcode	Creates Xcode project files for the project in the current path
vapor clean	Cleans up all temporary files
vapor fetch	Fetches the project's dependencies (but do not update)

Useful CLI Commands	Usage
`vapor update`	Updates all dependencies of the current project
`vapor cloud [command]`	Executes a Vapor Cloud command
`vapor heroku [command]`	Executes a Heroku command
`vapor [provider] [command]`	Executes a provider's command
`brew upgrade vapor`	Upgrades Vapor on macOS
`sudo apt-get update; sudo apt-get install vapor`	Upgrades Vapor on Ubuntu

Getting help on a specific Vapor command

You can also get detailed information on a specific Vapor CLI command by inserting the command before the `--help` flag. For example, you use the following command to learn more about the `vapor new` feature:

```
$ vapor new --help
```

Vapor then prints out the detailed usage information about the new toolbox command:

```
Usage: vapor new <name> [--template] [--branch] [--tag] [--web] [--auth] [-
-api]
Creates a new Vapor application from a template.
 Use --template=repo/template for github templates
 Use --template=full-url-here.git for non github templates
 Use --web to create a new web app
 Use --auth to create a new authenticated API app
 Use --api (default) to create a new API
Arguments:
 name The application's executable name.
Options:
 --template The template repository to clone.
 Default: https://github.com/vapor/api-template.
 --branch An optional branch to specify when cloning
 --tag An optional tag to specify when cloning
 --web Sets the template to the web template:
https://github.com/vapor/web-template
 --auth Sets the template to the auth template:
https://github.com/vapor/auth-template
 --api (Default) Sets the template to the api template:
https://github.com/vapor/api-template
```

Exploring the Kitura CLI

Most of the CLI features in Kitura are encompassed in **Kitura Application Generator** (**KAG**), which allows you to configure a new Kitura project in a question and answer way. If you just need a basic starter project, you can simply use the `kitura init` command:

Useful CLI Commands	Usage
kitura init	Creates a basic starter project
kitura create	Creates an application using KAG

The rest of this section will cover the usage of KAG.

Using KAG

The `kitura create` command will launch Kitura's powerful application generator. If you don't want to customize the boilerplate for your Kitura project, you can simply skip this tool and use `kitura init` to create a basic starter project.

Once you've launched the application generator using the `kitura create` command, it's going to take a few minutes for KAG to extract dependent packages. Then, you'll be prompted for the name and directory of your project:

```
Initialization prompts? What's the name of your application? newWorld?
Enter the name of the directory to contain the project: newWorld
```

In the previous output, you use `newWorld` as your application name and choose `newWorld` as the directory name for your project.

Next, choose either one of the project types:

```
Select type of project: (Use arrow keys)
  Scaffold a starter
Generate a CRUD application
```

The scaffolded application option allows you to create a boilerplate with frontend and backend-for-frontend features you can choose.

The CRUD application option assumes your web service to have a data model and the application generator will provide endpoints to perform CRUD (Create, Retrieve, Update, and Delete) operations for your data.

Let's choose to build a scaffolded application here. You'll use a CRUD application boilerplate only if you want to create a Kitura application that serves as a backend database server.

Selecting a scaffolded application

For a scaffolded application, the application generator allows you to choose from one of the three preset options:

- Basic Preset:
  - Embedded metrics dashboard
  - Docker files

- Web Preset:
  - Static web file serving
  - Embedded metrics dashboard
  - Docker files

- Backend for Frontend (BFF) Preset:
  - Static web file serving
  - Swagger UI
  - Embedded metrics dashboard
  - Docker files

The **Basic Preset** adds embedded metrics dashboard capability to gather application and system metrics and adds several Docker files for easy deployment of your project using container technology.

The **Web Preset** is a superset to Basic Preset and has additional file structure for serving static web content.

The **Backend for Frontend (BFF) Preset** adds Swagger UI to the Web Preset. Swagger UI is also known as an Open API (https://www.openapis.org), which is an industry initiative to create vendor-neutral and open specification for providing technical metadata for RESTful APIs. RESTful API stands for a programmatic interface using representational state transfer (REST) technology. We will cover the topic more in Chapter 12, *Deploying to Cloud* when we discuss API Gateway.

For the newWorld application, choose the Basic Preset.

Choosing additional services

Once you have selected one of the presets, the application generator will prompt you to select which additional services you want to include:

Generate Boilerplate for Services:

- [ ] Cloudant / CouchDB
- [ ] Redis
- [ ] MongoD
- [ ] PostgreSQL
- [ ] ElephantSQL
- [ ] Object Storage
- [ ] AppID
- [ ] Auto-scaling
- [ ] Watson Conversation
- [ ] Alert Notifications
- [ ] Push Notification

Skip all of these additional services for the `newWorld` application. Also, select default options for the rest of the prompts.

Now, KAG is ready to create the project for you. The output looks like the following:

```
   create .swiftservergenerator-project
... [deleted]
create Jenkinsfile
Apple Swift version 4.1.2 (swiftlang-902.0.54 clang-902.0.39.2)
Target: x86_64-apple-darwin17.4.0
Fetching https://github.com/IBM-Swift/Kitura.git
... [deleted]
Compile Swift Module 'newWorld' (1 sources)
Linking ./.build/x86_64-apple-macosx10.10/debug/newWorld
swift build command completed
generated: ./newWorld.xcodeproj
generate .xcodeproj command completed
Next steps:Change directory to your app
$ cd /Users/fyeung1/Downloads/Packt/ch3/kitura/newWorld
Run your app
$ .build/debug/newWorld
```

As you can see, KAG will create a basic boilerplate project similar to that generated by `kitura init`. However, KAG allows you to add more features to the starting project. You'll find it very useful to start a new project quickly.

Summary

In this chapter, you've been provided with step-by-step instructions on how to install both Vapor Toolbox and the Kitura CLI on Mac or Linux. Whether Mac or Linux, your system is now ready for some serious server-side Swift project development. You've also learned the usage of some of the most useful command-line tools offered by the Swift Package Manager, Vapor Toolbox, and the Kitura CLI. In the next chapter, you're going to explore these tools to develop your first web applications using the Vapor and Kitura frameworks.

Building Your First Web App

3

This chapter takes you directly to server-side Swift coding with detailed instructions on creating a new web app project from a template provided in the web framework. You'll be guided to create, build, run, and test a Hello World! web app using Vapor 3.0. The files and directories in a typical Vapor web app will be reviewed, and their usages will be further explained. After that, you'll learn how to expand the features of the web app by adding more new routes to handle additional requests from client. You will continue your journey to create a similar Hello World! web app with the Kitura web framework. After going through an exercise showing you how to build a simple web app with both Vapor and Kitura, you'll take note of the similarities between the two web frameworks and appreciate the different approaches taken by them.

Before we move ahead, let's take a look at the topics that will be covered in this chapter:

- Creating an app using Vapor CLI
- Reviewing source code in Vapor boilerplate
- Adding more routes in Vapor
- Creating an app using Kitura CLI
- Reviewing source code in Kitura boilerplate
- Adding more routes in Kitura

Creating an app using Vapor CLI

By now, you should have the Vapor Toolbox installed on your system. Let's start creating a Hello World application using a boilerplate project provided by Vapor Toolbox.

Creating a hello world app from a template

Use the `vapor new` command to create a new project from the default template:

```
# Step 1: Create helloWorld app from the default template
vapor new helloWorld
```

You'll see the following output on the Terminal:

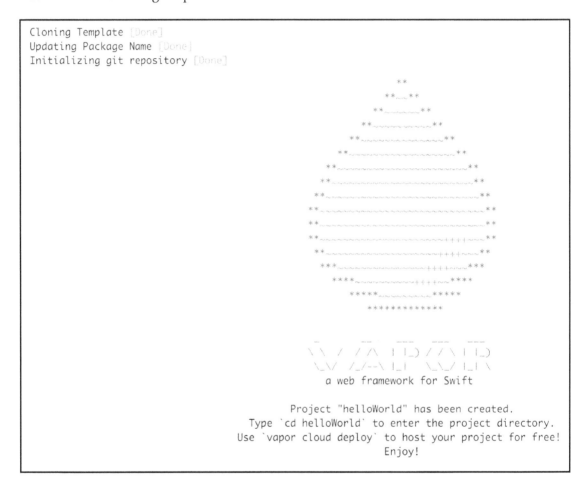

Vapor created the project `helloWorld` and put it in a new directory with the same name.

Building the hello world app

Your `helloWorld` Vapor app is already functional.

Enter the project directory and type in the `vapor build` command to build the `helloWorld` app:

```
# Step 2: Build the current project
cd helloWorld
vapor build
```

The first command, `cd` is to change the current directory to the `helloWorld` directory. The second command tells Vapor to start fetching and installing all the dependencies and then building the project itself.

The building process may take a few minutes:

```
No .build folder, fetch may take a while...
Fetching Dependencies [Done]
 Building Project [Done]
```

Since you are building the application for the first time, the Swift compiler will create the `.build` folder in your current directory to store all installed dependencies, temporary files, and executables.

Running the hello world app

Now you are ready to use the `vapor run` command to execute the app in the current directory:

```
# Step 3: Run the app in the current directory
vapor run
```

Your `helloWorld` app will be running:

```
Running helloWorld ...
 [ INFO ] Migrating 'sqlite' database (FluentProvider.swift:28)
 [ INFO ] Preparing migration 'Todo' (MigrationContainer.swift:50)
 [ INFO ] Migrations complete (FluentProvider.swift:32)
 Running default command: .build/debug/Run serve
 Server starting on http://localhost:8080
```

To see your app in action, launch your web browser and go to the
URL `http://localhost:8080/hello`:

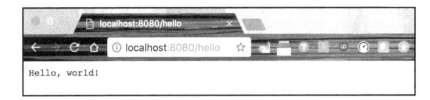

The `hello` path in the URL is the name of a route that is handled in the application to print
out the string `Hello, world!`.

If you want to stop the execution of the application, use the *Ctrl + C* command in the
Terminal.

Converting to the Xcode project on a Mac

As explained before, you can optionally take advantage of the powerful editing and
debugging features of Xcode if you use macOS. The Vapor Toolbox CLI provides a
convenient way for you to generate an Xcode project file from a generic Vapor project.

1. In the current directory of your Vapor project, run the following Vapor Toolbox
   CLI command:

```
# Step 4: Generate Xcode project files
vapor xcode
```

2. After a few minutes, Xcode project files will be generated. When you are
   prompted with the question **Open Xcode project?**, Press *Y* to open your project
   in Xcode:

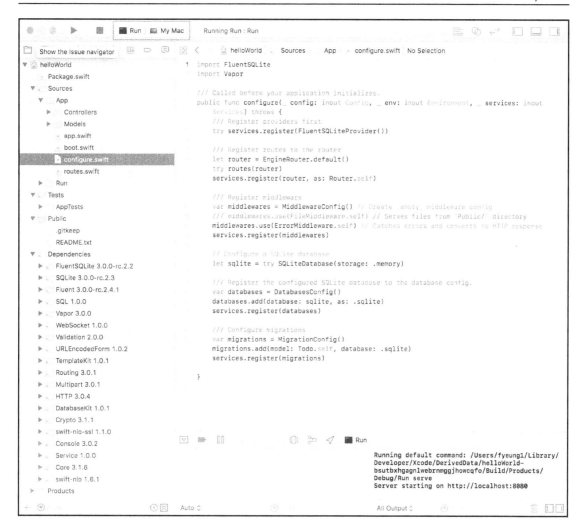

3. From the toolbar at the top left corner of Xcode, select the **Run** scheme and **My Mac** device. Then, click on the Play button (*command + R*) at the top left of Xcode to build and run your Xcode project. You should see the message **Running Run : Run** at the top.

Open the URL `http://localhost:8080/hello` again in your web browser; you should see the **Hello, world!** message. It confirms that Xcode is running your `helloWorld` Vapor app.

Reviewing source code in Vapor boilerplate

The following diagram gives you an overview of the boilerplate generated from Vapor's default template:

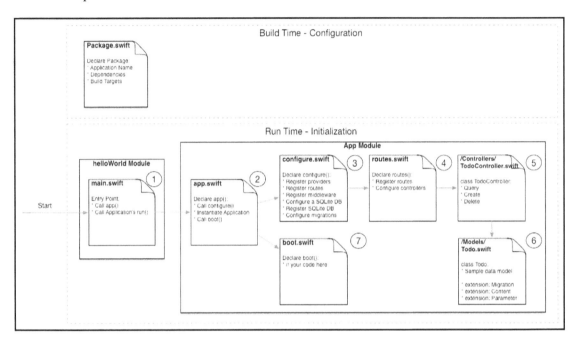

The `Package.swift` is used by Swift Package Manager during build time to configure your project's package. The package description comprises essential information such as application name, dependencies on other packages, and different build targets supported in your project.

There are three modules in the project: `helloWorld`, `App`, and `AppTests`. (The diagram only shows the `helloWorld` and `App` modules, but the `AppTests` module will be soon reviewed in the next chapter.) The functions and classes in the files in `helloWorld` and `App` modules are invoked in the following order:

1. The `helloWorld` executable contains a single entry point in `main.swift` that calls `app()` to create an application instance and invokes the instance's `run()` method to boot your app server.
2. The `App` module contains all of your server application logic. The `app()` function in `app.swift` first calls `configure()` to register all services properly, then it will create an application instance, followed by a call to `boot()`.

3. `configure()` in `configure.swift` registers all services required for your application:routes, middleware, Fluent providers, SQLite database, and migrations.

4. The `routes()` in `routes.swift` is called to register routes and configure controllers that handle all the requests routed to them.

5. Vapor includes a sample controller, `TodoController` class in `/Controllers/TodoController.swift`, in the default project to show how to interact with the data model and perform operations such as query, create, and delete.

6. The data model, `Todo` class in `/Models/Todo.swift`, is a sample model subclassing from `SQLiteModel`. It is also extended to support migration, content, and parameter to take advantage of the rich built-in features offered by Vapor.

7. The `boot()` in `boot.swift` has no any code implementation. It is a placeholder for you to put any initialization code after the application instance is created.

See Appendix A: `Vapor Boilerplate Project`, for a more detailed review of the files generated in a Vapor boilerplate project.

Adding more routes in Vapor

This section will show you how to add more routes in Vapor:

1. Open the `routes.swift` file from Project Navigator on Xcode's left panel and add the following code to the line right before the closing brace at the bottom:

```
. . .
router.get("greet", String.parameter) { req -> String in // [1]
    let guest = try req.parameters.next(String.self) // [2]
    return "Hi \(guest), greetings! Thanks for visiting us." // [3]
}
. . .
```

2. The preceding code does three things:
    1. Add a new route using `greet` as the first parameter from the path components and specifying the second parameter to be a string.
    2. Extract the guest string from the request's next item in its parameters list.
    3. Interpolate the guest string in the string returning to the client.

If you build and run your project again, you can see the following output by directing your web browser to `http://localhost:8080/greet/Neil`. Take note that the path is case-sensitive. For example, the *N* in *Neil* is capitalized:

3. Now, you can add another route to show how your application will respond to different requests. Add the following code to the line right after the greet route but before the final ending brace:

```
. . .
router.get("student", String.parameter) { req -> String in
    let studentName = try req.parameters.next(String.self) // [1]
    let studentRecords = [ // [2]
        "Peter" : 3.42,
        "Thomas" : 2.98,
        "Jane" : 3.91,
        "Ryan" : 4.00,
        "Kyle" : 4.00
    ]
    if let gpa = studentRecords[studentName] { // [3]
        return "The student \(studentName)'s GPA is \(gpa)" // [4]
    } else {
        return "The student's record can't be found!" // [5]
    }
}
. . .
```

4. The new route, `student`, will be added. Depending on the `student`'s name, the logic handling the route will respond differently:
    1. Assign the next item on the request's parameters list to be the student name `studentName`
    2. Create a new array `studentRecords` that contains key-value pairs for the student's names and their GPA
    3. Unwrap the `studentRecords` using a student's name
    4. Format `queryResponse` with a student's name and their GPA
    5. Format `queryResponse` if the student's record can't be found

If you point your web browser to `localhost:8080/student/Jane`, you'll get an output text that looks like this:

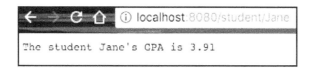

Alternatively, you can run the `curl` command in a Terminal:

```
$ curl "http://localhost:8080/student/Jane"
The student Jane's GPA is 3.91
```

The student's name in client's request is used to check against the keys in an array with key-value pairs. You'll see in future chapters how we create controllers to implement logic in processing such query. The array of key-value pairs can be also replaced with a database for data recording and retrieval.

Creating an app using Kitura CLI

After your first Hello World application in Vapor, let's do the same using Kitura CLI to create a similar Hello World application in Kitura.

Creating a hello world app from a default template

1. First, create a new directory called `helloWorld` and change the directory to `helloWorld`:

    ```
    # Step 1a: Create a new directory for your project
    $ mkdir helloWorld
    $ cd helloWorld
    ```

    Kitura CLI will use the current directory's name to create your project and put all the files in the same directory.

2. Next, use the `kitura init` command to create a new project from the default Kitura template:

    ```
    # Step 1b: Create helloWorld app using the default Kitura template
    $ kitura init
    ```

This step not only creates the project by fetching dependencies and setting up the project environment for you but also builds the project right away. It takes Kitura several minutes to fetch dependencies and build the `helloWorld` project for you:

```
create .swiftservergenerator-project
 create .gitignore
 create .swift-version
 create LICENSE
 create Sources/Application/InitializationError.swift
 create Sources/Application/Application.swift
 create spec.json
 create Tests/ApplicationTests/RouteTests.swift
 create Tests/LinuxMain.swift
 create Sources/Application/Metrics.swift
 create Sources/Application/Routes/HealthRoutes.swift
 create README.md
 create Sources/Application/Routes/.keep
 create iterative-dev.sh
 create Sources/kitura/main.swift
 create Package.swift
 create cli-config.yml
 create Dockerfile
 create Dockerfile-tools
 create .dockerignore
 create manifest.yml
 create .cfignore
 create .bluemix/toolchain.yml
 create .bluemix/deploy.json
 create .bluemix/scripts/container_build.sh
 create .bluemix/scripts/kube_deploy.sh
 create .bluemix/pipeline.yml
 create chart/kitura/Chart.yaml
 create chart/kitura/templates/deployment.yaml
 create chart/kitura/templates/service.yaml
 create chart/kitura/templates/hpa.yaml
 create chart/kitura/templates/istio.yaml
 create chart/kitura/templates/basedeployment.yaml
 create chart/kitura/values.yaml
 create chart/kitura/bindings.yaml
 create Jenkinsfile
 Apple Swift version 4.1.2 (swiftlang-902.0.54 clang-902.0.39.2)
 Target: x86_64-apple-darwin17.4.0
 Fetching https://github.com/IBM-Swift/HeliumLogger.git
 Fetching https://github.com/IBM-Swift/CloudEnvironment.git
 Fetching https://github.com/RuntimeTools/SwiftMetrics.git
 Fetching https://github.com/IBM-Swift/Health.git
 swift build command completed
 Updating https://github.com/IBM-Swift/HeliumLogger.git
```

```
 Updating https://github.com/IBM-Swift/Health.git
 Updating https://github.com/RuntimeTools/SwiftMetrics.git
 Updating https://github.com/IBM-Swift/CloudEnvironment.git
 generate .xcodeproj command completed
 Next steps:
Change directory to your app
$ cd /Users/fyeung1/Code/kitura
Run your app
$ .build/debug/kitura
```

After the build of the Kitura application is successful, the command outputs the recommended **next steps** for running the application.

Running your Kitura app from a Terminal

When the building process finishes, you are ready to launch the app server and test it with a web browser or the `curl` command in the Terminal.

Launch the debug version of your `helloWorld` app:

```
# Step 2a: Run the app from Terminal
$ .build/debug/helloWorld
```

Alternatively, you can run the `swift run` command to launch the application:

```
# Step 2b: Run the app from Terminal
$ swift run
```

Running your Kitura app from Xcode

Unlike Vapor Toolbox, which takes an additional step to create Xcode project files, the Kitura init command automatically creates Xcode project file for you. If you don't want to launch the app from the Terminal, you can open the Xcode project file and run it from Xcode:

```
# Step 2b: Open helloWorld.xcodeproject to launch Xcode
$ open ./helloWorld.xcodeproj
```

The Xcode screen looks as follows:

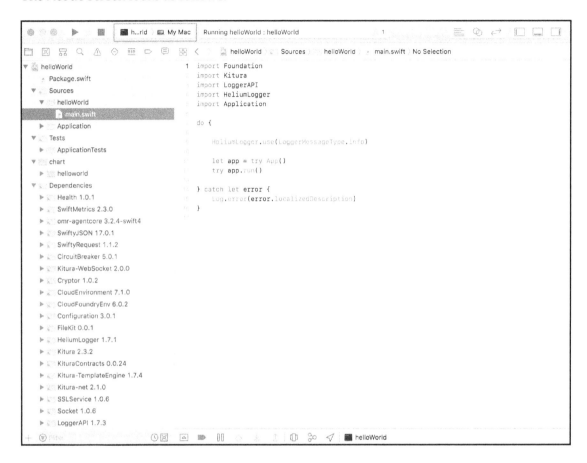

From the toolbar at the top-left corner of Xcode, select the **helloWorld** scheme and then **My Mac** device. After clicking on the **Play** button (*command + R*), you should see the message **Running helloWorld : helloWorld** at the top.

Testing the app with a web browser client

Once your `helloWorld` app server is running, you can use a web browser and go to the URL `http://localhost:8080`.

If you see a screen that looks as follows, it confirms that your Kitura build environment has been set up correctly and that the `helloWorld` Kitura application is running as expected:

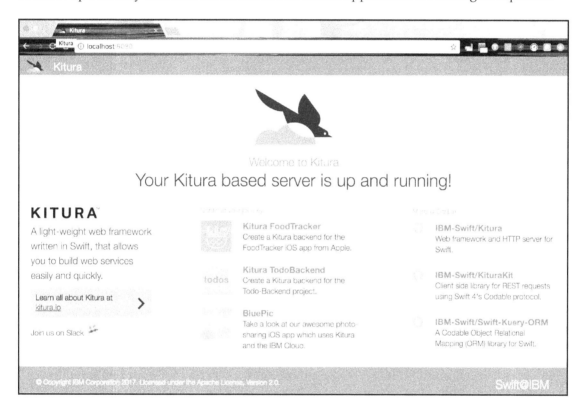

Reviewing source code in Kitura boilerplate

The following diagram illustrates the source code files generated from the last section:

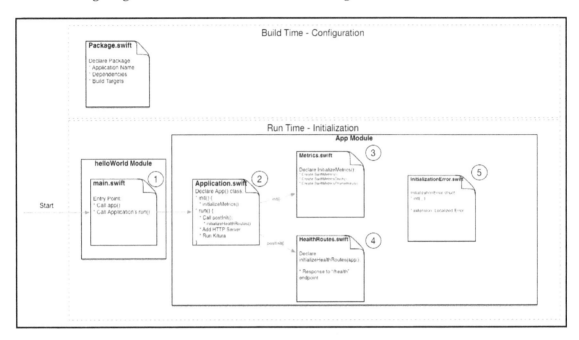

The `Package.swift` is used in the same way as that in a Vapor project. Your application's name, required package dependencies, and different build targets are configured in this manifest file.

A typical Kitura project is partitioned in a similar fashion as in a Vapor project; an application executable module, a test-executable module, and a core application module with all of your application logics:

1. There is only one Swift file in the `helloWorld` executable module. It serves as an entry point for your project and does several things: It configures Kitura's Helium logger to be used in this project, creates an `App()` instance, and calls the instance's `run()` function. The entry point is implemented in a do-try-catch block to catch any runtime errors in your project. In `run()`, it first calls the `postInit()` function, then it will configure a HTTP server and start running a Kitura application instance.

2. The `App()` class used in the `main.swift` file's do-try-catch block is defined in `Application.swift`. Before an instance of `App()` is being constructed, the initializer function `init()` will be called. The `init()` function will in turn call `initializeMetrics()`.

3. The `initializeMetrics()` function is implemented in `Metrics.swift`. It creates three metrics monitoring instances: a `SwiftMetrics` to gather performance metrics, a `SwiftMetricsDash` to enable a dashboard web page that displays the performance metrics, and a `SwiftMetricsPrometheus` to allow the performance metrics to be used in application clusters monitoring tool.

4. In the basic template, the `postInit()` function in `main.swift` sets up only one endpoint: Health Route, by calling the `initializeHealthRoutes(app:)` function that is defined in `HealthRoutes.swift`. `initializeHealthRoutes(app:)` handles the response to the `/health` endpoint. Any routes such as this Health Route are initialized after an app instance is created, but before a Kitura server is started.

5. `Initialization.swift` contains only one struct `InitializationError()` that is inherited from `Error()` struct. It gives you a chance to modify error messages when there is an error during initialization.

See Appendix B: `Kitura Boilerplate Project`, for a more detailed review of the files generated in a Kitura boilerplate project.

Adding more routes in Kitura

You can add more routes to your project as follows:

1. Open `Application.swift` in Xcode and add the following code to the line right after `initializeHealthRoutes(app: self)` in the `PostInit()` function:

```
. . .
// add after initializeHealthRoutes(app: self)
router.get("/greet") { request, response, next in // [1]
    if let guest = request.queryParameters["guest"] { // [2]
        response.send("Hi \(guest), greetings! Thanks for visiting us.") // [3]
    } else {
        response.send("Hi stranger, It's nice meeting with you.")
    }
}

router.get("/student/:name") { request, response, next in // [4]
```

```
let studentName = request.parameters["name"]!

let studentRecords = [ // [5]
    "Peter"  : 3.42,
    "Thomas" : 2.98,
    "Jane"   : 3.91,
    "Ryan"   : 4.00,
    "Kyle"   : 4.00
]

var queryResponse : String

if let gpa = studentRecords[studentName] {
    queryResponse = "The student \(studentName)'s GPA is \(gpa)" //
[6]
} else {
    queryResponse = "The student's record can't be found!"
}
response.send(queryResponse) // [7]
. . .
```

2. Similar to what you have done in the `helloWorld` Vapor project, the preceding code adds two routes, `greet` and `student`, to your Kitura project and processes them in the following ways:
    1. [1] Add the path `greet` with the query parameter guest
    2. [2] Retrieve the guest parameter from the request using `queryParameters()`
    3. [3] Send a response using `response.send()`
    4. [4] Add the path student followed by the path parameter's name
    5. [5] Create a dictionary with a name and GPA key-value pairs
    6. [6] Use the name as a key to retrieve the GPA and customize the response
    7. [7] Send the response with a customized message using `response.send()`

The first endpoint handles a request with query parameter and returns a response like this:

```
$ curl "http://localhost:8080/greet?guest=Neil"
Hi Neil, greetings! Thanks for visiting us. Unfortunately, there is
nothing too much to see here.
```

The second endpoint handles a request with path parameter and returns the following response:

```
$ curl "http://localhost:8080/student/Jane"
The student Jane's GPA is 3.91
```

There are three parameters that are passed to a router's closure: **request**, **response**, and **next in**.

- The request parameter contains all the information about the incoming HTTP request. The `/greet` endpoint demonstrates a path with query parameters, that is, `localhost:8080/greet?guest=Neil`, you can use the request's `queryParameter()` to retrieve it. Kitura also allows you to use a path with a parameter, as shown in the `/student` endpoint. A path parameter is the parameter name prefixed with a colon. In the preceding code, you use the request object's parameters array to retrieve the path parameter. If you want, you can add as many path parameters as you want, as long as each path parameter is unique.

- The response parameter provides you with a flexible way to return data going out to the requestor. In this example, your response is simply a string message. However, you can also include status code, formatted headers, `[String: Any]` dictionary, or even a JSON object in your response.

- The next parameter is the `next` handler that should be invoked for the route. Kitura allows more than one handler for each endpoint. To let the next handler have an opportunity to run its code, you need to call `next()` right before you have finished using your router code:

```
. . .
router.get("/greet") { request, response, next in
    if let guest = request.queryParameters["guest"] {
        response.send("Hi \(guest), greetings! Thanks for visiting
us.")
    } else {
        response.send("Hi stranger, It's nice meeting with you.")
    }
    next() // [1]
}
router.get("/greet") { request, response, next in
    response.send(" Unfortunately, there is nothing too much to see
here.")
}
. . .
```

In the preceding code, there are two handlers for the /greet endpoint. The next() call at [1] is added to the first handler of the /greet endpoint so the second handler of the /greet endpoint has a chance to handle the request. The output will look like this:

Try removing the next() statement and you will see that the second handler no longer works.

Summary

You've started doing a lot of hands-on coding in this chapter. First, you learned how to use the vapor new command to create a Hello World application from a boilerplate project. You moved on to add more routes to the application, and then used the commands vapor build and vapor run to build and run the application. Next, you did the same exercise with Kitura CLI; you used kitura init to construct a starter boilerplate, added the same routes as you did in Vapor, then used swift build and swift run commands to build and run your Kitura application. Overall, this is a good introductory chapter to some hands-on coding with Vapor and Kitura. In the next chapter, let's learn some good techniques for debugging and testing your server-side Swift projects.

Debugging and Testing

4

A seasonal developer spends far more time on debugging and testing code than writing code, in a typical software project. This chapter introduces the basics of writing tests for a server-side Swift project and recommends the best practice in debugging server-side Swift code. When it comes to a web development framework, both the Vapor and Kitura frameworks offer very good testing and debugging support. You are going to learn how to use the test framework in Swift and logging features in Vapor and Kitura to help debugging and error-proofing your code.

This chapter covers writing tests for server-side Swift projects as well as debugging in server-side Swift.

The following is a list of topics on debugging for server-side Swift:

- Using the Logging API in a Vapor project
- Using the Logger API in a Kitura project
- Debugging using the HTTP traffic monitoring tool

Writing tests for server-side Swift projects

Writing tests is an important part in server-side Swift development. A server-side test is different from that of a client side test because server-side code involves a lot of querying different APIs by clients, or writing calls to other backend cloud services or microservices. You need to write tests that intercept calls dynamically. To do that, you instantiate and run a server instance, then you simulate the runtime environment using known data and match the output with the expected result.

If the data required for a test is not available, you can make up something using fake data or simulated data. A test is passed only if the results are validated and matched with your expectation. You don't just test if a feature works correctly when presented with valid data. You should also check if a feature fails gracefully and consistently with invalid data. Graceful failure is part of the overall user experience for your server product.

When writing each test, keep in mind that each test is independent from each other. One test cannot rely on the result from another test. This approach is called **unit testing**. Sometimes it is helpful to construct helper methods to handle repetitive steps common to all unit tests. It is okay to repeat some operations in every unit test so that each test is totally decoupled from each other. You'll see shortly that there are good coding techniques that promote code re-using in writing tests in Swift.

Besides unit tests, there is another kind of test called an **integration test**. Integration testing is useful when you want to validate how different methods work correctly together. Since more business logic is involved in integration testing, you can expect to have more complicated test cases. Therefore, it is beneficial for you to have good coverage in unit tests. Unit testing helps you identify problems earlier and reduce the need for complicated debugging efforts for the defects discovered later in integration testing.

Preparing a test executable target

In general, you want to create two executable targets for your project: one for the main application and another for the test application. Since Swift builds and runs one application at a time, you have to make your code testable by splitting the code into an application and library. The library will contain most of your business logic. The test executable file is separated from the main executable file. Both executable targets will be dependent on the core library you've just created.

In `Package.swift` of your Vapor 3 boilerplate project, you can see a test executable target defined:

```
.testTarget(name: "AppTests", dependencies: ["App"])
```

This test target is named `AppTests` and it is dependent on a library called `App`.

You can add more test targets to a project by inserting a new test target into `Package.swift`. You simply choose one of the targets to run the tests contained in the target.

Writing tests using XCTest

The following diagram illustrates how you can build a test using the `XCTest` framework in Swift:

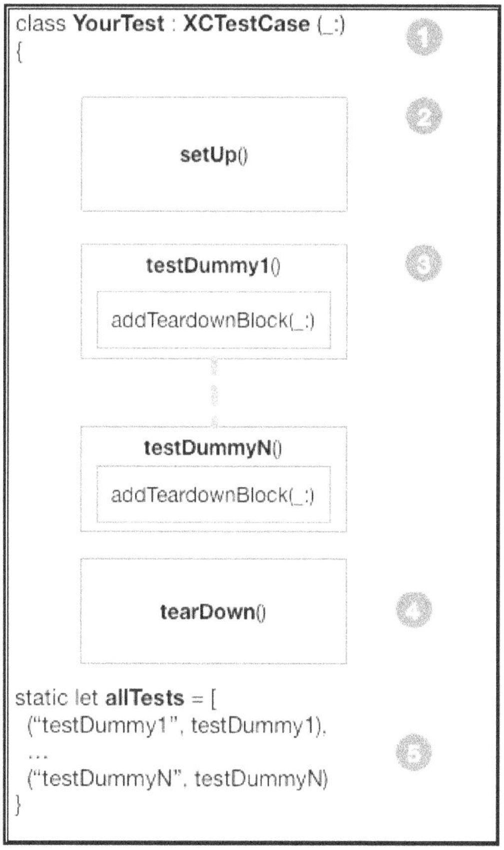

When running tests, XCTest finds all the test classes in our application. Each test class is a subclass of XCTestCase [1]. XCTest runs the setUp() method [2] and then all of the class's test methods.

Each test method [3] that implements a test always has the prefix *test*, takes no parameters, and returns no values. A test method may have an optional block called addTeardownBlock(_:) for us to add additional cleanup code. This is useful if we need to destroy a resource created locally in the test method.

If XCTest runs out of all the test methods, it will run the class teardown method [4] and move on to the next class. This process is repeated until all test classes are executed.

The static array allTests [5] is an object XCTest used to know which tests to execute. It is there to keep the tests compatible for a Linux environment. If you would like to run a Swift test in Linux, you'll need to create the LinuxMain.swift file that calls allTests. The LinuxMain.swift file shown here is automatically generated by Kitura CLI:

```
// LinuxMain.swift file for Linux
import XCTest

@testable import ApplicationTests

XCTMain([
    testCase(RouteTests.allTests),  // [1]
    ])
```

LinuxMain.swift acts as the test runner for Linux platforms. It calls XCMain(_:) which lists all your test cases [1].

Checking out test cases in a Vapor boilerplate project

Now that you've learned the basic workflow of how XCTest runs tests, it makes sense for you to check out the default test cases in a Vapor boilerplate project. The default test case template in a Vapor project gives you a bare-bones implementation of tests without any testing logic. It serves as a simple starting point for you to add more real tests to your project.

File: `/Tests/AppTests/AppTests.swift`

```swift
import App
import XCTest // [1]

final class AppTests: XCTestCase { // [2]
 func testNothing() throws { // [3]
 // add your tests here
 XCTAssert(true) // [4]
 }

 static let allTests = [ // [5]
 ("testNothing", testNothing)
 ]
}
```

The following is a list of what the preceding bare-bones source code does:

1. Imports the XCTest module
2. Declares a new class by subclassing from XCTestCase
3. Defines the first test function with a test prefix
4. Adds a dummy assertion that always turns out to be true
5. Defines a static array that contains all test functions

The macro XCTAssert() in [4] asserts a given Boolean expression to be true. Swift actually provides many different macros for test assertions. Next, you'll check out some of the assertion macros useful for your tests.

Learning useful assertion macros

Swift test assertions are useful in checking expected results in test methods. There is a family of macros similar to XCTAssert() to help evaluate any given conditions. Each macro optionally allows a literal NSString to describe what happens when there is a failure. For XCTAssert(), a failure is when the Boolean expression == false:

Macro	Usage
XCTAssertTrue()	Assert an expression to be true
XCTAssertFalse()	Assert an expression to be false
XCTAssertNil()	Assert an expression to be nil
XCTAssertNotNil()	Assert an expression to be not nil
XCTAssertEqual()	Assert two expressions to have the same value

Macro	Usage
XCTAssertNotEqual()	Assert two expressions to have the different value
XCTAssertEqualObjects()	Assert two objects to be equal
XCTAssertNotEqualObjects()	Assert two expressions to be different
XCTAssertGreaterThan()	Assert the value of one expression to be greater than another
XCTAssertGreaterThanOrEqual()	Assert the value of one expression to be greater than or equal to another
XCTAssertLessThan()	Assert the value of one expression to be less than another
XCTAssertLessThanOrEqual()	Assert the value of one expression to be less than or equal to another
XCTAssertThrows()	Assert an expression to throw an NSException
XCTAssertNoThrows()	Assert an expression not to throw an NSException
XCTAssertThrowsSpecific()	Assert an expression to throw an NSException with a specific name
XCTAssertNoThrowsSpecific()	Assert an expression not to throw an NSException with a specific name

Adding a unit test to your project

Now you're ready to add your own unit tests to the Vapor 3 project you created in the last chapter. Previously, you added a new route called "student" and your web application allows a user to query for a student's record that was stored in the array `studentRecords`. You can add a unit test to `AppTests.swift` and check if this feature works as expected:

```
@testable import App // [1]
import XCTest
import Vapor // [2]

final class AppTests: XCTestCase {
    func testNothing() throws {
        // add your tests here
        XCTAssert(true)
    }
    func testStudent() throws { // [3]
        let myApp = try app(Environment.testing) // [4]
        let studentRecords = [ // [5]
            "Peter" : 3.42,
            "Thomas" : 2.98,
            "Jane" : 3.91,
            "Ryan" : 4.00,
            "Kyle" : 4.00
        ]
```

```
            for (studentName, gpa) in studentRecords { // [6]
                let query = "/student/" + studentName;
                let request = Request(http: HTTPRequest(method: .GET,
                                                        url: URL(string:
query)!),
                                    using: myApp) // [7]
                // [8]
                let response = try myApp.make(Responder.self).respond(to:
request).wait()
                guard let data = response.http.body.data else { // [9]
                    XCTFail("No data in response")
                    return
                }
                let expectedResponse = "The student \(studentName)'s GPA is
\(gpa)"
                // [10]
                if let responseString = String(data: data, encoding: .utf8) {
                    XCTAssertEqual(responseString, expectedResponse)
                }
            }
        }

    static let allTests = [
        ("testNothing", testNothing),
        ("testStudent", testStudent)
    ]
}
```

The following steps are used to unit test the /student route:

1. Add the @testable attribute to the import statement for a high level of access
2. Import the Vapor framework
3. Add the testStudent() test function
4. Create an app instance by calling the app() function
5. Copy studentRecords[] from the routes() function in routes.swift
6. Use a for loop to make queries for all students in studentRecords[]
7. Construct an HTTP request
8. Make the HTTP request and retrieve an HTTP response
9. Unwrap the data optional of the HTTP response
10. Assert the string of the HTTP response data to be the expected string

The `@testable` attribute in [1] is to elevate the access to the `App` module. Swift prevents an external entity from accessing anything declared as internal in a compiled module. If you elevate the access level to "public" for testability, it's going to reduce the benefits of type safety. Swift provides an alternative way to work around the access control problem of a module, if you enable the testability (use the `-enable-testing` compilation flag or set **Build Settings | Enable Testability** in Xcode) during its compilation. You'll be able to elevate the access when you add the `@testable` attribute to an import statement for the testing enabled module.

The implementation of a new test in [3] is straightforward. It illustrates the essential steps in making an HTTP request and handling its HTTP response. First, a new instance of app is created in [4] by calling the `app()` function in `app.swift`. Next, you copy the `studentRecords[]` array from `routes.swift` you used in the previous chapter and iterate each entry of the array for an HTTP request to the Vapor application. Since the request takes a definite time, you use the `wait()` function in [8] to make sure that you have received a valid HTTP response. In [10], the data of the HTTP response is then compared with the expected response.

Running unit tests in Xcode

Xcode automatically scans all of your `XCtestCase` tests with a prefix of *test*, for example, `testNothing()`, and links them to a specific test target. You can use a new scheme configured by Xcode to use that target and run it within Xcode.

In Xcode, use ⌘ + *U* or select from the menu **Product | Test** to run the tests in this test target:

The highlighted numbered sections in the image have a specific role.These roles are listed here:

1. The `AppTests` class is inherited from `XCTestCase`
2. The `testNothing()` function with the prefix `test` will be executed
3. Icons will show whether or not `AppTests` and `testNothing()` have been executed successfully
4. You can also run an individual test using the test's play button in Test Navigator

Use Test Navigator to give you an overview of all the available tests in a test target. It has a play button next to each individual test; you can choose to run a specific test individually.

Check the results of your test runs. In Xcode's console window, it prints out how many tests were run and how many of them failed.

Checking code coverage

Xcode includes a convenient feature for you to check the coverage of your tests. The test coverage metric measures how much of your code is covered by the unit tests already implemented in your project. This metric gives you confidence that any code changes you made will be adequately tested. Even though you may not find it too useful to have a perfect test coverage, you generally want to maintain a high percentage of code coverage throughout your development. In this way, it is less likely for you to break any code as you make progress in adding incremental enhancements to your project.

Turning on code coverage

The code coverage report option is not turned on by default because code coverage data collection incurs a performance penalty. You can turn on code coverage in the build target's scheme.

Click on the **helloWorldPackageTests** build target:

Then select the **Edit Scheme** option from the pull-down menu:

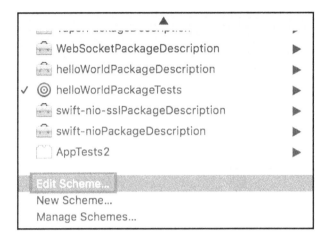

Choose the **Test** option from the left panel and enable the checkbox for the **Gather coverage for all targets** option at the bottom of the right panel:

Generating a coverage report

When you run all the unit tests again, a **code coverage report** will be generated:

1. Go to the Reports Navigator in Xcode and click on the { } **Coverage** item of the latest test:

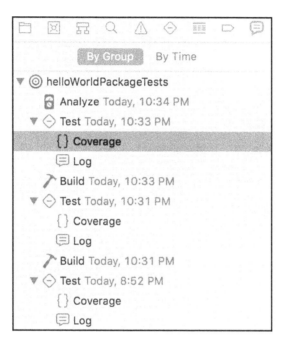

2. A list of modules and functions is displayed:

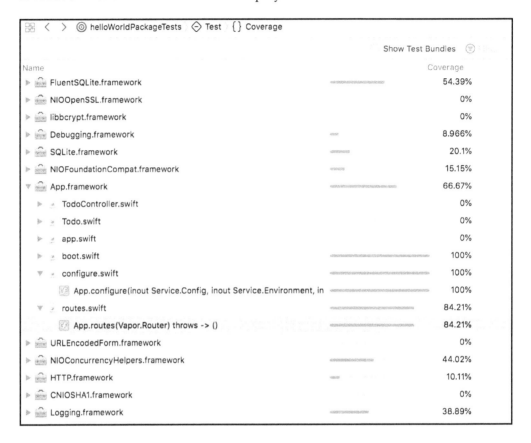

If you expand the item list of `App.framework`, you'll see the percentage of coverage of your unit tests.

3. Double-click on the `routes.swift` file and Xcode will take you to the source editor:

```
88  <      helloWorld    Sources    App    routes.swift    routes(_:)

       let todoController = TodoController()
       router.get("todos", use: todoController.index)
       router.post("todos", use: todoController.create)
       router.delete("todos", Todo.parameter, use: todoController.delete)

       router.get("greet", String.parameter) { req -> String in
           let guest = try req.parameters.next(String.self)
           return "Hi \(guest), greetings!  Thanks for visiting us."
       }

       router.get("student", String.parameter) { req -> String in
           let studentName = try req.parameters.next(String.self)

           let studentRecords = [
               "Peter" : 3.42,
               "Thomas" : 2.98,
               "Jane" : 3.91,
               "Ryan" : 4.00,
               "Kyle" : 4.00
           ]

32         var queryResponse : String

           if let gpa = studentRecords[studentName] {
               queryResponse = "The student \(studentName)'s GPA is \(gpa)"
           } else {
               queryResponse = "The student's record can't be found!"
           }
           return queryResponse
       }
   }
```

You'll notice that some code is highlighted in red to bring your attention to them. They are the lines of code that haven't been executed by your tests.

The lines of code that have been executed before are highlighted in green, with the number of executions listed on the right. For example, in our `testStudent()` unit test, the "student" route is executed five times. It corresponds to the number of element pairs in `studentRecords[]`.

Your goal is to increase the code coverage by adding additional testing logic that invokes the highlighted code missed in your previous tests.

In ensuring the proper coverage of unit tests in your project, you want to have every public method covered by at least one corresponding test. Each time, after writing a test for each public method, you can run the tests again and check the coverage.

If you follow this approach to cover as much code as possible, you're going to bring the total percentage of test coverage up. It is a very good habit for you to add new unit tests right after each new feature you have added to the project. Typically, a developer spends twice the amount of time on writing tests or debugging than writing the code. By adding unit tests incrementally and in a disciplined fashion, you will be eventually saving more time by reducing the number of defects occurring during runtime.

Reviewing Kitura boilerplate tests

Writing tests for server-side Swift projects starting with the Kitura framework will be the same as what you've just learned with the Vapor framework, since both Kitura and Vapor use the same XCTest framework.

If you check out the boilerplate project created with kitura init, you will find more tests there. The first test, testGetStatic, shows you how to test a Kitura server running static content. The second test, testHealthRoute, demonstrates how to test the probing results of health on a Kitura server instance:

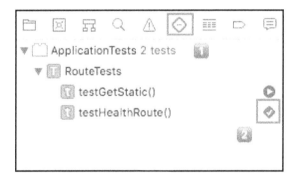

Now open the RouteTests.swift file, and you will see a typical XCTestCase implementation:

```
// ...
class RouteTests: XCTestCase { // [1]
    static var port: Int!
    static var allTests : [(String, (RouteTests) -> () throws -> Void)] {
// [2]
        return [
```

```
                ("testGetStatic", testGetStatic)
    override func setUp() { // [3]
        super.setUp()

        HeliumLogger.use()
        do {
            // ... [not shown]
            let app = try App()
            RouteTests.port = app.cloudEnv.port
            try app.postInit()
            Kitura.addHTTPServer(onPort: RouteTests.port, with: app.router)
            Kitura.start()
        } catch {
            XCTFail("Couldn't start Application test server: \(error)")
        }
    }

    override func tearDown() { // [4]
        Kitura.stop()
        super.tearDown()
    }

    func testGetStatic() { // [5]
        // ... [not shown]
    }
    func testHealthRoute() { // [6]
        // ... [not shown]
    }
}
private extension URLRequest { // [7]
    // ... [not shown]
}
```

If you put aside the implementation details in the preceding code, you'll see the high-level constructs of XCTestCase class clearly:

1. Declare RouteTests by subclassing from XCTestCase
2. Include all tests that contains all target tests (for LINUX compatibility)
3. Set up and run a new Kitura server instance
4. Stop and tear down the current server instance
5. Implement the logic for testing static content
6. Implement the probe for the current server instance's health
7. Use extensions to include implementation common to both tests

The `RouteTests` class takes advantage of `setUp()` and `tearDown()` methods in implementing a Kitura server instance used by each test. As explained before, each unit test will be independent from each other. You need to set up a new instance of the Kitura server each time a test is executed. The `setUp()` and `tearDown()` methods help you avoid writing repetitive code by reusing the server setup and teardown code.

Next, try to run the tests to see what results the two tests output. In Xcode, select the test target:

When you use the command + *U* command to run the test target in Xcode, the console window prints the following output:

```
[Mon May 28 11:52:56 2018] com.ibm.diagnostics.healthcenter.loader INFO: Swift Application Metrics
[2018-05-28T11:52:56.401-07:00] [VERBOSE] [Router.swift:108 init(mergeParameters:)] Router initialized
[2018-05-28T11:52:56.490-07:00] [VERBOSE] [Router.swift:108 init(mergeParameters:)] Router initialized
[2018-05-28T11:52:56.491-07:00] [INFO] [Metrics.swift:20 initializeMetrics(router:)] Initialized metrics.
2018-05-28 11:52:56.492194-0700 helloWorld[5820:23521410] CFPropertyListCreateFromXMLData(): Old-style plist parser: missing semicolon or
value in dictionary on line 1. Parsing will be abandoned. Break on _CFPropertyListMissingSemicolonOrValue to debug.
[2018-05-28T11:52:56.493-07:00] [VERBOSE] [Kitura.swift:104 run()] Starting Kitura framework...
[2018-05-28T11:52:56.493-07:00] [VERBOSE] [Kitura.swift:118 start()] Starting an HTTP Server on port 8080...
[2018-05-28T11:52:56.494-07:00] [INFO] [HTTPServer.swift:124 listen(on:)] Listening on port 8080
[2018-05-28T11:52:56.494-07:00] [VERBOSE] [HTTPServer.swift:125 listen(on:)] Options for port 8080: maxPendingConnections: 100,
allowPortReuse: false
```

Handling asynchronous tests

Given the non-blocking asynchronous communication model in most of the server-side frameworks, each test often involves an asynchronous call to an API method. The callback of an asynchronous call contains the results of a test run. This means that the validation of the returned results of a test happen at an undetermined time later. You need to take precautionary measures to ensure that the thread for validating the result doesn't terminate prematurely.

The Kitura test boilerplate code shows you how to handle a non-blocking asynchronous situation elegantly:

```
func testGetStatic() {
    let printExpectation = expectation(description: "The /route will serve
static HTML content.") // [1]

    URLRequest(forTestWithMethod: "GET")?
        .sendForTestingWithKitura { data, statusCode in // [2]
            if let getResult = String(data: data, encoding:
String.Encoding.utf8){ // [3]
                XCTAssertEqual(statusCode, 200)
                XCTAssertTrue(getResult.contains("<html"))
                XCTAssertTrue(getResult.contains("</html>"))
            } else {
                XCTFail("Return value from / was nil!")
            }
            printExpectation.fulfill() // [4]
        }

    waitForExpectations(timeout: 10.0, handler: nil) // [5]
}
```

In this code, `XCTestCase` uses the class `XCTestExpectation` to help facilitate the communication to you when asynchronous test tasks are complete:

1. Creates a new expectation
2. Uses an `URLRequest` extension function to process the HTTP request/response
3. Receives the HTTP response result asynchronously
4. Marks an expectation instance as fulfilled
5. Waits for the expectation to finish

You use the method `expectation(description:)` in [1] to create a new expectation with an associated description. The method returns an instance of `XCTestExpectation` that you can use. The description in the string will be displayed in the test log for this expectation to help diagnose failures.

When the asynchronous tasks in your test are done, call the expectation instance's `fulfill()` method in [4] to signal that the expectation is fulfilled.

To instruct `XCTestCase` not to end your test prematurely, you call `waitForExpectation(timeout:handler:)` in [5] and specify how much time you want to wait.

Using extensions for functions common to all tests

Besides the `setUp()` and `tearDown()` methods in the Kitura test boilerplate code, you'll also find the same code reusing strategy in the extension `URLRequest`. Extensions in Swift add new functionality to an existing class for which you do not have access to the source code. In the `URLRequest` extension, the Kitura test boilerplate code extends the class `URLRequest` in the Swift Foundation library to include URL parsing and handling code specific to the Kitura server environment:

```
private extension URLRequest { // [1]
    // [2]
    init?(forTestWithMethod method: String, route: String = "", body: Data?
= nil) {
        if let url = URL(string: "http://127.0.0.1:\(RouteTests.port)/" +
route){ // [3]
            self.init(url: url)
            addValue("application/json", forHTTPHeaderField: "Content-
Type")
            httpMethod = method
            cachePolicy = .reloadIgnoringCacheData
            if let body = body {
                httpBody = body
            }
        } else {
            XCTFail("URL is nil...")
            return nil
        }
    }

    func sendForTestingWithKitura(fn: @escaping (Data, Int) -> Void) { //
[4]

        guard let method = httpMethod, var path = url?.path, let headers =
allHTTPHeaderFields else {
            XCTFail("Invalid request params")
            return
        }

        if let query = url?.query {
            path += "?" + query
        }

        let requestOptions: [ClientRequest.Options] = [.method(method),
.hostname("localhost"), \
                                        .port(8080), .path(path),
```

```
.headers(headers)]

        let req = HTTP.request(requestOptions) { resp in

            if let resp = resp, resp.statusCode == HTTPStatusCode.OK ||
resp.statusCode ==
HTTPStatusCode.accepted {
                do {
                    var body = Data()
                    try resp.readAllData(into: &body)
                    fn(body, resp.statusCode.rawValue)
                } catch {
                    print("Bad JSON document received from Kitura-
Starter.")
                }
            } else {
                if let resp = resp {
                    print("Status code: \(resp.statusCode)")
                    var rawUserData = Data()
                    do {
                        let _ = try resp.read(into: &rawUserData)
                        let str = String(data: rawUserData, encoding:
String.Encoding(rawValue:
String.Encoding.utf8.rawValue))
                        print("Error response from Kitura-Starter:
\(String(describing: str))")
                    } catch {
                        print("Failed to read response data.")
                    }
                }
            }
        }
        if let dataBody = httpBody {
            req.end(dataBody)
        } else {
            req.end()
        }
    }
}
```

The following explains what this extension does:

1. Declares an extension to `URLRequest`
2. Includes a failable initializer
3. Wraps the URL optional and retrieves its associated networking parameters
4. Implements a function that constructs an HTTP request and processes its corresponding HTTP response

The `init?()` method in [2] is called a failable initializer. It means that the initialization can fail. For example, failure may occur when the networking parameters are incorrect or when a required external resource is not present. The pass/fail condition is checked when the supplied URL optional is unwrapped and validated.

The function in [4] is used by each test when sending an HTTP request and waiting for its HTTP response. It is a manifestation of the **Separation of Concerns** concept so each test can focus on validating the test results while the `URLRequest` extension function can focus on handling the HTTP request/response.

Debugging in a server-side Swift project

There are in general two types of errors: one occurs in runtime and the other takes place during code compilation. Runtime errors are expensive because they are difficult to track and tackle. Swift enforces strong type checking to reduce the chance of your mistake slipping through compilation error checking and become a runtime error. Unit tests with good code coverage also help you discover problems during development time. However, when a runtime error does occur, you'll need a better strategy to cope with it.

This is especially true for a server-side project because it is hard to reproduce the same condition that caused a runtime error to happen when there could be so many different kinds of networking conditions and situations. Normally, you'll set breakpoints in your code for some conditions which you suspect to have caused an error, and then inspect the state of your code when an error did get triggered. In a server-side project, not all conditions are reproducible if a condition is caused by some external factors, such as the available capacity in the network infrastructure or the network bandwidth availability in the data center, which are out of your control.

Given the nature of problems common to server projects, there are some debugging techniques that could be more useful than others. Logging is one of those debugging techniques that is useful for a server-side Swift project. A logging framework provides useful utility functions that allow you to record, manage, and store useful logging information in your project. When a runtime error occurs, it allows you to trace back the steps that lead to a failure.

Using the Logging API in a Vapor project

Vapor has its own pluggable logger framework. Since the Logging module is part of Vapor's Console package, it is included in all Vapor projects by default. You'll have access to all **Logging APIs** after you include `import Vapor` in a Swift file.

Vapor's Logging module includes the `Logger` protocol that declares common interfaces for all logger implementations. One example is **SwiftyBeaver Logger** for Vapor 3.0, `https://swiftybeaver.com/`. In Vapor 3.0, it includes a simple implementation, `PrintLogger` for the `Logger` protocol that prints out logging information on the Terminal screen.

The Logging module is intended to provide logging information while your Vapor app is running. It offers different log levels for you to classify different types of log messages:

Log Level	Usage
verbose	For logging messages including unimportant information
debug	For logging a diagnostic message for debugging
info	For logging an informational message
warning	For logging a warning message that needs your attention
error	For logging an error message
fatal	For logging a fatal error message

Typical Vapor `Logger` usage looks like this:

```
let logger = try container.make(Logger.self)
logger.info("Logger created!")
```

You can get an instance of `Logger` from any container in Vapor. A container in Vapor refers to a collection of registered services on an event loop and which are prescribed with specific configurations and environments.

Some common containers are application, request, and response. For example, you can get a `Logger` instance from Application:

```
let logger = try app.make(Logger.self)
```

Where `app` is an instance of your application.

Using the Logger API in a Kitura Project

Similarly, Kitura provides a unified interface for different kinds of logger implementations. Kitura uses the `LoggerAPI` as the Logging API throughout its implementation. In a typical Kitura project, `HeliumLogger` is often used. `HeliumLogger` is a lightweight implementation of `LoggerAPI` and it is available as an open source project.

If you use `kitura init` to create a boilerplate for your project, you do not need to import `LoggerAPI` and `HeliumLogger` specifically, as the packages have already been included as dependencies in your Kitura project.

You'll find the import `LoggerAPI` and import `HeliumLogger` statements at the beginning of `main.swift`:

```
...
// main.swift
import LoggerAPI
import HeliumLogger

do {
    HeliumLogger.use(LoggerMessageType.info) // [1]
...
} catch let error {
    Log.error(error.localizedDescription) // [2]
}
```

This code snippet shows how `LoggerAPI` and `HeliumLogger` are used in your project:

1. `HeliumLogger` is configured to use `LoggerMessageType.info`
2. Calls `Log.error()` to log an error message

The `LoggerMessageType` is an enum consisting of the following message types:

Message type	Usage
entry	For logging entering into a function
exit	For logging exiting a function
debug	For logging a diagnostic message for debugging
verbose	For logging messages including unimportant information
info	For logging informational messages
warning	For logging a warning message that needs your attention
error	For logging an error message

The message types are listed in ascending order of severity levels. If you choose to use a message type with a higher severity level, messages with lower severity will not be shown. Consider the `verbose` severity level:

```
HeliumLogger.use(LoggerMessageType.verbose)
```

When the `verbose` severity level is chosen, the `debug` messages will not be shown because the `debug` message type has a lower severity level.

If you change the `HeliumLogger` message type setting from `LoggerMessageType.info` to `LoggerMessageType.verbose` in [1] and rebuild your project using *command + R*, you're going to see additional information logged and printed on screen with the **[VERBOSE]** message type:

```
. . .
 [Mon Jun 25 11:31:32 2018] com.ibm.diagnostics.healthcenter.loader INFO:
Swift Application Metrics
 [2018-06-25T11:31:32.154+08:00] [VERBOSE] [Router.swift:108
init(mergeParameters:)] Router initialized
 [2018-06-25T11:31:32.200+08:00] [VERBOSE] [Router.swift:108
init(mergeParameters:)] Router initialized
 [2018-06-25T11:31:32.200+08:00] [INFO] [Metrics.swift:20
initializeMetrics(router:)] Initialized metrics.
 [2018-06-25T11:31:32.201+08:00] [VERBOSE] [Kitura.swift:104 run()]
Starting Kitura framework...
 [2018-06-25T11:31:32.201+08:00] [VERBOSE] [Kitura.swift:118 start()]
Starting an HTTP Server on port 8080...
 [2018-06-25T11:31:32.202+08:00] [INFO] [HTTPServer.swift:124 listen(on:)]
Listening on port 8080
 [2018-06-25T11:31:32.202+08:00] [VERBOSE] [HTTPServer.swift:125
listen(on:)] Options for port 8080: maxPendingConnections: 100,
allowPortReuse: false
```

Throughout your project, you can log different types of logging messages. Some examples are:

```
Log.warning("The input parameter is out of range!")
Log.debug("Variable x increments by 100.")
Log.error("Bummer! Something is not working well.")
```

Logging is a useful server-side development technique. Since your server application will be deployed and running on a hosted server remotely in a data center, logging is perhaps one of the best ways to detect problems and find out their root causes.

Debugging using the HTTP traffic monitoring tool

If the logging information leads you to believe that an error was caused by a specific network condition, you shall take a further step to investigate the networking cause. Since all server-side Swift frameworks accept HTTP requests and return HTTP responses, you'll find the HTTP traffic monitoring tool useful.

Debugging using Postman

One of such tools is **Postman** which you'll find very handy for all of your server-side Swift projects. You can download the tool at `https://www.getpostman.com/`.

The following screenshot shows you how to use Postman to analyze the HTTP response of a request using HTTP `GET` and the parameter `localhost:8080/student/Ryan`:

Run your *helloWorld* application for either Vapor or Kitura in the background. A response is available at the bottom after clicking on the **Send** button to send out the HTTP request you've created. You can check the headers as well as the body of the HTTP response from the server application.

Debugging using the curl command in the Terminal

Another tool is the `curl` command that you can use to make HTTP requests in the Terminal.

Run your `helloWorld` application for Vapor with `curl`:

```
$ curl "http://localhost:8080/student/Jane"
```

Here is the output you expected:

The student Jane's GPA is 3.91

When `verbose` mode is enabled with the `-v` flag, `curl` will give out more information on the HTTP request and response:

```
$ curl -v "http://localhost:8080/student/Jane"
* Trying ::1...
* TCP_NODELAY set
* Connected to localhost (::1) port 8080 (#0)
> GET /student/Jane HTTP/1.1
> Host: localhost:8080
> User-Agent: curl/7.55.1
> Accept: */*
>
< HTTP/1.1 200 OK
< content-type: text/plain; charset=utf-8
< content-length: 30
< date: Wed, 21 Nov 2018 06:46:44 GMT
<
* Connection #0 to host localhost left intact
The student Jane's GPA is 3.91
```

The `curl` command is extremely powerful. As you'll see in the next chapter, you can specify a `curl` command with HTTP `POST` and JSON data:

```
$ curl --header "Content-Type: application/json"   --request POST   --data
'{"id":"2","title":"New Test","content":"New Content"}'
http://localhost:8080/journal/
```

Summary

In this chapter, you learned how to write tests for server-side Swift applications using the XCTest framework. Sample tests are provided in Vapor and Kitura boilerplate projects, giving you a head start in adding unit tests to your project. In addition, you learned how to run unit tests in Xcode and use the code coverage feature in Xcode to improve your code's overall coverage. Next, you learned about the logging frameworks in Vapor and Kitura, and then HTTP traffic monitoring tools, such as Postman and `curl`. These unit tests and debugging techniques for server-side Swift projects are useful as you develop complex server-side Swift projects in the next chapters.

5
Setting Up Routes and Controllers

This chapter dives into the details of handling custom requests with **routes** and **controllers**. A *route* in a web framework is an object used to represent a custom request embedded in a URL, and a *controller* is the component that contains the business logic to handle the request routed to it. You'll learn how to add custom routes for requests, create controllers to handle the routes, and construct responses for the requests. You'll manipulate custom parameter types and process a group of routes in a collection. Finally, you'll learn how to take advantage of the `Codable` an class in Swift to encode and decode complex **JavaScript Object Notation** (**JSON**) objects in easy way.

Let's take a look at the topics covered in this chapter:

- Adding custom routes in a Vapor project
- Adding custom routes in a Kitura project

Adding custom routes in a Vapor project

In a typical model–view–controller architecture, you'll consciously separate data from the controller code that handles the data and from the view that represents a snapshot of the data. The data structure of your custom data is defined by its model. Routes are the endpoints for a client to query for the data:

Component	Usage	Recommended path in Vapor
Model	Description of data	`Sources/App/Models/`
View	Representation of data	`Resources/Views/`
Controller	Business logic of data	`Sources/App/Controllers`
Routes	Endpoints for data querying	`Sources/App/Routes`

In this chapter, you'll learn how to define the model of custom data used in a new application called `myJournal`, which is a server-side Swift power web application for personal journals.

Modeling your data with content type

As a starter, use the following commands in the Terminal to create a new application `myJournal` from Vapor's boilerplate project:

```
$ vapor new myJournal
$ cd myJournal
$ vapor xcode
```

Create a new directory, `/Sources/App/Models`, in Xcode, and add a new Swift file, `Entry.swift`, to the newly created directory:

```
// Entry.swift
import Vapor

struct Entry {
    var id: String // [1]
    var title: String?
    var content: String?
    init(id: String, title: String? = nil, content: String? = nil) {
        self.id = id
        self.title = title
        self.content = content
    }
}
```

`Entry` is a simple structure representing a journal entry. It has three fields and an initializer. The `id` string field is a **Universal Unique Identifier** (**UUID**) that will uniquely identify an `Entry` item.

Vapor 3 offers the `Content` type for you to parse and serialize specific data types conveniently. `Content` is built upon `Codable` to take advantage of the new data-handling infrastructure introduced in Swift 4.0. `Codable` makes encoding and parsing JSON extremely easy.

To add the implicit JSON format conversion to your data structure, you simply make sure your data structure conforms to the `Content` type:

```
struct Entry: Content {
    ...
}
```

In addition to JSON, the `Content` type can be used to represent various other format types, such as `protobuf`, `URLEncodedForm`, and `multipart`. You can parse and serialize content of all supported types using the same API in Vapor.

Vapor would parse the following HTTP request sent to your application:

```
POST /new HTTP/1.1
Content-Type: application/json
{
    "id": "999",
    "title": "My First Day at College",
    "content": "Met with a lot of people."
}
```

The key names and data types of input data exactly matches with that of the struct you've created.

Every HTTP request has a content container. When you conform `Entry` to `Content` type, Vapor will be able to decode the HTTP request message and create a new `Entry` object that represents the decoded content.

The following code shows how to process a request via an HTTP POST:

```
router.post("new") { req -> Future<HTTPStatus> in
    return req.content.decode(Entry.self).map { entry in
        print("Appended a new entry: \(entry)")
        return HTTPStatus.ok
    }
}
```

The `decode()` function returns a future for `HTTPStatus`. `Future` is the value you'll receive at a later time when an asynchronous process is complete. Decoding content from a request is considered to be asynchronous because it takes time to process the multiple parts decomposed from the content.

The following shows how a HTTP GET request is handled:

```
router.get("get") { req -> Entry in
    return Entry(id: "999", title: "First Day", content: "Lots of fun")
}
```

It will return JSON-encoded data of `Entry` and adds a default HTTP response with a `200 OK` status code.

Using controller for logical operations

For simplicity, your `myJournal` application persists data in memory. You'll use database operations for permanent data storage later on.

Even though you are not using a database operation, you'll implement the typical **Create**, **Read**, **Update**, and **Delete** (**CRUD**) operations for your data. Create the `JournalController.swift` file in the `/Sources/App/Controllers` directory:

```
// Journal controller
import Vapor

final class JournalController {
    var entries : Array<Entry> = Array() // [1]
    //: Get total number of entries
    func total() -> Int { // [2]
        return entries.count
    }
    //: Create a new journal entry
    func create(_ entry: Entry) -> Entry? { // [3]
        entries.append(entry)
        return entries.last
    }
    //: Read a journal entry
    func read(index: Int) -> Entry? { // [5]
        if let entry = entries.get(index: index) {
            return entry
        }
        return nil
    }
    //: Update the journal entry
    func update(index: Int, entry: Entry) -> Entry? { // [6]
        if let entry = entries.get(index: index) {
            entries[index] = entry
            return entry
        }
        return nil
    }
    //: Delete a journal entry
    func delete(index: Int) -> Entry? { // [7]
        if let _ = entries.get(index: index) {
            return entries.remove(at: index)
```

```
        }
        return nil
    }
}

extension Array {
    func get(index: Int) -> Element? { // [4]
        if index >= 0 && index < count {
            return self[index]
        }
        return nil
    }
}
```

The `journalController` class performs the following operations:

- Declares an array to hold all the instances of `Entry` in memory
- Returns the number of entries in the array
- Appends a new `Entry` item to the array
- Adds a safe `get(index:)` function to the `Array` extension that checks for bounds
- Retrieves an `Entry` item identified by a zero-based index from the array
- Replaces a current item in the array with the supplied `Entry` item
- Deletes an item from the array

An array in `[1]` will be used as in memory persistence and holds the references for all `Entry` instances. The `total()` method in `[2]` gives out the total number of entries in the array. In `[4]`, a safe `get(index:)` function is implemented as an extension to `Array`. It checks for the given index against the bounds of entries array. The functions in `[3]`, `[5]`,`[6]` and `[7]` implement the CRUD operations on the array.

Using Vapor's route collection

Vapor allows you to use **route collection** in managing the collection of related routes. With route collection, you can divide your routes and let one sub-router that implements `RouteCollection` protocol handle a segment of routes. Each sub-router doesn't need to handle all routes, as it is responsible for the routes that it can handle only.

In /Sources/App/routes.swift, instantiate a RouteCollection and register it with the router:

```
import Vapor

/// Register your application's routes here
public func routes(_ router: Router) throws {

    let journalRoutes = JournalRoutes()
    try router.register(collection: journalRoutes)
}
```

Create the Routes directory under /Sources/App and add JournalRoutes.swift to this new directory:

```
// JournalRoutes.swift
import Vapor

struct JournalRoutes : RouteCollection { // [1]
    let journal = JournalController() // [2]
    func boot(router: Router) throws { // [3]
      // to be implemented later
    }
    // Add route handlers here // [4]
}
```

All the routes and their handlers will go to this new file. The JournalRoutes struct does several things:

1. Implements the RouteCollection protocol
2. Creates an instance of JournalController that works with in-memory persistence
3. Adds the boot(router:) function to for one-time set up. Routes will be implemented here
4. Adds the rest of the route handlers right after the boot(router:) function

Even though the implementation of RouteCollection is straightforward, it is extremely useful for organizing your routes into different functional areas. For example, you may want to use RouteCollection to conveniently designate user access level to different content areas.

Grouping related routes

You'll find it convenient to group all routes for `JournalController` together. Vapor actually offers **route grouping** exactly for that.

Add the following route handlers to the `JournalRoutes` struct in the `/Sources/App/Routes/JournalRoutes.swift` file you've just created:

```
import Vapor

struct JournalRoutes : RouteCollection {
    let journal = JournalController()
    func boot(router: Router) throws {
        let topRouter = router.grouped("journal") // [1]
        topRouter.get(use: getTotal)
        topRouter.post(use: newEntry)
        let entryRouter = router.grouped("journal", Int.parameter) // [2]
        entryRouter.get(use: getEntry)
        entryRouter.put(use: editEntry)
        entryRouter.delete(use: removeEntry)
    }
    // Add route handlers here // [3]
```

The `JournalRoutes` struct lays out two groups of routes, as follows:

1. It creates the route group `/journal` for routes that retrieve all entries with HTTP GET and posts a new entry with HTTP POST
2. It creates the second route group, `/journal/Int.parameter`, for routes that retrieve an entry with HTTP GET, updates an entry with HTTP UPDATE, and removes an entry with HTTP DELETE
3. It adds all the required route-handler functions right after the `boot(router:)` function

The first route group in [1] tells Vapor to direct all URL requests to `/journal`, while the second group in [2] directs all requests to `/journal/Int.parameter` itself. The path, `Int.parameter`, is a dynamic parameter. The closures in a route group can access this dynamic parameter using `req.parameters.next()`.

Implementing route handlers

Next, you will implement the handlers used in both route groups.

Retrieving all entries

Append the `getTotal()` function to the line right after `boot(router:)`:

```
func getTotal(_ req: Request) -> String {
    let total = journal.total()
    print("Total Records: \(total)")
    return "\(total)"
}
```

The function simply calls the `JournalController total()` function and return the total count of entries.

Creating a new entry with a unique ID

Following `getTotal()`, add the following handler for creating a new entry:

```
func newEntry(_ req: Request) throws -> Future<HTTPStatus> { // [1]
    let newID = UUID().uuidString // [2]
    return try req.content.decode(Entry.self).map(to: HTTPStatus.self) {
entry in // [3]
        let newEntry = Entry(id: newID,
                            title: entry.title,
                            content: entry.content) // [4]
        guard let result = self.journal.create(newEntry) else { // [5]
            throw Abort(.badRequest) // [6]
        }
        print("Created: \(result)")
        return .ok // [7]
    }
}
```

The `newEntry(_ req:)` function handles the creation of a new entry in several steps:

1. Constructs a throwable function that returns a Future of `HTTPStatus`
2. Uses Swift's `UUID()` to create a unique ID for the new entry
3. Decodes the JSON object embedded in an HTTP request and serializes to an entry instance
4. Instantiates a new entry object using the new ID
5. Invokes the `create()` function of `RouteController` to add the new entry object to in-memory storage
6. Throws an `Abort` if the last step returns nil
7. Returns `HTTPStatus.ok` when reaching the end of the function

In `[4]`, whatever ID that has been submitted is simply ignored, since the `id` field is always over-written with a new UUID. This guarantees that the `id` is unique, and this is very useful for you to debug the CRUD operations you've implemented.

The `Abort` in `[6]` is a default implementation of the `AboutError` protocol. Vapor always displays any error code specified in `Abort` to the end user, even in production mode where most error messages are suppressed.

Retrieving an entry

The handlers in the route group `/journal/Int.parameter` deal with a specific entry. The first handler belonging to this route group is `getEntry()`:

```
func getEntry(_ req: Request) throws -> Entry {
    let index = try req.parameters.next(Int.self) // [1]
    let res = req.makeResponse() // [2]
    guard let entry = journal.read(index: index) else {
        throw Abort(.badRequest)
    }
    print("Read: \(entry)")
    try res.content.encode(entry, as: .formData) // [3]
    return entry
}
```

There are several interesting steps in the preceding implementation:

1. Retrieve the index of an `Entry` object, using the `req.parameters.next()` command
2. Create a response instance by calling the `makeResponse()` method
3. Serialize the `Entry` object that conforms to `Content` into a JSON object and return

All handlers in this route group use the same `req.parameters.next()` command in `[1]` to work with a specific `Entry` object. The line at `[3]` demonstrates how easy it is to serialize a data model into a JSON object once the model conforms to the `Content` protocol.

Updating an entry

The handler for updating an entry is the second handler belonging to the
`/journal/Int.parameter` route group:

```
func editEntry(_ req: Request) throws -> Future<HTTPStatus> {
    let index = try req.parameters.next(Int.self)
    let newID = UUID().uuidString
    return try req.content.decode(Entry.self).map(to: HTTPStatus.self) {
entry in // [1]
        let newEntry = Entry(id: newID,
                             title: entry.title,
                             content: entry.content)
        guard let result = self.journal.update(index: index, entry:
newEntry) else {
            throw Abort(.badRequest)
        }
        print("Updated: \(result)")
        return .ok
    }
}
```

The line at [1] shows that the JSON object is decoded and serialized into an `Entry` object,
and then an array containing `HTTPStatus` is returned from the mapping of a result using
`map(to:)`.

Deleting an entry

The last handler in the `/journal/Int.parameter` route group implements the deletion of
an entry using the element's index:

```
func removeEntry(_ req: Request) throws -> HTTPStatus {
    let index = try req.parameters.next(Int.self)
    guard let result = self.journal.delete(index: index) else {
        throw Abort(.badRequest)
    }
    print("Deleted: \(result)")
    return .ok
}
```

Testing the routes

Build and run your Vapor application:

```
$ vapor build
$ vapor run
```

You can check all the route handlers using Postman. For example, create a HTTP POST request to `localhost:8080/journal/` while your Vapor application is running locally:

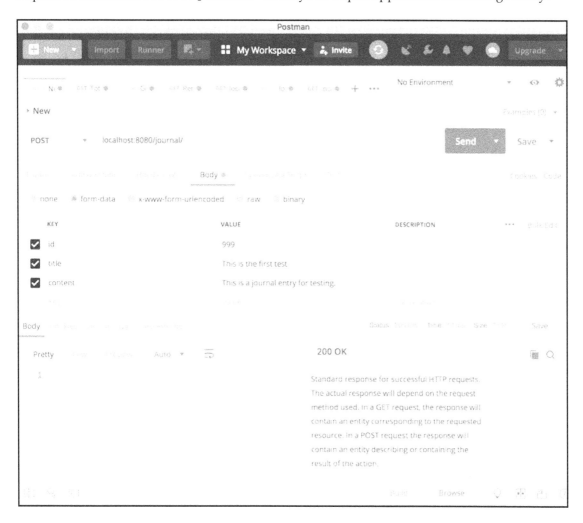

Alternatively, you can use the `curl` tool to make a request in the Terminal:

```
$ curl --header "Content-Type: application/json"   --request POST   --data
'{"id":"2","title":"New Test","content":"New Content"}'
http://localhost:8080/journal/
```

The output of the two tests looks like the following:

```
Server starting on http://localhost:8080
Created: Entry(id: "4BCDD028-ECF0-4D43-81FD-2C8318781480", title:
Optional("11111"), content: Optional("111111"))
Created: Entry(id: "85EC887F-D0D5-4E10-A3B7-A76E0AF3D654", title:
Optional("New Test"), content: Optional("New Content"))
```

Adding custom routes in a Kitura project

Kitura offers powerful route-handling features similar to what you've learned about in the previous Vapor project. All Kitura versions since Kitura 2.0 take advantage of `Codable` in Swift 4.1 for JSON encoding and parsing, in a way similar to `Content` type in Vapor. In previous versions prior to Kitura 2.0, you would need to use a third-party library such as `SwiftyJSON` and write more tedious code for JSON encoding and decoding.

Just as `Codable` routing dramatically simplifies the handling of JSON-encoded data from a client's HTTP requests in the server, Kitura also provides a connector called `KituraKit` that mirrors `Codable` routing in the implementation of a client. With `KituraKit`, it simplifies the programming for JSON encoding and decoding via a concept called a client/server `Contract`.

Next, you'll conform your data model to `Codable`, implement `Controller` for logical operations, adding `Codable` routes, and handling Kitura routes.

Modeling Codable data

You can run the following commands on the Terminal to create your `myJournal` application from the Kitura boilerplate project:

```
$ mkdir myJournal
$ cd myJournal
$ kitura init
$ swift run
$ open ./myJournal.xcodeproj
```

Create a new directory, `/Sources/Application/Models`, and add a new Swift file, `Entry.swift`, to the directory:

```
import Foundation

struct Entry: Codable {

  var id: String
  var title: String?
  var content: String?

  init(id: String, title: String? = nil, content: String? = nil) {
  self.id = id
  self.title = title
  self.content = content
  }
}
```

The implementation of the `Entry` data structure is similar to that in the `myJournal` Vapor project. While Kitura's `Entry` implements `Codable` protocol directly, Vapor's `Entry` implements `Content`, which builds on top of `Codable`.

Using controllers for logical operations

Create the `/Source/Application/Controllers` directory and add the same `JournalController.swift` you have used in your `myJournal` Vapor project to this new directory:

File: `/Sources/Application/Controllers/JournalController.swift`:

```
import Foundation

final class JournalController {
    var entries : Array<Entry> = Array()
    //: Get total number of entries
    func total() -> Int {
        return entries.count
    }
    //: Create a new journal entry
    func create(_ entry: Entry) -> Entry? {
        entries.append(entry)
        return entries.last
    }
    //: Read a journal entry
    func read(index: Int) -> Entry? {
```

```
            if let entry = entries.get(index: index) {
                return entry
            }
            return nil
        }
        //: Update the journal entry
        func update(index: Int, entry: Entry) -> Entry? {
            if let entry = entries.get(index: index) {
                entries[index] = entry
                return entry
            }
            return nil
        }
        //: Delete a journal entry
        func delete(index: Int) -> Entry? {
            if let _ = entries.get(index: index) {
                return entries.remove(at: index)
            }
            return nil
        }
    }

    extension Array {
        func get(index: Int) -> Element? {
            if index >= 0 && index < count {
                return self[index]
            }
            return nil
        }
    }
```

As you can see, the implementation of `JournalController` is agnostic to either the Vapor or Kitura framework. The *JournalController.swift* file here is **identical** to the same file in your previous Vapor project. Refer to the previous sections if you are looking for more details of the `JournalController` class.

Implementing Codable routing

Now, you can proceed to implement route handlers that work with the controller's CRUD operations. Create another new directory, `/Sources/Application/Routes`, and add the following `JournalRoute.swift` file to it:

```
import Foundation
import Kitura
```

```
struct JournalRoutes {

    let journal = JournalController()
    func newEntry(entry: Entry, completion: (Entry?, RequestError?) -> Void
) {
        let newID = UUID().uuidString
        if let result = journal.create(Entry(id: newID,
                                             title: entry.title,
                                             content: entry.content)) {
            print("Created: \(result)")
            completion(result, nil)
        } else {
            completion(Entry(id: "-1"), nil)
        }
    }

    func editEntry(id: Int, new: Entry, completion: (Entry?, RequestError?)
-> Void ) -> Void {
        let newID = UUID().uuidString
        if let result = journal.update(index: id,
                                       entry: Entry(id: newID,
                                                    title: new.title,
                                                    content: new.content))
{
            print("Updated: \(result)")
            completion(result, nil)
        } else {
            completion(nil, .notFound)
        }
    }
    func getEntry(index: Int, completion: (Entry?, RequestError?) -> Void )
{
        if let entry = journal.read(index: index) {
            completion(entry, nil)
            return
        }
        completion(nil, .notFound)
        return
    }

    func removeEntry(id: Int, completion: (RequestError?) -> Void ) -> Void
{
        if let result = self.journal.delete(index: id) {
            print("Deleted: \(result)")
            completion(nil)
            return
        }
        completion(.notFound)
```

```
        }
    }
```

The previous code is the implementation of four Codable CRUD routes. The Codable routing function that handles a HTTP POST request for a new entry takes in two arguments: an `Entry` object, and a `completion` closure:

```
func newEntry(entry: Entry, completion: (Entry?, RequestError?) -> Void ) {
        let newID = UUID().uuidString
        if let result = journal.create(Entry(id: newID,
                                              title: entry.title,
                                              content: entry.content)) {
            print("Created: \(result)")
            completion(result, nil)
        } else {
            completion(Entry(id: "-1"), nil)
        }
    }
```

When the provided `Entry` object is successfully added to the in-memory array, the `newEntry(entry:completion:)` function calls `completion()`, which then automatically sends the HTTP response back to the client.

If an entry exists, an additional argument for the ID of existing entry is required. For the `editEntry(id:new:completion:)` function, it takes three arguments, the `id` of an existing `Entry` object, a new `Entry` object that is going to replace the existing one, and a `completion` closure:

```
func editEntry(id: Int, new: Entry, completion: (Entry?, RequestError?) ->
Void ) -> Void {
    let newID = UUID().uuidString
    if let result = journal.update(index: id,
                                   entry: Entry(id: newID,
                                                title: new.title,
                                                content: new.content)) {
        print("Updated: \(result)")
        completion(result, nil)
    } else {
        completion(nil, .notFound)
    }
}
```

The `editEntry(id:new:completion:)` function simply calls
`JournalController.update(index:entry:)` to update the object in the in-memory
array with the specified index. The function calls a `completion()` closure with an optional
of `Entry` when the `Entry` object is successfully updated; otherwise, it calls a
`completion()` closure with `nil` and `.notFound` error code.

The next two functions, `getEntry(id:completion:)` and
`removeEntry(id:completion)`, are also applicable to an existing `Entry` object so they
both take in `id` and `completion` as arguments. The `getEntry(id:completion:)`
function calls `JournalController.read(index)` to retrieve the existing `Entry` object:

```
func getEntry(index: Int, completion: (Entry?, RequestError?) -> Void ) {
    if let entry = journal.read(index: index) {
        completion(entry, nil)
        return
    }
    completion(nil, .notFound)
    return
}
```

Similarly, the `removeEntry(id:completion:)` function calls
`JournalController.delete(index)` to delete the existing `Entry` object from the in-
memory array:

```
func removeEntry(id: Int, completion: (RequestError?) -> Void ) -> Void {
    if let result = self.journal.delete(index: id) {
        print("Deleted: \(result)")
        completion(nil)
        return
    }
    completion(.notFound)
}
```

That's all the route handlers you're going to use. Next, you'll move on to define the
endpoints.

Handling Kitura routes

Finally, you can put everything together by specifying all the endpoints that connect routes
to handlers.

In the `postInit()` method of the `App` class, you're going to tell the router to direct appropriate HTTP requests to the CRUD Codable routes defined in `JournalRoutes.swift`:

```
func postInit() throws {
    let journalRoutes = JournalRoutes() // [1]
    // Endpoints
    initializeHealthRoutes(app: self)
    router.get("/journal") { _, response, _ in // [2]
        let total = journalRoutes.getTotal()
        response.send("\(total)")
    }
    router.post("/journal", handler: journalRoutes.newEntry) // [3]
    router.get("/journal", handler: journalRoutes.getEntry) // [4]
    router.put("/journal", handler: journalRoutes.editEntry) // [5]
    router.delete("/journal", handler: journalRoutes.removeEntry) // [6]
}
```

The following operations are added to the previous code:

1. Instantiate the `JournalRoutes` object
2. Define a normal route handling closure
3. Direct the handling of HTTP POST /journal to `newEntry()` of `JournalRoute`
4. Direct the handling of HTTP GET /journal to `getEntry()` of `JournalRoute`
5. Direct the handling of HTTP PUT /journal to `editEntry()` of `JournalRoute`
6. Direct the handling of HTTP DELETE /journal to `removeEntry()` of `JournalRoute`

Both normal and Codable routing handlers are implemented. Since the normal route handling in [2] doesn't require its response data to be `Codable`, we can use a string in `response.send()`. The handlers in [3-6] direct route handling to the functions that use `Codable` data directly.

You can check Kitura's route handlers using Postman. For route handling in Kitura, it expects the HTTP request data to be URL encoded. Make sure that you choose the second option, as shown in the following screenshot:

Summary

In this chapter, you learned how to add custom routes and controllers to your Vapor and Kitura applications. For simplicity, in-memory storage was used in both applications, but the controller classes can be later adopted to work with databases, which we will see in `Chapter 8`, *Employing the Storage Framework*. Both Vapor and Kitura make their data models conform to the `Codable` for `Encodable` and `Decodable` protocols, making the handling of JSON conversion to data models extremely easy. In the next chapter, you'll continue to build upon the routes and controllers code you have and apply template engines to create and render web pages automatically.

6
Working with Template Engines

This chapter introduces you to two templating engines: **Leaf** for Vapor and **Stencil** for Kitura. Templating languages allow you to work with content automatically generated by a script. For dynamic content, you'll learn how template engines help to accelerate development for dynamic web pages. Dynamic content creation is useful when presenting results of data generated at run-time and that are not known beforehand. For static content, you'll learn how templating engines help to ensure a consistent structure, such as headers and footers, and appearance characteristics, such as color scheme and background. You'll further get introduced to the nuts and bolts of the Leaf and Stencil templating languages and learn how to use variables and tags in template scripts to communicate information between Swift classes and script functions.

Let's take a look at the topics covered in this chapter:

- Using the Leaf templating engine in Vapor
- Templating with Stencil in a Kitura project

Using the Leaf templating engine in Vapor

Leaf is Vapor's official templating engine and it was created specifically for Vapor. With the template engine, you'll find it easy to pass information from the Swift source code to the Leaf template. The compiled templating source code will then be used to render the final HTML content automatically for you.

There are many different reasons for using a template language. First, you can use templates to help reuse code that's shared across multiple web pages. Next, you can use various tagging syntax to help generate code dynamically and programmatically. Finally, you can embed one template into another and doing so helps you accelerate the development of content.

You will continue the `myJournal` project from the previous chapter and use the Leaf template engine to enhance the project's features.

Configuring the Leaf templating engine

In order to use Leaf template engine in your Vapor project, you're required to configure for it using the Swift Package Manager.

In `Package.swift`, add the Leaf template engine as one of the package dependencies and include Leaf in the `App` build target:

```
// swift-tools-version:4.0
import PackageDescription

let package = Package(
    name: "myJournal",
    dependencies: [
        //  A server-side Swift web framework.
        .package(url: "https://github.com/vapor/vapor.git", from: "3.0.0"),
        //  Swift ORM (queries, models, relations, etc) built on SQLite 3.
        .package(url: "https://github.com/vapor/fluent-sqlite.git", from:
"3.0.0"),
        // Leaf template engine
        .package(url: "https://github.com/vapor/leaf.git", from: "3.0.0")
    ],
    targets: [
    .target(name: "App", dependencies: ["FluentSQLite", "Vapor", "Leaf"]),
    .target(name: "Run", dependencies: ["App"]),
    .testTarget(name: "AppTests", dependencies: ["App"])
    ]
)
```

You'll typically put your Leaf template files in the `/Resources/Views` directory. You won't find this directory if you start your project from Vapor's boilerplate code. Create this directory now.

In `configure.swift`, add the code to register and configure the Leaf templating engine:

```
// File: configure.swift
import Leaf . // [1]
...
public func configure(_ config: inout Config, _ env: inout Environment, _
services: inout Services) throws {
    ...
    /// Register Leaf templating engine
    try services.register(LeafProvider())  // [2]
    ...
    config.prefer(LeafRenderer.self, for: ViewRenderer.self) // [3]
}
```

Don't forget to import the Leaf package [1] at the beginning of `configure.swift`. In `configure()`, use `services.register()` function to register the Leaf templating engine [2] and add the `config.prefer()` line towards the end of the `configure()` function [3].

The Leaf templating engine is ready for you to use.

Using the basic functions of the Leaf templating engine

After registering and configuring for the Leaf templating engine, you're about to explore some basic functions offered by Leaf.

Follow these steps to render the main page using Leaf:

1. First, you need to import the Leaf module into your file. Add this line to `routes.swift`:

   ```
   import Leaf
   ```

2. The following shows you the basic syntax of rendering a Leaf template from a route:

   ```
   router.get { req -> Future<View> in // [1]
       let leaf = try req.make(LeafRenderer.self) // [2]
       let context = [String: String]() // [3]
       return leaf.render("main", context) // [4]
   }
   ```

   There are four steps involved in rendering a page:

   1. Return a future view object in a route's closure
   2. Get a handler to the Leaf templating engine from a container
   3. Create a `Context` dictionary used to pass parameters into the template
   4. Render the specific Leaf template file with the `Context` dictionary

   Since the rendering of a template takes some time, Leaf always renders a template asynchronously and returns the `Future` of `View` [1]. The HTTP request is a `Container` in Vapor, so you are able to retrieve a `leaf` handler from `req` [2]. The dictionary in [3] is a flexible and direct way for you to pass parameters into the templating engine during the rendering of the template [4].

Following the same four-step processing, you can now modify the `getTotal()` route handler in `/Sources/App/Routes/JournalRoutes.swift` from *Chapter 5, Setting up Routes and Controllers*. Instead of returning `String` as the HTTP response, you now add `count` to the context of template rendering:

```
...
import Leaf

struct JournalRoutes : RouteCollection {
...
    func getAll(_ req: Request) throws -> Future<View> {
        let total = journal.total()
        let leaf = try req.make(LeafRenderer.self)
        let context = ["count": total]
        return leaf.render("main", context)
    }
...
}
```

3. Create the corresponding `main.leaf` file in the `/Resources/Views` directory:

```
<!DOCTYPE html>
<html lang="en">
<head>
<meta charset="utf-8" />
<title>Hello World</title>
</head>
<body>
<h1>Hello World</h1>
Count: #(count)
</body>
</html>
```

It looks like a normal HTML page, except that you see `tag #(count)`, which instructs the Leaf templating engine to replace it with the count value passing in via `Context`.

4. Use your web browser and direct it to `localhost:8080/journal/total`:

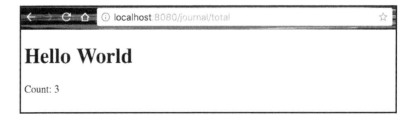

Viola! Your `myJournal` application now returns a real web page for your client's request.

Using variables and tags in Leaf templating

The Leaf templating engine uses the `#` token to represent a tag, as seen in `#(count)` from the previous HTML code. The Leaf tag has general syntax: `#Name( Args ){ Body }`, where `Name` is the tag's name, `Arg` is a list of expected arguments, and `Body` is an optional element that often includes additional content.

Vapor provides many useful tagging usages and they are summarized in the following:

Tag	Usage	
`#capitalize(Var)`	Converts `Var` into capitals	`#capitalize(title)`
`#uppercase(Var)`	Converts `Var` into all uppercase	`#uppercase(title)`
`#lowercase(Var)`	Converts `Var` into all lowercase	`#lowercase(title)`
`#if(Condition)`	Executes only if `Condition` is met	`#if(title) {` `The title is #(title) }`
`#contains(Array, Val)`	Returns `true` if `Val` is contained in `Array`	`#if(contains(users,` `"John")) { Welcome! }`
`#for(Var in Array) {}`	Loops `Var` over `Array`	`#for(user in users){` `#(user) }`
`#count(Array)`	Returns the number of items in `Array`	`We have #count(users)` `participants`
`#set(Tag){}`	Sets up a tag to be used by Leaf	`#set("title"){ Welcome to` `My Home }`
`#get(Tag)`	Gets the content associated with `Tag`	`#get("title")`
`#embed(Page)`	Inserts another `Page` into the current one	`#embed("footer")`

Setting a variable

Use `#set(){}` to declare a new tag (variable). For example, you can set the title of a page, as follows:

```
\#set("title") { Welcome to my home page }
```

Working with context

The `context` dictionary allows you to pass custom data to the renderer for `main.leaf`:

```
let context = ["title": "Welcome to my homepage", "user": "John Doe"]
return try leaf.make("main", context)
```

The previous code will expose `title` and `user` to your Leaf template.

In `main.leaf`, you can use the `title` and `user` tags passed in using `Context`:

```
<h1>#(title)</h1>
<p>Greetings, #(user). Welcome to my homepage.</p>
```

Looping through a collection

To loop through a collection, you can use the `#for` tag. For example, you can pass three users in `Context`:

```
let context = ["users": ["John", "Angus", "Mary"]]
```

In the HTML code, you can loop through an array of items using Leaf's `#for` tag:

```
<h2>Event Participants</h2>
#for(user in users){ <li>#(user)</li> }
```

Within the `#for` loop, you could use the following loop variables to handle more complex situation:

- `isFirst`: `true` if the current iteration is the first one
- `isLast`: `true` if the current iteration is the last one
- `index`: `count` of the current iteration

The following HTML sample code shows how to use the `isLast` variable to format the last user in a list:

```
This year's participants are
#for(user in users){
  #if(isLast) { and #(user). }
  else { #(user), }
```

Checking conditions

Vapor template uses `#if(){} else {}` to check a `condition`, as in the following example:

```
#set("guest") { John }
#if(user == guest) {
  You're welcome.
} else {
  Sorry, this site is not open to public.
}
```

When the tag is part of your condition, you can omit # for the inner tag, like this:

```
#if(lowercase(user) == lowercase(guest)) {
  ...
}
```

Embedding other templates

Leaf also allows you to insert another Leaf template into your template file using the `#embed` tag:

```
#embed("another")
```

When doing this, you should omit the template's file extension.

A common practice for template embedding is to include header and footer templates in each of your pages:

```
#embed("header")
#embed("footer")
```

This makes it easy for updating and propagating changes to all of your web pages.

You can also automate the creation of a child page using a master template:

```
#set("user") { <b>John Doe</b> }
#embed("master")
```

`master.leaf` may look like this:

```
<html>
<head><title>Welcome to My Homepage</title></head>
<body>Hi #get(user), have a great day!</body>
</html>
```

You can use `#set()` to set up and assign a variable, then use `#get()` to retrieve it later on.

Adding more Leaf templates

Now you can add more Leaf templates to the `myJournal` application:

1. Create header and footer templates that will be shared by every other web pages. The following is a sample header template:

```
//File: header.leaf
<!DOCTYPE html>
<html lang="en">
<head>
<meta charset="utf-8" />
<title>#(title)</title>
</head>
<body>
```

Similarly, following is a sample footer template:

```
// footer.leaf
<hr>
<center>
#(title) Application by #(author)
</center>
</body>
</html>
```

2. Modify the `main.leaf` template to embed both the header and footer templates:

```
// main.leaf
#embed("header")
<h1>#(title)</h1>
Count: #(count)
#embed("footer")
```

3. In the `getTotal()` route handler, add `title`, `author`, and `count` to the `context` dictionary for the templating engine:

```
// journalroutes.swift
let title = "My Journal"
let author = "Angus"
func boot(router: Router) throws {
...
    func getTotal(_ req: Request) throws -> Future<View> {
        let total = journal.total()
```

```
        let count = "\(total)"
        let leaf = try req.make(LeafRenderer.self)
        let context = ["title": title, "author": author, "count":
count]
        return leaf.render("main", context)
    }
...
```

4. Execute `localhost:8080/journal/total` again to check everything is running as expected:

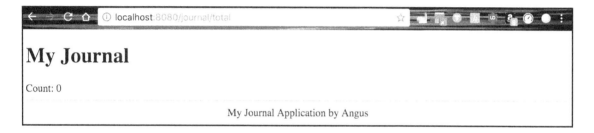

Displaying all journal entries

You can further enhance the `getTotal()` feature by turning it into a main page that displays all journal entries in a single web page:

1. Create the `JournalContext` struct that is `Encodable`:

```
struct JournalRoutes : RouteCollection {
...
    struct JournalContext : Encodable {
        let title: String
        let author: String
        let count: String
        let entries: [Entry]
    }
...
}
```

You use the `Encodable` struct to represent all parameters you pass into the Leaf templating engine. The last parameter is the entire dictionary of `Entry`.

2. Add a new function, `readAll()`, in your `JournalController()` class:

```
//: Read all journal entries
func readAll() -> [Entry] {
    return entries
}
```

3. In `getTotal()`, it simply passes everything including the `entries` dictionary to the Leaf engine:

```
func getTotal(_ req: Request) throws -> Future<View> {
    let total = journal.total()
    let entries : [Entry] = journal.readAll()
    let count = "\(total)"
    let leaf = try req.make(LeafRenderer.self)
    let context = JournalContext(title: title, author: author,
count: count, entries: entries)
    return leaf.render("main", context)
}
```

4. You use the `#for()` tag to loop through each item of entries, displaying each item's `title` and `content`:

```
// main.leaf
#embed("header")
<h1>#(title)</h1>

#for(entry in entries) {
    <hr>
    <h2>#(entry.title)</h2>
    #(entry.content)
}
#embed("footer")
```

5. The result looks like the following screenshot:

Completing the features

Following the similar steps in the previous example, you can complete the template rendering for all other CRUD routes:

1. The updated JournalRoutes is shown in the following:

```
import Vapor
import Leaf

struct JournalRoutes : RouteCollection {
    let journal = JournalController()
    let mainPage = "/journal/all"
    let title = "My Journal"
    let author = "Angus"
    struct JournalContext : Encodable {
        let title: String
        let author: String
        let count: String
        let entries: [Entry]
    }
    struct EntryContext : Encodable {
        let title: String
        let author: String
```

```
            let index: Int
            let entry: Entry
        }
        func boot(router: Router) throws {
            let topRouter = router.grouped("journal")
            topRouter.get("", use: getAll)
            topRouter.get("all", use: getAll)
            topRouter.get("create", use: createEntry)
            topRouter.post("new", use: newEntry)
            let entryRouter = router.grouped("journal", Int.parameter)
            entryRouter.get("get", use: getEntry)
            entryRouter.post("edit", use: editEntry)
            entryRouter.get("remove", use: removeEntry)
        }
        func getAll(_ req: Request) throws -> Future<View> {
            let total = journal.total()
            let entries : [Entry] = journal.readAll()
            let count = "\(total)"
            let leaf = try req.make(LeafRenderer.self)
            let context = JournalContext(title: title, author: author,
count: count, entries: entries)
            return leaf.render("main", context)
        }
        func createEntry(_ req: Request) throws -> Future<View> {
            let leaf = try req.make(LeafRenderer.self)
            let context = ["title": title, "author": author]
            return leaf.render("new", context)
        }
        func newEntry(_ req: Request) throws -> Future<Response> {
            let newID = UUID().uuidString
            return try req.content.decode(Entry.self).map(to:
Response.self) { entry in
                if let result = self.journal.create(Entry(id: newID,
                                                    title:
entry.title,
                                                    content:
entry.content)) {
                    print("Created: \(result)")
                }
                return req.redirect(to: self.mainPage) // [1]
            }
        }
        func getEntry(_ req: Request) throws -> Future<View> {
            let index = try req.parameters.next(Int.self)
            let leaf = try req.make(LeafRenderer.self)
            var entry = Entry(id: "-1")
            if let result = journal.read(index: index) {
                entry = result
```

```
        }
        let context = EntryContext(title: title, author: author,
index: index, entry: entry)
        return leaf.render("entry", context)
    }
    func editEntry(_ req: Request) throws -> Future<Response> {
        let index = try req.parameters.next(Int.self)
        return try req.content.decode(Entry.self).map(to:
Response.self) { entry in
            if let result = self.journal.update(index: index,
                                              entry: Entry(id:
entry.id,
                                                            title:
entry.title,
content: entry.content)) {
                print("Updated: \(result)")
            }
            return req.redirect(to: self.mainPage)
        }
    }

    func removeEntry(_ req: Request) throws -> Response {
        let index = try req.parameters.next(Int.self)
        if let result = self.journal.delete(index: index) {
            print("Deleted: \(result)")
        }
        return req.redirect(to: mainPage)
    }
}
```

2. Once a new entry has been added to your local storage, as shown in the
   `newEntry()` function [1], you can redirect the response to the main page like
   this:

```
return req.redirect(to: self.mainPage)
```

3. Now add all of the templates for the main page, as shown in the following. First is the header template:

```
// header.leaf
<!DOCTYPE html>
<html lang="en">
<head>
<meta charset="utf-8" />
<title>#(title)</title>
</head>
<body>
```

This is followed by the footer template:

```
// footer.leaf
<hr>
<center>
#(title) Application by #(author).
</center>
</body>
</html>
```

And then there's the main template:

```
// main.leaf
#embed("header")
<h1>#(title)</h1>

[   <a href="/journal/create">Add New Entry</a>  ]
<P>
#for(entry in entries) {
    <hr>
    <h2>#(entry.title)</h2>
    #(entry.content)
    <BR> [   <a href="./#(index)/get">Edit</a>  |   <a
href="./#(index)/remove">Remove</a>  ]
    <BR> <em>Index:#(index) out of #(count); ID: #(entry.id);</em>
}
#embed("footer")
```

The rendering output of the main page looks like the following screenshot:

There are links for adding a new entry or editing/removing each existing entry.

4. The **Add New Entry** link takes a user to a form for submitting new entries for `title` and `content`:

```
// new.leaf
#embed("header")
<h1>Create a Journal Entry</h1>
<form action="/journal/new/" method="post">
<input name="id" type="hidden" value="-1" />
<input name="title" type="text" placeholder="Enter title here" />
<P>
<textarea name="content" placeholder="Enter your journal content
here..." rows="5">

</textarea>
<P>
<button type="submit" class="btn btn-lg btn-
primary">Submit</button>
</form>
#embed("footer")
```

The previous code is a simple HTML form that contains different types of elements, including a hidden text field for `id`, a text field for `title`, a `textarea` for `content`, and a **Submit** button.

When rendered, the `new.leaf` template displays a form for a user to enter the title and content:

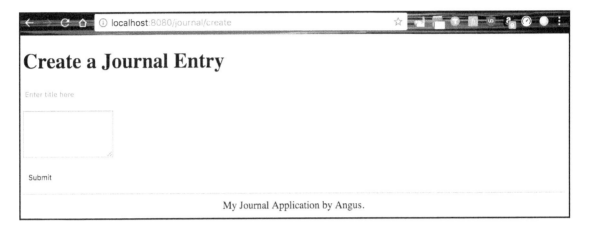

After form submission, the user will be redirected to the main page.

5. If the user clicks on the **Edit** link underneath an entry, another form will be used:

```
// entry.leaf
#embed("header")
<h1>Edit a Journal Entry</h1>
<form action="/journal/#(index)/edit/" method="post">
<input name="id" type="hidden" value=#(entry.id)" />
<input name="title" type="text" value="#(entry.title)" />
<P>
<textarea name="content" rows="5">
#(entry.content)
</textarea>
<P>
<button type="submit" class="btn btn-lg btn-
primary">Submit</button>
<BR>
<em>Index:#(index); ID: #(entry.id)</em>

#embed("footer")
```

The HTML form for editing an entry is similar to that of creating an entry, except that all of the input and textarea elements will be populated with the original values.

The output of `entry.leaf` template is rendered as follows:

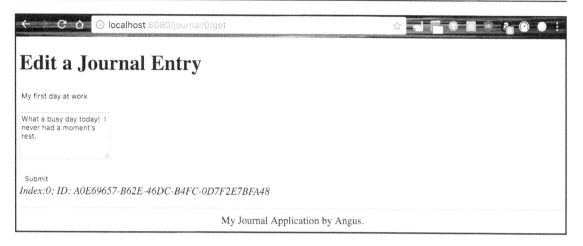

The hidden `id` input field is populated with the actual `id` value of entry that the user selected so the updated entry will continue to use the same ID even after updating. The form will also be populated with the current title and content.

That's all. Now you have a quite functional web application that allows users to submit a new journal entry and edit or remove an existing entry.

Templating with Stencil in a Kitura project

Unlike Vapor, which adopts Leaf as its own templating engine, Kitura allows support for multiple templating engines through its `TemplateEngine` protocol. Kitura's templating engine API provides a unified interface for multiple templating engines. Currently three templating engines are included in Kitura:

- Stencil
- Mustache
- Markdown

You'll learn about Stencil extensively in this chapter because Stencil has the best coverage and support among the three templating engines in the Kitura's developer community. Stencil works similarly to Vapor's Leaf in generating dynamic frontend web pages. The templating engine scans for variables and tags in a template file and replaces them with actual values or places control flows that render filtered content. Given Stencil's maturity, it offers a richer set of features such as loops, conditions, blocks, filters, and tags. Like Vapor's Leaf, Stencil is also easy to extend its features by adding your own custom filters and tags.

While the template is useful for your Kitura project, it is also limited in programmability. So, don't add too much data handling logic to your template code. Limit your template code to handle mainly displaying logic.

Learning the basic functions of the Stencil templating engine

The Stencil templating engine replaces variables and tags in a template file with actual values in runtime or places control flows that render filtered content.

All Stencil template files have the `*.stencil` file extension. Typically, you'll start a Stencil template file from a HTML file and instrument the HTML syntax with Stencil variables, tags, and filters. For communicating to the template from your Swift code, you'll pass a context to a template when calling the function to render the template file. The context contains values for variables and data structures that will be used in the template.

Using variables and tags in Stencil templating

Stencil uses double curly braces like : `{{ Var }}` for a variable that prints to the template output. For example, Stencil looks up the variable `title` in the context and evaluates it:

```
<title>{{ title }}</title>
```

Stencil also uses `{% ... %}` for tags and `{# ... #}` for comments.

The following tag allows you to have a loop through every element in the `entries` array:

```
{% for entry in entries %}
  {{ entry.title }}
{% endfor %}
```

The following comment will be ignored and not included in the rendering of the template:

```
{# This comment will be hidden. #}
```

Summarizing useful filters and tags in Stencil

The following table is a list of useful built-in filters in Stencil:

Filter	Description	Usage
`{{`**`Var`**`|capitalize}}`	Converts `Var` into capitals	`{{"hobbies"|capitalize}}`
`{{`**`Var`**`|uppercase}}`	Converts `Var` into uppercase	`{{"hobbies"|uppercase}}`
`{{`**`Var`**`|lowercase}}`	Converts `Var` into lowercase	`{{"hobbies"|lowercase}}`
`{{`**`Var`**`|default:`**`Str`**`}}`	Uses `Str` if `Var` not found	`{{name|default:"nobody"}}`
`{{`**`Array`**`|join:", "}}`	Joins an `Array` of items	`{{entries|join:", " }}`, `entries` is an array
`{{`**`String`**`|split:", "}}`	Splits a `String` into substrings by separator	`{{"Apple, Orange, Pear"|split:", " }}`

The following table is a list of useful built-in tags:

Tag	Description	Usage
`{% for `**`Var`**` in `**`Array`**` %}` **`Block`**`{% endfor %}`	Loop `Var` over `Array`	`{% for entry in entries %}` ID is `entry.id {% endfor %}`
`{% if `**`Var`**` %}` **`Block`**`{% endif %}`	if condition	`{% if entry %}` ID is `entry.id {% endif %}`
`{% include `**`Str`**` %}`	Include another template	`{% include "header.html" %}`
`{% extends `**`Str`**` %}`	Extends the template from a parent template	`{% extends "base.html" %}`
`{% filter `**`Var`**` %}` **`Block`** `{% endfilter %}`	Filters the contents of a block	`{% filter lowercase|captialize %}` Text goes to here: `{% endfilter %}`

The functionality of some of these tags can be further expanded. For example, the `if` built-in tag can be combined with the `and`, `or`, and `not` operators:

```
{% if A and B %}
    Both A and B are present.
{% endif %}

{% if not A or B %}
    None of A or B is there.
{% endif %}
```

Configuring the Stencil templating engine

With the introduction of Stencil template language in the previous section, you're now ready to add code to your myJournal Kitura application.

First of all, you're required to add Stencil as a dependency for your project. You can start with the same myJournal project from the last chapter. To add Stencil to your project, open the Package.swift file in Xcode and add the Stencil package to the dependencies and target arguments as shown in the following code:

```
// swift-tools-version:4.0
import PackageDescription

let package = Package(
    // ...
        .package(url:
"https://github.com/IBM-Swift/Kitura-StencilTemplateEngine.git", from:
"1.10.0"),
    ],
    targets: [
        .target(name: "myJournal", dependencies: [ .target(name:
"Application"), "Kitura" , "HeliumLogger", "KituraStencil"]),
        // ...
    ]
)
```

Next, you'll develop code that works with Stencil templates and implement those templates.

Developing code working with Stencil templates

After configuring your project for Stencil template engine, there are a couple of steps to take before you can use Stencil.

First, you need to import the KituraStencil module into your Application.swift file. Add this line after the import Dispatch statement:

```
import KituraStencil
```

Next, you need to tell Kitura to use the default Stencil templating engine since Kitura has three built-in templating engines you can choose from.

Add this line before you call initializeHealthRoutes(app: self):

```
router.setDefault(templateEngine: StencilTemplateEngine())
```

Adding Stencil templates to your Kitura project

Since your project has been configured for the Stencil templating engine, you can now add several Stencil templates that you'll need later. All of the templates should be placed under the `Views` folder in a Kitura project.

First of all, add the header and footer templates that are shared by other Stencil templates.

Add the `/Views/header.stencil` template:

```
<!DOCTYPE html>
<html lang="en">
<head>
<meta charset="utf-8" />
<title>{{ title }}</title>
</head>
<body>
```

Also, add the `/Views/footer.stencil` template:

```
<hr>
<center>
{{ title }} Application by {{ author }}.
</center>
</body>
</html>
```

Now, add the `/Views/main.stencil` template:

```
% include "header.stencil" %}

<h1>{{ title }}</h1>

[  <a href="/journal/create">Add New Entry</a> ]
<P>
{% for entry in entries %}
<hr>
<h2>{{ entry.title }}</h2>
{{ entry.content }}
<BR> [  <a href="/journal/get/{{ forloop.counter0 }}">Edit</a> |  <a
href="/journal/remove/{{ forloop.counter0 }}">Remove</a> ]
<BR> <em>Index:{{ forloop.counter0 }} out of {{ count }}; ID: {{ entry.id
}};</em>
{% endfor %}

{% include "footer.stencil" %}
```

The `main.stencil` template is used to render the main web page, which lists all of your journal entries using the `for` loop syntax, `{% for entry in entries %}`.

Next, you need a template that renders a form for the user to create a new journal entry.

Add the `/Views/new.stencil` template:

```
{% include "header.stencil" %}
<h1>Create a Journal Entry</h1>
<form action="/journal/new" method="post" enctype="application/x-www-form-
urlencoded" target="/journal/all">
<input name="id" type="hidden" value="-1" />
<input name="title" type="text" placeholder="Enter title here" />
<P>
<textarea name="content" placeholder="Enter your journal content here..."
rows="5">

</textarea>
<P>
<button type="submit" class="btn btn-lg btn-primary">Submit</button>
</form>
{% include "footer.stencil" %}
```

When creating a new entry, the `id` field will be automatically generated. In the **Create a Journal Entry** form, the value of the hidden `id` input element will be simply ignored. After a new entry is submitted and created, Kitura will take you back to the main screen.

The last template you're going to need is a form for the user to edit a journal entry.

Add the `/Views/entry.stencil` template:

```
{% include "header.stencil" %}
<h1>Edit a Journal Entry</h1>
<form action="/journal/edit/{{ index }}" method="post"
enctype="application/x-www-form-urlencoded">
<input name="id" type="hidden" value="{{ entry.id }}" />
<input name="title" type="text" value="{{ entry.title }}" />
<P>
<textarea name="content" rows="5">
{{ entry.content }}
</textarea>
<P>
<button type="submit" class="btn btn-lg btn-primary">Submit</button>
</form>
<BR> <em>Index:{{ index }}; ID: {{ entry.id }};</em>
{% include "footer.stencil" %}
```

Those are all of the templates you will need. Next, you'll learn how to interact with the Stencil templates from your Swift source code.

Displaying all journal entries

With all of the templates in place, you can now proceed to add all of the required routes and their handler functions:

1. Create a new file, `JournalRoutes.swift`, in the `/Application/Routes` directory.

2. Add the following code to the newly create file:

```
// file: /Application/Routes/JournalRoutes.swift
import Foundation
import KituraStencil
import Kitura

func initializeJournalRoutes(app: App, journal: JournalController)
{ // [1]
    let mainPage = "/journal/all" // [2]
    let title = "My Journal" // [3]
    let author = "Angus" // [4]
    struct JournalContext : Encodable { // [5]
        let title: String
        let author: String
        let count: String
        let entries: [Entry]
    }

    app.router.get("/journal/all") { ... } // [6]
    app.router.get("/journal/create") { ... }
    app.router.post("/journal/new") { ... }
    app.router.get("/journal/get/:index?") { ... }
    app.router.post("/journal/edit/:index?") { ... }
    app.router.get("/journal/remove/:index?") { ... }
}
```

3. The new file has the following design steps:
    1. Implement the `initializeJournalRoute(app, journal)` function that takes in the application's context and a reference to the persistence encapsulated in `JournalController`
    2. Declare the master return path
    3. Declare the `title` setting
    4. Declare the `author` setting

5. Declare the `JournalContext Encodable` structure
6. Process different routes

The `JournalContext Encodable` structure in [5] previously is used to store and pass context into the template. You'll see how `JournalContext` is filled and gets passed to `response.render()` during the rendering of a template:

```
app.router.get("/journal/all") { _, response, _ in
        let total = journal.total() // [1]
        let entries : [Entry] = journal.readAll() // [2]
        let count = "\(total)"
        let context = JournalContext(title: title,
                                     author: author,
                                     count: count,
                                     entries: entries) // [3]
    do {
        try response.render("main", with: context) // [4]
    } catch let error {
        response.send(error.localizedDescription)
    }
  }
}
```

4. The previous `Display All` code does the following:
    1. Queries `JournalController` for the total number of entries
    2. Gets all entries into an array
    3. Instantiates a new `JournalContext` object initialized with appropriate data
    4. Gets response to render the main.stencil template with the `Encodable` structure `context`

The raw route handling allows you to work with lower level operations compared to the codable route handling using the objects request, response, and next. In the previous code, you have used `response` to render a template page but didn't have a chance to use `request` and `next`. As you can see, these two objects are marked with _ in the function's arguments.

5. When rendering the `Display All` route, you'll see a web page similar to the following:

Completing the features

You'll continue to finish the other five routes in `initializeJournalRoutes()`. The `/journal/create` route will display a form for the user to create a new entry and its companion route, `/journal/new`, will process the form. For an existing entry, the `/journal/get/:index?` route will display a form for the user to make changes to an existing form and the `/journal/edit/:index?` route will process the changes. Lastly, the `/journal/remove/:index?` route will delete an existing entry and bring you back to the main page.

Creating a new journal entry

This route renders a new form so a user can submit a new entry:

```
app.router.get("/journal/create") { request, response, next in
        response.headers["Content-Type"] = "text/html; charset=utf-8"
```

```
        try response.render("new", context: ["title": title, "author":
    author])
        }
```

It doesn't do too much except tell the response to render the `new.stencil` template. The follow web page will be generated if you point your web browser to `localhost8080:/journal/create`:

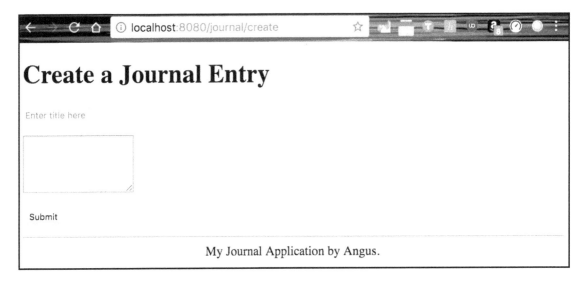

Once the form's data is filled and submitted to `/journal/new` via `HTTP POST`, the data will be processed accordingly to create a new entry in `JournalController`:

```
    app.router.post("/journal/new") { request, response, next in
        guard let entry = try? request.read(as: Entry.self) // [1]
            else {
                return try response.status(.unprocessableEntity).end()
        }

        let newID = UUID().uuidString // [2]
        if let result = journal.create(Entry(id: newID,
                                             title: entry.title,
                                             content: entry.content)) { //
    [3]
            print("Created: \(result)")
            try response.redirect(mainPage) // [4]
        }
    }
```

The previous piece of code creates a new entry in the following steps:

1. An `Optional` of the `Entry Codable` data structure is read from the request object and unwrapped
2. A new ID is created using Swift's `UUID` utility function
3. A new `Entry` object is created and fed into the `create()` function of `JournalController`
4. This redirect the response to the default path stored in `mainPage`

This route handler simply processes the HTTP request it has, creates a new UUID, and then delegates the creation of a new entry to `JournalController`.

Editing a journal entry

Similarly, an existing entry can be edited and updated. The following route handling code renders a form filled with your requested entry:

```
app.router.get("/journal/get/:index?") { request, response, next in
    guard let index = request.parameters["index"] else {
        return try response.status(.badRequest).send("Missing entry
index").end()
    }
    guard let idx = Int(index) else {
        return try response.status(.badRequest).send("Invalid entry
index").end()
    }
    guard let entry = journal.read(index: idx) else {
        return try response.status(.unprocessableEntity).end()
    }
    try response.render("entry", context: ["title": title, "author":
author, "index": idx, "entry": entry])
}
```

Kitura allows you to pass the URL parameter to your route handling code. Use the `":index?"` format to encode a URL parameter. To retrieve the parameter, you use `request.parameters["index"]` in your Swift code.

The `entry.stencil` template is used to render the form:

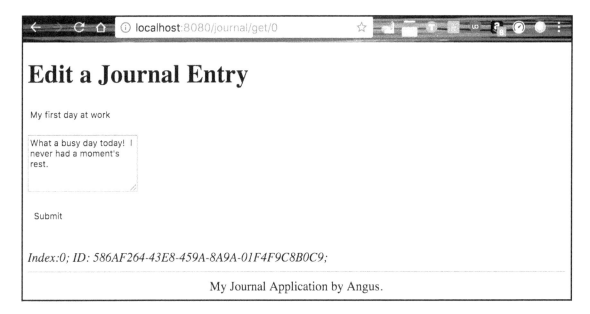

Once the user submits the form, the filled data in the form will be used to replace the entry data by `index`:

```
app.router.post("/journal/edit/:index?") { request, response, next in
    guard let index = request.parameters["index"] else {
        return try response.status(.badRequest).send("Missing entry
index").end()
    }
    guard let idx = Int(index) else {
        return try response.status(.badRequest).send("Invalid entry
index").end()
    }
    if let entry = try? request.read(as: Entry.self) {
        if let result = journal.update(index: idx, entry: entry) {
            print("Updated: Entry[\(index)]: \(result)")
            try response.redirect(mainPage)
        }
    }
    try response.status(.unprocessableEntity).end()
}
```

The implementation is similar to the route handling code used to create a new entry. It uses the `update()` function of `JournalController` to replace the entry by `index`.

Removing a journal entry

Finally, the following code demonstrates how the entry is removed:

```
app.router.get("/journal/remove/:index?") { request, response, next in
    guard let index = request.parameters["index"] else {
        return try response.status(.badRequest).send("Missing entry
index").end()
    }
    guard let idx = Int(index) else {
        return try response.status(.badRequest).send("Invalid entry
index").end()
    }
    if let entry = journal.delete(index: idx) {
        print("Deleted: Entry[\(index)]: \(entry)")
        try response.redirect(mainPage)
    }
    try response.status(.unprocessableEntity).end()
}
```

The route handling process follows the similar step to decipher the URL parameter from `request`. Then it calls `JournalController.delete()` to update the deletion of that entry by `index`.

Summary

In this chapter, you learned all of the basic coding techniques you need to work with templating engines. For your Vapor project, you learned how to set up the Leaf templating engine and create Leaf templates. You also modified your code from the previous chapter to work with the Leaf templates. In the second part of this chapter, you continued your coding exercise with Kitura's Stencil templating engine. You were introduced to the usage of Stencil and then proceeded to create Stencil templates and add code that works with them.

In the next chapter, you are going to learn how to make the rendered web pages more professional-looking with Bootstrap.

Bootstrapping Your Design 7

Bootstrap is an open source frontend framework, developed by Twitter, to add pre-designed components to your web pages, making it easy to beautify your web content, even if you are not a digital artist. You can buy components in various styles developed by professional artists from Bootstrap marketplaces and add purchased stylish components to your web app for rapid design and development. This chapter will introduce you to the Bootstrap framework, consisting of a collection of CSS and JavaScript libraries, and explain how the Bootstrap framework allows you to build responsive websites easily. You'll follow step-by-step instructions for inserting Bootstrap components into your templates and learn how to beautify different UI elements in your template with Bootstrap. At the end, you'll learn how to include Bootstrap in your project when you are ready to deploy your web apps.

The following topics will be covered in this chapter:

- Getting started with the Bootstrap framework
- Using Bootstrap for a Vapor application
- Using Bootstrap for Kitura

Getting started with the Bootstrap framework

You've learned about Leaf and Stencil templating engines in `Chapter 6`, *Working with Template Engines*. The templating engines provide you with a very convenient way to interact and render raw HTML pages. But that is not sufficient if you want to deliver a professional-looking design for your web content. For professional-looking design, you'll have to leverage a frontend component library for web styling. One of the most popular web styling component libraries is Bootstrap, an open source library from Twitter. It provides enhanced styling and interactivity features for frontend user interface development. In addition, Bootstrap is highly optimized for mobile devices.

A Bootstrap application builds on top of existing web technologies, such as HTML for web content, CSS for styling, JavaScript and jQuery for scripting, and Sass for stylesheet language. Bootstrap adds a complete portfolio of UI components:

- Layout: Grid, Breakpoints, Z-Index, Code, Images, Tables, and Figures
- UI elements: Button, Badge, Dropdown, Form, Input, Progress, NavBar, and Tooltips
- Utilities: Border, Carousel, Colors, Display, Position, Sizing, Spacing, Vertical Align, and Visibility

While this is not a complete list of components in Bootstrap, it does show an extended coverage of UI components by the Bootstrap library. You're encouraged to visit Bootstrap's official website for examples, detailed documentation, and other useful information: `https://getbootstrap.com`.

Setting up for Bootstrap

There are different ways to set up your project in preparation for use of the Bootstrap component library. You may download the official version of CSS and JavaScript libraries and include them as part of your third-party library dependency. A recommended approach, however, is to skip the download, and use the **Bootstrap CDN service** to deliver a cached version of compiled and minimized CSS and JavaScript files. Most web browsers have been optimized, so popular libraries such as Bootstrap are available almost immediately.

For simplicity, we'll use the CDN approach in this chapter.

Inserting the stylesheet

It's actually very easy to set up your web project for Bootstrap. First, add this stylesheet link to your header section, marked with `<head>`, before all other stylesheets. It instructs the web browser to load the Bootstrap stylesheet first:

```
<link rel="stylesheet"
href="https://stackpath.bootstrapcdn.com/bootstrap/4.1.2/css/bootstrap.min.
css" integrity="sha384-
Smlep5jCw/wG7hdkwQ/Z5nLIefveQRIY9nfy6xoR1uRYBtpZgI6339F5dgvm/e9B"
crossorigin="anonymous">
```

As you can see, the stylesheet is downloaded directly from `stackpath.bootstrapcdn.com`.

Adding dependency for JavaScript files

Next up, we'll add the following three scripts to the end of the body section, right before `<body>`:

```
<script src="https://code.jquery.com/jquery-3.3.1.slim.min.js"
integrity="sha384-
q8i/X+965DzO0rT7abK41JStQIAqVgRVzpbzo5smXKp4YfRvH+8abtTE1Pi6jizo"
crossorigin="anonymous"></script>
<script
src="https://cdnjs.cloudflare.com/ajax/libs/popper.js/1.14.3/umd/popper.min
.js" integrity="sha384-
ZMP7rVo3mIykV+2+9J3UJ46jBk0WLaUAdn689aCwoqbBJiSnjAK/l8WvCWPIPm49"
crossorigin="anonymous"></script>
<script
src="https://stackpath.bootstrapcdn.com/bootstrap/4.1.2/js/bootstrap.min.js
" integrity="sha384-
o+RDsa0aLu++PJvFqy8fFScvbHFLtbvScb8AjopnFD+iEQ7wo/CG0xlczd+2O/em"
crossorigin="anonymous"></script>
```

The first two scripts are used by Bootstrap:

1. **jQuery** is a small and fast library that helps HTML document traversal and processing extremely easy
2. **Popper** is a positioning engine that makes it possible to position an element near a reference element

The last one is the Bootstrap script, which is also available from `stackpath.bootstrapcdn.com`.

That's all required that's for you to start using Bootstrap in your web project!

Using a starter template in Bootstrap

Listed here is a starter template that you can use as a basis for your own work:

```
<!doctype html>
<html lang="en">
  <head>
    <!-- Required meta tags -->
    <meta charset="utf-8">
    <meta name="viewport" content="width=device-width, initial-scale=1,
shrink-to-fit=no">

    <!-- Bootstrap CSS -->
    <link rel="stylesheet"
```

```
href="https://stackpath.bootstrapcdn.com/bootstrap/4.1.2/css/bootstrap.min.
css" integrity="sha384-
Smlep5jCw/wG7hdkwQ/Z5nLIefveQRIY9nfy6xoR1uRYBtpZgI6339F5dgvm/e9B"
crossorigin="anonymous">

    <title>Hello, world!</title>
  </head>
  <body>
    <h1>Hello, world!</h1>

    <!-- Optional JavaScript -->
    <!-- jQuery first, then Popper.js, then Bootstrap JavaScript  -->
    <script src="https://code.jquery.com/jquery-3.3.1.slim.min.js"
integrity="sha384-
q8i/X+965DzO0rT7abK41JStQIAqVgRVzpbzo5smXKp4YfRvH+8abtTE1Pi6jizo"
crossorigin="anonymous"></script>
    <script
src="https://cdnjs.cloudflare.com/ajax/libs/popper.js/1.14.3/umd/popper.min
.js" integrity="sha384-
ZMP7rVo3mIykV+2+9J3UJ46jBk0WLaUAdn689aCwoqbBJiSnjAK/l8WvCWPIPm49"
crossorigin="anonymous"></script>
    <script
src="https://stackpath.bootstrapcdn.com/bootstrap/4.1.2/js/bootstrap.min.js
" integrity="sha384-
o+RDsa0aLu++PJvFqy8fFScvbHFLtbvScb8AjopnFD+iEQ7wo/CG0xlczd+2O/em"
crossorigin="anonymous"></script>
  </body>
</html>
```

The starter HTML template begins with the `<!DOCTYPE>` tag to specify the HTML5 language and version. The HTML template is divided into the header section, `<head></head>`, and the body section, `<body></body>`. You'll put all of your meta tags, CSS, and links for fonts and images in the header section. For enhanced performance, the JavaScript files are usually placed at the bottom of the document, just before the closing tag, `</body>`.

In the header, there is a responsive viewport meta tag added for optimized mobile-display rendering:

```
<meta name="viewport" content="width=device-width, initial-scale=1, shrink-
to-fit=no">
```

This line allows mobile web browsers to render Bootstrap elements appropriately. Bootstrap follows the principle of "mobile first", so the design of all user interface elements have been optimized and tested for an array of major mobile devices.

Next, you're going to use a couple of major features that Bootstrap has to offer.

Using basic Bootstrap components

Bootstrap offers a big collection of responsive frontend components for your web user interface. The library is organized into four categories:

- Layout
- Content
- Component
- Utilities

You'll learn how to use Bootstrap's grid system to organize the layout, then apply `jumbotron`, the navigation bar, form controls, and glyphicons to the web content.

Organizing content into grids

Bootstrap wraps web content into its basic layout element, called containers. The container layout is required for its powerful grid system, so you'll see the container syntax extensively in any Bootstrap empowered web content. Here are the basics of container usage:

1. A basic container has the following syntax:

```
<div class="container">
  <!-- Content here -->
</div>
```

2. You can specify a container to occupy the entire width of the viewport using container-fluid:

```
<div class="container-fluid">
  <!-- Content here -->
</div>
```

3. With the container layout, you can organize a web page into several sections:

```
<body>
<section class="sec1" id="sec1">
<div class="container">
   <!-- Section 1 goes to here -->
   Container 1
</div>
</section>
<section class="sec2" id="sec2">
<div class="container">
```

```
      <!-- Section 2 goes to here -->
      Container 2
   </div>
   </section>
   . . .
   <section class="secN" id="secN">
   <div class="container">
      <!-- Section N goes to here -->
      Container N
   </div>
   </section>
   </body>
```

4. To illustrate the effect of the preceding container code for you, a CSS file has been used to create the following diagram, with a colored bounding box for each container:

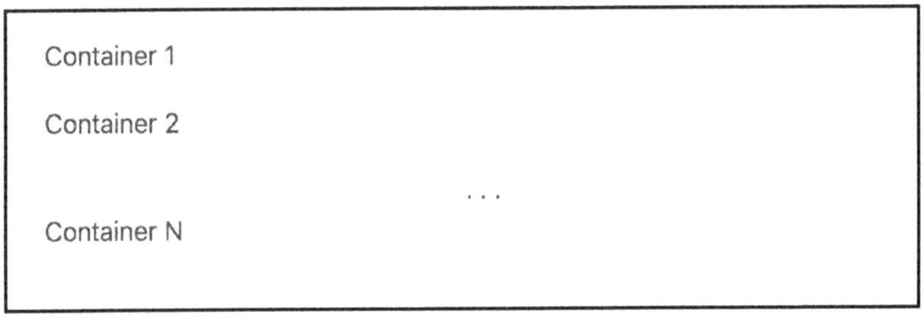

5. With Bootstrap's grid system, you can layout and align content with containers, rows, and columns. For example, the following layout code arranges the content in a container into one row and three columns:

```
<div class="container">
  <div class="row">
    <div class="col-4">
      One of three columns
    </div>
    <div class="col-4">
      One of three columns
    </div>
    <div class="col-4">
      One of three columns
    </div>
  </div>
</div>
```

The result looks like this:

One of three columns	One of three columns	One of three columns

6. Bootstrap divides a row into roughly 12 columns. For three equally-spaced columns, you'll assign four original columns to each new column using `"col-4"`. There are also other grid options, such as `.col-sm`, `.col-md`, `.col-lg`, and `.col-xl`, for small, medium, large, and extra-large columns.

7. To create an equal-width multi-row grid, you can insert a `.w-100` to the column break, as shown here:

```
<div class="container">
  <div class="row">
    <div class="col-6">
      first column of first row
    </div>
    <div class="col-6">
      second column of first row
    </div>
    <div class="w-100"></div>
    <div class="col-6">
      first column of second row
    </div>
    <div class="col-6">
      second column of second row
    </div>
  </div>
</div>
```

And here is the result:

first column of first row	second column of first row
first column of second row	second column of second row

Displaying a jumbotron with parallax animation

A `jumbotron` is a big banner that draws the viewer's attention to special information in your web content. You'll typically add a `jumbotron` at the beginning of a page for heading information, as shown here:

```
<!--Jumbotron-->
<div class="jumbotron banner-align-top" id="myBanner">
```

```
    <div class="banner-background text-center" style="background-image:
url(img/pier.png);">
        <div class="container text-center" id="banner-size">
          <h2 class="banner-title">My Journal</h2>
          <h3 class="banner-subtitle">The Path of Heart!</h3>
        </div>

    </div>
</div>
```

The `jumbotron` banner is marked with a pair of `<div class="jumbotron"></div>` tags. A background image, `pier.png`, is used. When rendering, the banner look like this when scrolling down the web page:

The following is the CSS stylesheet used for the banner:

```
/*----------- BANNER ---------*/

header {
    padding-bottom:40px;
}

.banner-align-top {
    padding:0;
}
```

```
.banner-background {
    text-align:center;
    background-position:center center;
    background-repeat:no-repeat;
    background-size:cover;
    background-attachment:fixed;
    overflow:hidden;
}

#banner-size {
    height:600px;
    padding-top:160px;
}

.banner-title {
    font-family:sans-serif;
    font-size:72px;
    line-height:1;
    font-weight:300;
    color:#fff
}

.banner-subtitle {
    font-family:sans-serif;
    font-size:30px;
    line-height:1.4;
    font-weight:300;
    color:#fff;
}
```

The .banner-background has a fixed background-attachment attribute. This creates a parallax visual effect, as if the background image is fixed while the foreground content is moving up, when scrolling down the web page.

Adding a navigation bar

A navigation bar consists of navigation menu items in a tray, typically at the top of a web page. To use a navigation bar, we wrap a section with .navbar and use parameters such as .navbar-expand{-sm|-md|-lg|xl}, fixed-top, and scrolling-navbar. The navigation bar is attached to the top and is fluid (taking up the maximum allowable width) by default:

```
<nav class="navbar navbar-expand-lg navbar-dark fixed-top scrolling-
navbar">
    <div class="container">
        <a class="navbar-brand" href="#"><strong>myJournal</strong></a>
```

```
        <button class="navbar-toggler" type="button" data-toggle="collapse"
data-target="#myNavbar" aria-controls="myNavbar" aria-expanded="false"
aria-label="Toggle navigation">
            <span class="navbar-toggler-icon"></span>
        </button>
        <div class="collapse navbar-collapse" id="myNavbar">
            <ul class="navbar-nav mr-auto">
                <li class="nav-item active">
                    <a class="nav-link" href="#">Home <span class="sr-
only">(current)</span></a>
                </li>
                <li class="nav-item">
                    <a class="nav-link" href="#">Admin</a>
                </li>
                <li class="nav-item">
                    <a class="nav-link" href="#">About</a>
                </li>
            </ul>
        </div>
    </div>
</nav>
```

The navigation bar is collapsible, so the menu items will be hidden when the width of web page is reduced:

A toggle button, marked with the `<button></button>` tag, is used to expand the list of menu items. The menu items will be listed vertically when the view is toggled on:

Using form controls

Bootstrap customizes the feel and look of a form with form controls. Form controls enforce more or less consistent rendering of form displays across different user devices.

Here is an example of Bootstrap's form style:

```html
<!--form-->
<section class="form" id="myForm">
<div class="container">
  <div class="row">
    <div class="col-lg-12">
      <div class="heading">
        <h2>Submit a New Entry</h2>
      </div>
    </div>
  </div>
</div>
<div class="container max-width">
  <div class="row">
  <div class="done">
    <div class="alert alert-success"> <!-- [1] -->
      <button type="button" class="close" data-dismiss="alert">X</button>
      Your message has been submitted.
    </div>
  </div>
    <div class="col-md-12">
        <form>
            <fieldset class="form-group">
                <input type="text" class="form-control" id="title"
placeholder="Title">
            </fieldset>

            <fieldset class="form-group">
                <textarea class="form-control" rows="3" id="content"
placeholder="Content"></textarea>
            </fieldset>
            <button type="submit" class="contact submit">Submit</button>
        </form>
    </div>
  </div>
</div>
</section>
```

The form has a text input field for title and a textarea element for content. Both of them are styled with the .form-control class. The example also shows how the form uses a Bootstrap Alert component to display a success message with alert alert-success [1] if the form has been submitted successfully.

The following are the style elements for the form:

```css
/*----------- FORM ---------*/
input.form-control {
    background:#ccddcc;
    border:solid 1px #557755;
    color:#000000;
    padding:15px 30px;
    margin-right:3%;
    margin-bottom:30px;
    outline:none;
    border-radius: 3;
}

textarea.form-control {
    background:#ccddcc;
    color:#000000;
    border:solid 1px #557755;
    padding:15px 30px;
    margin-bottom:40px;
    outline:none;
    height:200px;
    border-radius: 3;
}

button.entryform.submit {
    background:#557755;
    font-family: sans-serif;
    color:#fff;
    font-size:1em;
    font-weight:400;
    text-align:center;
    margin:0;
    border:none;
    border-radius:3px;
    padding:15px 45px;
}

button.entryform.submit:hover {
    background:#339933;
}
```

```
.form-control:focus{
    border-color: #339933;
    outline: 0;
}

.done {
    display:none;
}
```

The rendering of this Bootstrap form control looks like the following:

Reusing glyphicons

Bootstrap 4.0 does not include any glyphicon library by default. However, it recommends several libraries. One of the recommended glyphicon libraries is **Font Awesome**. Visit Font Awesome's official website at `https://fontawesome.com` and search for the icon you would like to use in your project. The site even offers a cheat sheet for its massive icon library, making finding the right icon for your project extremely easy and effortless.

To include Font Awesome in your project, you need to do the following:

1. You can include this CDN library in the header section of your HTML file for a cached version of the Font Awesome library:

```
<link rel="stylesheet"
href="https://use.fontawesome.com/releases/v5.2.0/css/all.css"
integrity="sha384-
hWVjflwFxL6sNzntih27bfxkr27PmbbK/iSvJ+a4+0owXq79v+lsFkW54bOGbiDQ"
crossorigin="anonymous">
```

2. Then you can use Font Awesome icons directly in your project. The following HTML code shows the usage of five glyphicons:

```
<!--footer-->
<section class="footer" id="footer">
  <div class="container">
    <div class="row">
      <div class="col-sm">
      <ul>
        <li><i class="fas fa-envelope"></i></li>
        <li><i class="fab fa-facebook"></i></li>
        <li><i class="fab fa-google-plus-g"></i></li>
        <li><i class="fab fa-linkedin"></i></li>
        <li><i class="fab fa-twitter"></i></li>
      </ul>
      <p>
      &copy; 2018 - Simply You<br>
      </p>
          </div>
      </div>
    </div>
</section>
```

When you reference an icon, you should specify its style prefix, followed by the icon's name prefixed with "*fa-*". There are two styles that are free of charge to you: style prefix "*fas*" for solid rendering style, and style prefix "*fab*" for brands style. In the preceding code, there is a "*fas*" icon type, followed by four "*fab*" icons.

3. The following CSS style attributes are used to format the footer user interface:

```
/*----------- FOOTER ---------*/
.footer {
    background:#557755;
    margin-top:100px;
    position:relative
}
```

```css
.footer .container {
    padding:60px 0 20px;
}

.footer ul {
    margin:0 auto;
    margin-bottom:30px;
    margin-top:10px;
    text-align:center;
    list-style-type:none;
    padding-left:0;
}

/* icon list */
.footer ul li {
  text-align:center;
    display:inline-block;
    background:rgba(0,0,0,0.2);
    color:#fff;
    line-height:45px;
    margin:0 4px;
    width:45px;
    height:45px;
    -webkit-border-radius:3px;
    border-radius:3px;
}

.footer ul li:hover {
    background:#339933;
}

/* Copyright */
.footer p {
    color:#fff;
    font-size:.9em;
    line-height:24px;
    font-weight:300;
    text-align:center;
    text-transform:uppercase;
}
```

The rendered footer looks like this:

Using Bootstrap for a Vapor application

After learning the basics of Bootstrap and choosing icons from the Font Awesome library, you can start putting everything together to upgrade the feel and look of web pages rendered by the Leaf templating engine.

To use Bootstrap in your Vapor project, you're required to use the file server middleware. Simply uncomment the following line in `configure.swift`:

```
middlewares.use(FileMiddleware.self) // Serves files from `Public/`
directory
```

1. The file server will make all the resource in `/Public` available for HTTP requests.
2. Create two subdirectories, `/css` and `/img`, under `/Public`.
3. Copy `custom.css` and `pier.png` from the resources for this chapter to `/Public/css` and `/Public/img`, respectively.
4. The CSS stylesheet will be included in `header.leaf`:

   ```
   <link rel="stylesheet" href="/css/custom.css">
   ```

   Remember the path for Vapor has to start with `/`. A common mistake is omitting it as `css/custom.css`.

5. The background image `pier.png` is used in the banner in `header.leaf`:

   ```
   <div class="banner-background text-center" style="background-image:
   url(/img/pier.png);">
   ```

That's it. You can now update all the five Leaf templates with the Bootstrap-enhanced web design that you finished in previous chapters.

Enhancing Leaf templates with Bootstrap

Now, apply the Bootstrap framework to the Leaf templates you created in `Chapter 6`, *Working with Templating Engines*. The application logics in the `myJournal` application from the last chapter largely remain unchanged. All changes in this chapter apply to the templates that will be rendered into web pages for client web browsers.

The rest of the Bootstrap enhanced Leaf templates are described in the following subsections.

header.leaf

First, upgrade the *header* template Bootstrap elements. Since the *header* template will be included by other templates, it reduces a lot of code that is common to every template:

```
<!DOCTYPE html>
<html lang="en">
<head>
<meta charset="utf-8" />
<title>#(title)</title>
<!-- Required meta tags -->
<meta charset="utf-8">
<meta name="viewport" content="width=device-width, initial-scale=1">

<!-- Bootstrap CSS -->
<link rel="stylesheet"
href="https://stackpath.bootstrapcdn.com/bootstrap/4.1.2/css/bootstrap.min.
css" integrity="sha384-
Smlep5jCw/wG7hdkwQ/Z5nLIefveQRIY9nfy6xoR1uRYBtpZgI6339F5dgvm/e9B"
crossorigin="anonymous">

<link rel="stylesheet"
href="https://use.fontawesome.com/releases/v5.2.0/css/all.css"
integrity="sha384-
hWVjflwFxL6sNzntih27bfxkr27PmbbK/iSvJ+a4+0owXq79v+lsFkW54bOGbiDQ"
crossorigin="anonymous">
<!-- Custom CSS -->
<link rel="stylesheet" href="/css/custom.css">

</head>

<body>
<!--wrapper start-->
<div class="wrapper" id="wrapper">
```

```html
<!--Banner-->
<header>

<!--Navbar-->
<nav class="navbar navbar-expand-lg navbar-dark fixed-top scrolling-
navbar">
<div class="container">
<a class="navbar-brand" href="#"><strong>myJournal</strong></a>
<button class="navbar-toggler" type="button" data-toggle="collapse" data-
target="#myNavbar" aria-controls="myNavbar" aria-expanded="false" aria-
label="Toggle navigation">
<span class="navbar-toggler-icon"></span>
</button>
<div class="collapse navbar-collapse" id="myNavbar">
<ul class="navbar-nav mr-auto">
<li class="nav-item active">
<a class="nav-link" href="#">Home <span class="sr-
only">(current)</span></a>
</li>
<li class="nav-item">
<a class="nav-link" href="#">Admin</a>
</li>
<li class="nav-item">
<a class="nav-link" href="#">About</a>
</li>
</ul>
</div>
</div>
</nav>


<!--Jumbotron-->
<div class="jumbotron banner-align-top" id="myBanner">
<div class="banner-background text-center" style="background-image:
url(/img/pier.png);">
<div class="container text-center" id="banner-size">
<h2 class="banner-title">My Journal</h2>
<h3 class="banner-subtitle">The Path of Heart!</h3>
</div>

</div>
</div>

</header>
```

Several new elements are added to the *header* template. First, links to Bootstrap and Font Awesome stylesheets are added. Next, Bootstrap's navigation bar element, which is used in every web page, is defined. Lastly, a `jumbotron` is added to display the banner on our web pages.

footer.leaf

Like the *header* template in `header.leaf`, the footer template in footer.leaf is used in every web page in this project. Change the footer template to the following:

```
<!--footer-->
<section class="footer" id="footer">
<div class="container">
<div class="row">
<div class="col-sm"> <!-- [1] -->
<ul>
<li><i class="fas fa-envelope"></i></li>
<li><i class="fab fa-facebook"></i></li>
<li><i class="fab fa-google-plus-g"></i></li>
<li><i class="fab fa-linkedin"></i></li>
<li><i class="fab fa-twitter"></i></li>
</ul>
<p>
&copy; 2018 - #(title) Application by #(author)<br>
</p>
</div>
</div>
</div>
</section>

</div><!--wrapper end-->


<!-- Optional JavaScript --> <-- [2] -->
<!-- jQuery first, then Popper.js, then Bootstrap JavaScript  -->
<script src="https://code.jquery.com/jquery-3.3.1.slim.min.js"
integrity="sha384-
q8i/X+965DzO0rT7abK41JStQIAqVgRVzpbzo5smXKp4YfRvH+8abTTE1Pi6jizo"
crossorigin="anonymous"></script>
<script
src="https://cdnjs.cloudflare.com/ajax/libs/popper.js/1.14.3/umd/popper.min
.js" integrity="sha384-
ZMP7rVo3mIykV+2+9J3UJ46jBk0WLaUAdn689aCwoqbBJiSnjAK/l8WvCWPIPm49"
crossorigin="anonymous"></script>
<script
src="https://stackpath.bootstrapcdn.com/bootstrap/4.1.2/js/bootstrap.min.js
```

```
" integrity="sha384-
o+RDsa0aLu++PJvFqy8fFScvbHFLtbvScb8AjopnFD+iEQ7wo/CG0xlczd+2O/em"
crossorigin="anonymous"></script>

</body>
</html>
```

The new *footer* template added a new row of icons [1]: Email, Facebook, Google, LinkedIn, and Twitter. You can add personalized links to these icons, so the user to your website can reach you. At the end of template and right before the </body> tag, a couple of links to the required JavaScript libraries in this project, including Bootstrap and Font Awesome, are added [2].

main.leaf

The main.leaf includes the header, footer, and main templates. It renders all journal entries in a single page, as follows:

```
#embed("header")
[  <a href="/journal/create">Add New Entry</a> ]
<P>
#for(entry in entries) {
<!--Section #(index)-->
<section class="sec#(index)" id="sec#(index)">
<div class="Container entry">
<h2>#(entry.title)</h2>
#(entry.content)
<BR> [  <a href="./#(index)/get">Edit</a> |  <a
href="./#(index)/remove">Remove</a> ]
    <BR> <em>Index:#(index) out of #(count); ID: #(entry.id);</em>
</div>
</section>
}
#embed("footer")
```

The Bootstrap-enhanced rendering looks like the following:

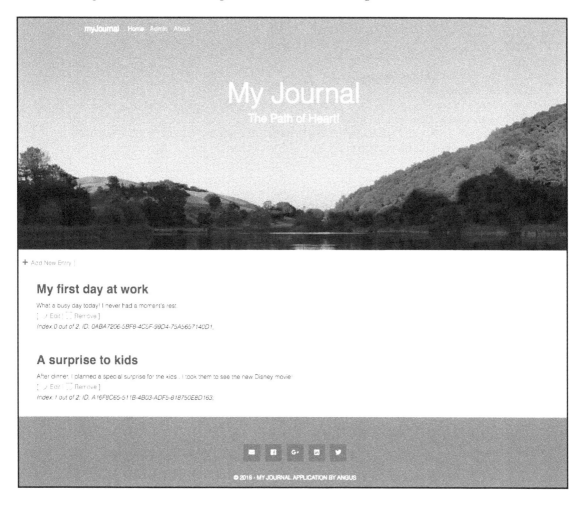

new.leaf

The `new.leaf` consists of a header, a footer, and a form:

```
#embed("header")
<!--form-->
<section class="form" id="myForm">
<div class="container">
<div class="row">
<div class="col-lg-12">
```

```
<div class="heading">
<h1>Create a Journal Entry</h1>
</div>
</div>
</div>
</div>
<div class="container max-width">
<div class="row">
<div class="done">
<div class="alert alert-success">
<button type="button" class="close" data-dismiss="alert">X</button>
Your message has been submitted.
</div>
</div>
<div class="col-md-12">
<form action="/journal/new/" method="post">
<fieldset class="form-group">
<input name="id" type="hidden" value="-1" />
<input type="text" class="form-control" name="title" placeholder="Enter
title here">
</fieldset>

<fieldset class="form-group">
<textarea class="form-control" rows="5" name="content" placeholder="Enter
your journal content here..."></textarea>
</fieldset>

<button type="submit" class="entryform submit">Submit</button>
</form>
</div>
</div>
</div>
</section>
#embed("footer")
```

The Bootstrap-enhanced rendering looks like the following:

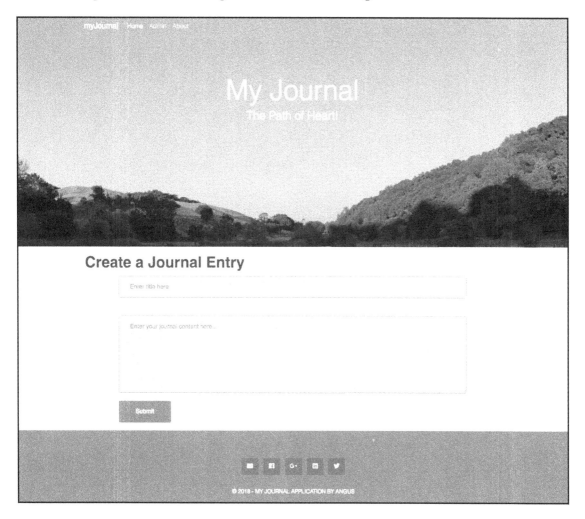

entry.leaf

The `entry.leaf` is similar to `new.leaf`. However, the existing entry's ID, title, and content are already filled in the form for you:

```
#embed("header")
<!--form-->
<section class="form" id="myForm">
<div class="container">
```

```
<div class="row">
<div class="col-lg-12">
<div class="heading">
<h1>Edit a Journal Entry</h1>
</div>
</div>
</div>
</div>
<div class="container max-width">
<div class="row">
<div class="done">
<div class="alert alert-success">
<button type="button" class="close" data-dismiss="alert">X</button>
Your message has been submitted.
</div>
</div>
<div class="col-md-12">
<form action="/journal/#(index)/edit/" method="post">
<fieldset class="form-group">
<input name="id" type="hidden" value=#(entry.id)" />
<input name="title" type="text" class="form-control" value="#(entry.title)"
/>
</fieldset>

<fieldset class="form-group">
<textarea class="form-control" rows="5" name="content">
#(entry.content)
</textarea>
</fieldset>

<button type="submit" class="entryform submit">Submit</button>
</form>
</div>
</div>
</div>
</section>
#embed("footer")
```

This'll be what it looks like when you edit an entry:

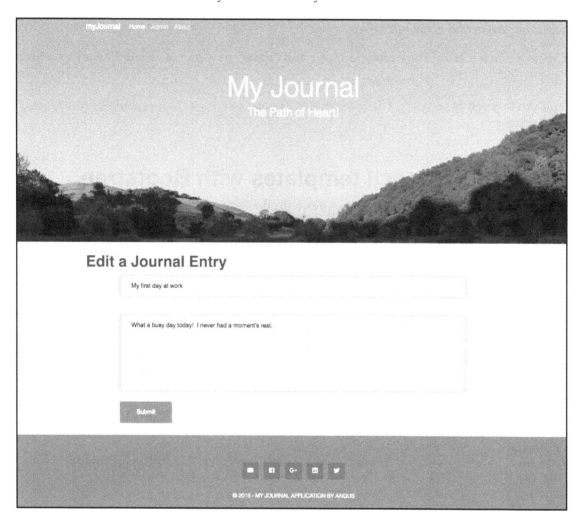

Using Bootstrap for Kitura

Enabling Bootstrap for Kitura is straightforward. Kitura serves all static web pages using the middleware `StaticFileServer`. In the `postInit()` function of the app, add the following line after `router.setDefault(templateEngine:)` in `/Sources/Application/Application.swift`:

```
router.get("/", middleware: StaticFileServer())
```

The static file server will look for all the resources under the folder called /public. Take note that while this folder, in a Vapor project, is capitalized as /Public, the folder name is a Kitura project and is not capitalized.

Create it at the top directory of myJournal and create /css and /img subdirectories under /pubic.

You can proceed to copy custom.css and pier.png to /public/css and /public/img, respectively.

Enhancing Stencil templates with Bootstrap

After updating all the five Stencil templates with Bootstrap, similar to what you've done for Vapor's Leaf templates, you will see the same rendered images and web content generated by Vapor 3.0.

header.stencil

The header.stencil contains the header elements shared by all web pages in the myJournal application:

```
<!DOCTYPE html>
<html lang="en">
<head>
<meta charset="utf-8" />
<title>{{ title }}</title>
<!-- Required meta tags -->
<meta charset="utf-8">
<meta name="viewport" content="width=device-width, initial-scale=1">

<!-- Bootstrap CSS -->
<link rel="stylesheet"
href="https://stackpath.bootstrapcdn.com/bootstrap/4.1.2/css/bootstrap.min.
css" integrity="sha384-
Smlep5jCw/wG7hdkwQ/Z5nLIefveQRIY9nfy6xoR1uRYBtpZgI6339F5dgvm/e9B"
crossorigin="anonymous">

<link rel="stylesheet"
href="https://use.fontawesome.com/releases/v5.2.0/css/all.css"
integrity="sha384-
hWVjflwFxL6sNzntih27bfxkr27PmbbK/iSvJ+a4+0owXq79v+lsFkW54bOGbiDQ"
crossorigin="anonymous">
<!-- Custom CSS -->
```

```
<link rel="stylesheet" href="/css/custom.css">

</head>

<body>
<!--wrapper start-->
<div class="wrapper" id="wrapper">

<!--Banner-->
<header>

<!--Navbar-->
<nav class="navbar navbar-expand-lg navbar-dark fixed-top scrolling-
navbar">
<div class="container">
<a class="navbar-brand" href="#"><strong>myJournal</strong></a>
<button class="navbar-toggler" type="button" data-toggle="collapse" data-
target="#myNavbar" aria-controls="myNavbar" aria-expanded="false" aria-
label="Toggle navigation">
<span class="navbar-toggler-icon"></span>
</button>
<div class="collapse navbar-collapse" id="myNavbar">
<ul class="navbar-nav mr-auto">
<li class="nav-item active">
<a class="nav-link" href="#">Home <span class="sr-
only">(current)</span></a>
</li>
<li class="nav-item">
<a class="nav-link" href="#">Admin</a>
</li>
<li class="nav-item">
<a class="nav-link" href="#">About</a>
</li>
</ul>
</div>
</div>
</nav>


<!--Jumbotron-->
<div class="jumbotron banner-align-top" id="myBanner">
<div class="banner-background text-center" style="background-image:
url(/img/pier.png);">
<div class="container text-center" id="banner-size">
<h2 class="banner-title">My Journal</h2>
<h3 class="banner-subtitle">The Path of Heart!</h3>
</div>
```

```
</div>
</div>

</header>
```

Similar to what you've done in the Vapor project, you are going to add the stylesheets for Bootstrap and Font Awesome, followed by a Bootstrap navigation bar and a `jumbotron`.

footer.stencil

Just like `header.stencil`, the `footer.stencil` file also contains the elements shared by all the web pages in this project:

```
<!--footer-->
<section class="footer" id="footer">
<div class="container">
<div class="row">
<div class="col-sm">
<ul>
<li><i class="fas fa-envelope"></i></li>
<li><i class="fab fa-facebook"></i></li>
<li><i class="fab fa-google-plus-g"></i></li>
<li><i class="fab fa-linkedin"></i></li>
<li><i class="fab fa-twitter"></i></li>
</ul>
<p>
&copy; 2018 - {{ title }} Application by {{ author }}<br>
</p>
</div>
</div>
</div>
</section>

</div><!--wrapper end-->


<!-- Optional JavaScript -->
<!-- jQuery first, then Popper.js, then Bootstrap JavaScript  -->
<script src="https://code.jquery.com/jquery-3.3.1.slim.min.js"
integrity="sha384-
q8i/X+965Dz00rT7abK41JStQIAqVgRVzpbzo5smXKp4YfRvH+8abtTE1Pi6jizo"
crossorigin="anonymous"></script>
<script
src="https://cdnjs.cloudflare.com/ajax/libs/popper.js/1.14.3/umd/popper.min
.js" integrity="sha384-
ZMP7rVo3mIykV+2+9J3UJ46jBk0WLaUAdn689aCwoqbBJiSnjAK/l8WvCWPIPm49"
```

```
crossorigin="anonymous"></script>
<script
src="https://stackpath.bootstrapcdn.com/bootstrap/4.1.2/js/bootstrap.min.js
" integrity="sha384-
o+RDsa0aLu++PJvFqy8fFScvbHFLtbvScb8AjopnFD+iEQ7wo/CG0xlczd+2O/em"
crossorigin="anonymous"></script>

</body>
</html>
```

This shared template adds a row of Font Awesome icons, followed by the CDN links to JavaScript libraries, such as Bootstrap, Popper, and jQuery.

main.stencil

The `main.stencil` file contains the template for displaying all journal entries in a single page:

```
{% include "header.stencil" %}
[ <a class="fas fa-plus-square" href="/journal/create"> Add New Entry</a> ]
<P>
{% for entry in entries %}
<!--Section {{ forloop.counter0 }}-->
<section class="sec{{ forloop.counter0 }}" id="sec{{ forloop.counter0 }}">
<div class="Container entry">
<h2>{{ entry.title }}</h2>
{{ entry.content }}
<BR> [ ID: {{ entry.id }}
: <a class="fas fa-edit" href="/journal/get/{{ forloop.counter0 }}">
Edit</a>
| <a class="fas fa-trash-alt" href="/journal/remove/{{ forloop.counter0
}}"> Remove</a> ]
</div>
</section>
{% endfor %}
Total: {{ count }};
{% include "footer.stencil" %}
```

The new main template replaces the *Edit* and *Remove* icons with those from Font Awesome. Apart from this change, the template remains the same as the main template you used in Chapter 6, *Working with Templating Engines*.

new.stencil

The new.stencil file contains the template that renders a web page with a submission form for creating a new journal entry:

```
{% include "header.stencil" %}
<!--form-->
<section class="form" id="myForm">
<div class="container">
<div class="row">
<div class="col-lg-12">
<div class="heading">
<h1>Create a Journal Entry</h1>
</div>
</div>
</div>
</div>
<div class="container max-width">
<div class="row">
<div class="done">
<div class="alert alert-success">
<button type="button" class="close" data-dismiss="alert">X</button>
Your message has been submitted.
</div>
</div>
<div class="col-md-12">
<form action="/journal/new" method="post" enctype="application/x-www-form-
urlencoded" target="/journal/all">
<fieldset class="form-group">
<input name="id" type="hidden" value="-1" />
<input type="text" class="form-control" name="title" placeholder="Enter
title here">
</fieldset>

<fieldset class="form-group">
<textarea class="form-control" rows="5" name="content" placeholder="Enter
your journal content here..."></textarea>
</fieldset>

<button type="submit" class="entryform submit">Submit</button>
</form>
</div>
</div>
</div>
</section>
{% include "footer.stencil" %}
```

The new template basically is the same as the one you used in the last chapter. It is still listed here for completeness.

entry.stencil

The template in the `entry.stencil` file is used to render an HTML form, populated with the elements of an existing journal entry:

```
{% include "header.stencil" %}
<!--form-->
<section class="form" id="myForm">
<div class="container">
<div class="row">
<div class="col-lg-12">
<div class="heading">
<h1>Edit a Journal Entry</h1>
</div>
</div>
</div>
</div>
<div class="container max-width">
<div class="row">
<div class="done">
<div class="alert alert-success">
<button type="button" class="close" data-dismiss="alert">X</button>
Your message has been submitted.
</div>
</div>
<div class="col-md-12">
<form action="/journal/edit/{{ index }}" method="post"
enctype="application/x-www-form-urlencoded" target="/journal/all">
<fieldset class="form-group">
<input name="id" type="hidden" value="{{ entry.id }}" />
<input name="title" type="text" class="form-control" value="{{ entry.title
}}" />
</fieldset>

<fieldset class="form-group">
<textarea class="form-control" rows="5" name="content">
{{ entry.content }}
</textarea>
</fieldset>

<button type="submit" class="entryform submit">Submit</button>
</form>
</div>
```

```
</div>
</div>
</section>
{% include "footer.stencil" %}
```

Again, there is no change required in the *Edit* template, since it is sufficient to leave Bootstrap code to the *header* and *footer* templates. This is another reason why you want to separate out all of the HTML and templating code that is common to all web pages in shared templates like *header* and *footer*.

The main screen of the `myJournal` for Kitura application is shown here:

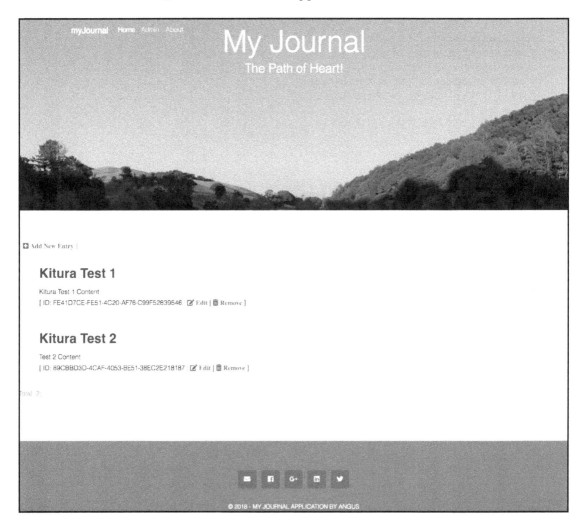

As you can see from the preceding screenshot, the Bootstrap-enhanced rendering output by myJournal for Kitura is almost indistinguishable from that of myJournal for Vapor.

Summary

In this chapter, you learned how to use the Bootstrap library to enhance the look and feel of rendered web pages by the myJournal applications you developed in Chapter 6, *Working with the Templating Engines*. Except for some minor details, the integration of Bootstrap into Leaf and Stencil templates is exactly the same. In the next chapter, you're going to replace the temporary local storage in the myJournal applications with a database.

8
Employing Storage Framework

This chapter encourages you to take advantage of the **Object Relational Mapping** (**ORM**) abstraction between the web application and the database to streamline your workflow when working with a database. One of the major benefits of using the ORM tool is that you don't have to deal with a database directly, avoiding the painful way of writing different querying commands specific to each type of database. Swift web frameworks support a number of database engines and sometimes you can use multiple databases in the same session.

In this chapter, you'll learn how to work with the Fluent abstraction framework in Vapor, and the Kuery framework in Kitura. You'll interact with your model in **Create**, **Retrieve**, **Update**, and **Delete** (**CRUD**) operations using these frameworks.

In this chapter, we will cover the following topics:

- Installing databases
- Working with the Fluent Framework in Vapor
- Working with the Database Abstraction Layer in Kitura

Installing databases

At the time of writing, both Vapor Fluent and Kitura Kuery support three popular implementations of relational databases: **PostgreSQL**, **SQLite**, and **MySQL**. A relational database uses a fixed-data format specified in the database's schema, compared to a non-relational (**NoSQL**) database, which doesn't require a fixed-data format. A relational database is much faster and more proven.

Installing PostgreSQL

PostgreSQL is the recommended native database driver for both Vapor and Kitura. The database is an open source project designed for enterprise use. PostgreSQL is designed for reliability, extensibility, and standards-compliance. Most cloud hosting services include PostgreSQL as one of the database provider options.

To use PostgreSQL on your system, you must install the PostgreSQL client locally. On macOS, use brew to install the PostgreSQL client and start the postgresql service:

```
$ brew install postgresql
$ brew services start postgresql
```

On Linux, use *apt-get* to install the PostgreSQL client and then start the service:

```
$ sudo apt-get install libpq-dev
$ sudo service postgresql start
```

If you have the pgAdmin 4 GUI client application installed on your system, you can also use it to launch and connect to a PostgreSQL database.

Installing SQLite

SQLite is an open source SQL database. It covers a reduced but essential feature set of the full SQL database. Since it is lightweighted and embedded, it has been chosen as the default database for mobile operating systems such as Android and iOS.

In Vapor, you can choose SQLite as either memory or file-based. That makes SQLite an ideal candidate for prototyping and testing your Fluent code. Once you are ready for production deployment, you can switch your database provider to one hosted on the cloud. Vapor uses its embedded SQLite so you do not need to install SQLite on your system.

Kitura's Kuery also position SQLite as a lightweight SQL implementation that is ideal for prototyping and testing your database's operation. Kuery requires you to install SQLite on your system:

1. On macOS, use `brew` to install `sqlite3`:

   ```
   $ brew install sqlite
   ```

   macOS provides an older version of `sqlite3`.

2. To instruct your project to use your installed `sqlite3`, add its path to your `.bash_profile`:

```
echo 'export PATH="/usr/local/opt/sqlite/bin:$PATH"' >>
~/.bash_profile
```

Remember to use `source ~/.bash_profile` to refresh your system with the change.

3. On Linux, use `apt-get` to install `sqlite3` and its static development library:

```
$ sudo apt-get install sqlite3 libsqlite3-dev
```

4. If SQLite is installed properly on your system, you can test it by running the following command on the Terminal:

```
$ sqlite3
```

5. You should get an output similar to the following:

```
SQLite version 3.20.1 2017-08-24 16:21:36
 Enter ".help" for usage hints.
 Connected to a transient in-memory database.
 Use ".open FILENAME" to reopen on a persistent database.
 sqlite>
```

By default, the SQLite instance will connect to a transient in-memory database unless you use the ".open FILENAME" command to explicitly open a persistent database.

Installing MySQL

MySQL is another database driver officially supported by both Vapor and Kitura; like SQLite and PostgresQL, it is also an open source database. MySQL is very popular because it is one of the main components in web services that is based on **LAMP** software stacks. LAMP stands for Linux, Apache Web Server, MySQL, and PHP Scripting Language. The MySQL database is available on most cloud hosting providers.
To have a MySQL database running on your system, install mysql with brew and start the mysql server:

```
$ brew install mysql
$ brew services start mysql
```

If you are using Linux, get the latest mysql package from one of the repositories, use `apt-get` to install it, and start mysql service:

```
$ wget https://repo.mysql.com//mysql-apt-config_0.8.4-1_all.deb
$ sudo dpkg -i mysql-apt-config_0.8.4-1_all.deb
$ sudo apt-get update
$ sudo apt-get install mysql-server libmysqlclient-dev
$ sudo service mysql start
```

To improve the security of your MySQL installation, run the following program:

```
$ mysql_secure_installation
```

Now you should have mysql installed and running on your system. Next, we'll see how to connect to a database from your code using an appropriate database driver.

Working with the Fluent Framework in Vapor

Fluent is Vapor's object-relational mapping (ORM) framework that abstracts the interaction with various database engines. By working with a single interface that abstracts many different database engines, your code will be more reusable and portable. With Fluent, you do not need to write low-level instructions, such as **structured query language** (**SQL**), to work with a database engine. Unlike the traditional way of querying a database using untyped arrays or dictionaries, Fluent build upon Swift's model-driven data-handling infrastructure and extends it to the querying of the database. This is a more natural way for you to interact with database using models.

Choosing a database driver

Fluent supports PostgreSQL, SQLite, and MySQL. You need to configure each database driver in order to use it properly in your Vapor project.

Using the PostgreSQL database driver

Let's start by using PostgreSQL database driver:

1. Add the `PostgreSQL` core as a dependency in your project's SPM package manifest file:

```
import PackageDescription
```

```
let package = Package(
    name: "MyJournal",
    dependencies: [
        ...
        .package(url: "https://github.com/vapor/fluent-
postgresql.git", from: "1.0.0"),
    ],
    targets: [
        .target(name: "App", dependencies: ["FluentPostgreSQL",
...]),
        .target(name: "Run", dependencies: ["App"]),
        .testTarget(name: "AppTests", dependencies: ["App"]),
    ]
)
```

2. After modifying `Package.swift`, remember to regenerate your Xcode project files to reflect the changes:

   ```
   $ vapor xcode
   ```

3. Register `PostgreSQLProvider` in `configure.swift` in order for the PostgreSQL driver to work properly:

   ```
   import PostgreSQL

   try services.register(PostgresSQLProvider())
   ```

4. When you register for PostgreSQL service, it automatically instantiates a database config struct using standard credentials.

5. You can configure for your PostgreSQL database manually and use it to create an instance of `PostgreSQLDatabase`:

   ```
   let config = PostgreSQLDatabaseConfig(hotname: "localhost",
                                         username: "admin",
                                         database: "myjournal",
                                         password: "password")
   let postgresql = try PostgreSQLDatabase(config: config)
   ```

   The preceding configuration code shows you how to set the database's credential.

6. Add the `PostgreSQLDatabase` instance to the list of databases you're going to support in your project:

   ```
   var databases = DatabasesConfig()
   databases.add(database: postgresql, as: .psql)
   services.register(databases)
   ```

These steps should get you set up for using PostgreSQL in your `myJournal` application.

Using the SQLite database driver

If you develop your project from Vapor's boilerplate project using the `vapor new` command, the SQLite database has already been configured and implemented. You can follow the steps here if you want to add SQLiteDatabase to your project from scratch:

1. To add the support of SQLite database, you need to add it as a dependency in your SPM package manifest file:

   ```
   import PackageDescription

   let package = Package(
    name: "MyJournal",
    dependencies: [
    ...
    .package(url: "https://github.com/vapor/fluent-sqlite.git", from:
   "3.0.0"),
    ],
    targets: [
    .target(name: "App", dependencies: ["FluentSQLite", ...]),
    .target(name: "Run", dependencies: ["App"]),
    .testTarget(name: "AppTests", dependencies: ["App"]),
    ]
   )
   ```

2. Update your Xcode project files with the changes you just made in Package.swift:

   ```
   $ vapor xcode
   ```

3. Register `FluentSQLiteProvider` in `configure.swift`:

   ```
   import FluentSQLite

   try services.register(FluentSQLiteProvider())
   ```

   Since SQLite is an embedded database and built on top of Vapor's `DatabaseKit`, you don't need to supply additional login credentials. You can choose either memory or file-based storage when setting up `SQLiteDatabase`.

4. Configure a memory-based SQLite database in `configure.swift`:

   ```
   let sqlite = try SQLiteDatabase(storage: .memory))
   ```

5. Alternatively, configure the database by specifying a local file to use:

```
let sqlite = try SQLiteDatabase(storage: .file(path:
"myjournal.sqlite"))
```

6. Add your `SQLiteDatabase` to one of the databases supported in your project:

```
var databases = DatabasesConfig()
databases.add(database: sqlite, as: .sqlite)
services.register(databases)
```

The SQLite default database identifier is `.sqlite`. Since Vapor allows you to use more than one database in a single project, you can add other databases to the services following the preceding code. While you can have a mixed database environment and configure each database separately, you cannot add or change database dynamically.

Using the MySQL database driver

The steps to configure MySQL are similar to the steps for configuring SQLite and PostgreSQL. Let's get started:

1. Add it as a dependency in `Package.swift`:

```
import PackageDescription

let package = Package(
    name: "MyJournal",
    dependencies: [
        ...
        .package(url: "https://github.com/vapor/fluent-mysql.git",
from: "3.0.0"),
    ],
    targets: [
        .target(name: "App", dependencies: ["FluentMySQL", ...]),
        .target(name: "Run", dependencies: ["App"]),
        .testTarget(name: "AppTests", dependencies: ["App"]),
    ]
)
```

2. Regenerate your Xcode project files after modifying `Package.swift`:

```
$ vapor xcode
```

3. Register `MySQLProvider` in `configure.swift`:

```
import MySQL

try services.register(MySQLProvider())
```

This will enable all of the services required for MySQL to work properly. It also assumes standard credentials.

4. If you want to override the default configuration, you can register a `MySQLDatabaseConfig` struct to your services:

```
let config = MySQLDatabaseConfig(hostname: "localhost",
                                 username: "admin",
                                 database: "myjournal",
                                 password: "password")
let mysql = try MySQLDatabase(config: config)

var databases = DatabasesConfig()
databases.add(database: mysql, as: .mysql)
services.register(databases)
```

That's all for adding and registering MySQL database in `myJournal` for Vapor.

Conforming to the Fluent Model

Fluent's model is the protocol that represents data used by Fluent when interacting with the database. Fluent takes advantage of data-model-centric features in the Swift library, such as `Codable`, which facilitates the handling of JSON objects, and extends the data model to support querying the database.

Creating a new Model

You can use either `struct` or `class` to conform to `Model`. Since `struct` is value-typed, a new copy of the `struct` model will be returned each time you query the database. Class is reference-typed so there won't be a new copy created when the `class` model is returned as the result for querying the database:

1. A new model looks like the following:

```
import FluentPostgreSQL
import Vapor
```

```
final class JournalEntry: PostgreSQLModel {
    var id: Int?
    var title: String
    var content: String
    init(id: Int? = nil, title: String, content: String) {
        self.id = id
        self.title = title
        self.content = content
    }
}
```

The final modifier prevents anyone from subclassing your model.

2. Specify the `id` field:

```
var id: Int?
```

Fluent uses `id` for the internal indexing of each data entry.

3. Add other data fields in your model:

```
var title: String
var content: String
```

4. Add an initializer for your model:

```
init(id: Int? = nil, title: String, content: String) {
    self.id = id
    self.title = title
    self.content = content
}
```

That's all you need for your data model. Next, you're going to explore some Fluent model helpers.

Creating Fluent Migrations

Fluent **Migration** provides you with convenient ways of creating a table for your model and making changes to your database's structure. The table description for your model is called a database schema. Migrations help you prepare a database schema for your model. You can also use them to make normal queries to your database.

There is a shortcut for declaring database migrations for your model. To conform Model to Migration, add an extension to conform to Migration:

```
extension JournalEntry: Migration {}
```

Fluent can infer the schema of your model automatically.

Add the following to tell Migration to create a table:

```
var migrations = MigrationConfig()
migrations.add(model: JournalEntry.self, database: .psql)
services.register(migrations)
```

In the preceding code, `PostgreSQLDatabase` is added to your model's migrations.

Migration just needs to run this once when a table is created. Fluent supports a mixed environment, so you can use more than one database in your project. If you have more than one database, you need to set up each database migration properly.

Using Fluent Model Helpers

Fluent provides many other convenient Model Helper protocols for database providers in Vapor.

For example, you may want to conform your model to `Codable` by extending your model to the **Content** type:

```
extension JournalEntry: Content {}
```

Vapor 3.0 supports many `Content` types (JSON, Multipart, protobuf) and treats them the same for encoding and decoding the content.

As another example, you may want to support a dynamic component in your route path with the `Parameter` extension:

```
extension JournalEntry: Parameter {}
```

Your model, with all the Fluent model helpers, now looks like the following:

```
import FluentPostgreSQL
import Vapor

final class JournalEntry: PostgreSQLModel {
    var id: Int?
    var title: String
    var content: String
    init(id: Int? = nil, title: String, content: String) {
        self.id = id
        self.title = title
        self.content = content
    }
```

```
}

extension JournalEntry: Migration { }
extension JournalEntry: Content { }
extension JournalEntry: Parameter { }
```

Next, you're going to use the `JournalEntry` model defined here to handle CRUD operations.

Implementing CRUD operations for Vapor

Fluent Model supports basic CRUD methods. Based on the same `myJournal` code you used in last chapter, you'll replace the in-memory persistence with the Fluent model using `SQLiteDatabase` and modify the route handlers to call CRUD methods directly.

Implementing the create operation

To create a new item for an instance of your model in the database, call the `.save(on:)` method:

```
func newEntry(_ req: Request) throws -> Future<Response> {
    return try req.content.decode(JournalEntry.self).flatMap { entry in
        return entry.save(on: req)
    }.transform(to: req.redirect(to: self.mainPage))
}
```

When the `save()` method completes, Fluent will automatically have filled in its `id` with a new, unique value, and it's safe to return.

In order for Fluent to work properly, you're required to remove the default ID in `new.leaf`:

```
<input name="id" type="hidden" value="-1" />
```

Now, let's proceed to implementing the *Read* operation.

Implementing the read operation

To read all of your records in a database, use `query(on:)` to query the database and `all()` to list all of them:

```
func getAll(_ req: Request) throws -> Future<View> {
    return JournalEntry.query(on: req).all().flatMap(to: View.self) {
```

```
entries in
        let context = JournalContext(title: self.title,
                                     author: self.author,
                                     count: String(entries.count),
                                     entries: entries)
        let leaf = try req.make(LeafRenderer.self)
        return leaf.render("main", context)
    }
}
```

If you know the ID of an item, you can use `find(_:on:)` instead of `query(on:)`. The following code shows you how to retrieve an item by its `id`:

```
func getEntry(_ req: Request) throws -> Future<View> {
    let id = try req.parameters.next(Int.self)
    return JournalEntry.find(id, on: req).flatMap(to: View.self) { entry in
        guard let entry = entry else { throw Abort(.notFound) }
        let leaf = try req.make(LeafRenderer.self)
        let context : EntryContext
        context = EntryContext(title: self.title,
                               author: self.author,
                               entry: entry)
        return leaf.render("entry", context)
    }
}
```

In the preceding code, the `.notFound` status code will be set in HTTP Response if an entry can't be found after calling `JournalEntry.find(_:on:)`.

Implementing the update operation

Continue to implement the update operation that works with an existing entry:

```
func editEntry(_ req: Request) throws -> Future<Response> {
    let id = try req.parameters.next(Int.self)
    return try req.content.decode(JournalEntry.self).flatMap { updated in
        return JournalEntry.find(id, on: req)
                           .flatMap(to: JournalEntry.self) { original in
                               guard let original = original else { throw
Abort(.notFound) }

                               original.title = updated.title
                               original.content = updated.content
                               return original.save(on: req)
        }
    }.transform(to: req.redirect(to: self.mainPage))
}
```

The update method matches the existing item associated with an instance of your model, makes any necessary changes, and then saves it back to the database.

Implementing the delete operation

The delete method is similar to the update method by matching with an existing entry. Once found, you'll call `delete(on:)` to remove it the item from the database:

```
func removeEntry(_ req: Request) throws -> Future<Response> {
    let id = try req.parameters.next(Int.self)
    return JournalEntry.find(id, on: req).flatMap { entry in
        guard let entry = entry else { throw Abort(.notFound) }
        return entry.delete(on: req).transform(to: req.redirect(to:
self.mainPage))
    }
}
```

After an entry is successfully deleted, the user will be redirected to the application's main screen.

Working with the Database Abstraction Layer in Kitura

Swift-Kuery-ORM is an ORM Framework that simplifies your interaction with the database using model objects. Similar to Vapor's Fluent, Swift-Kuery-ORM provides you with a single interface for many different database engines and relieves you from the burden of writing tedious low-level queries to the database. The framework itself is built on top of Swift-query, which is a lower-level abstraction layer that allows you to customize SQL queries for the database. Normally it is sufficient for you to use Swift-Kuery-ORM only for the persistence of model objects with your server, but you can always switch to Swift-Kuery when you have to customize SQL queries.

Choosing a database driver

Kitura Kuery supports SQLite, PostgreSQL, and MySQL. For each database driver, you need to add the dependencies to Swift Package Manager and import the ORM and database plugin packages into your Kitura project.

Using the PostgreSQL database driver

Follow these steps to use PostgreSQL in your project:

1. Add `SwiftKueryORM` and `SwiftKuerySQLite` to the dependencies and targets in your application's `Package.swift`:

```
import PackageDescription

let package = Package(
    name: "myJournal",
    dependencies: [
      .package(url: "https://github.com/IBM-Swift/Kitura.git",
.upToNextMinor(from: "2.5.0")),
      .package(url:
"https://github.com/IBM-Swift/HeliumLogger.git",
.upToNextMinor(from: "1.7.1")),
      .package(url:
"https://github.com/IBM-Swift/CloudEnvironment.git", from:
"8.0.0"),
      .package(url:
"https://github.com/RuntimeTools/SwiftMetrics.git", from: "2.0.0"),
      .package(url: "https://github.com/IBM-Swift/Health.git",
from: "1.0.0"),
      .package(url:
"https://github.com/IBM-Swift/Kitura-StencilTemplateEngine.git",
from: "1.8.0"),
      .package(url:
"https://github.com/IBM-Swift/Swift-Kuery-ORM.git",
.upToNextMinor(from: "0.3.1")),
      .package(url:
"https://github.com/IBM-Swift/Swift-Kuery-PostgreSQL.git", from:
"1.2.0"),
      ],
      targets: [
      .target(name: "myJournal", dependencies: [ .target(name:
"Application"), "Kitura" , "HeliumLogger", "KituraStencil"]),
      .target(name: "Application", dependencies: [ "Kitura",
"CloudEnvironment","SwiftMetrics","Health", "SwiftKueryORM",
"SwiftKueryPostgreSQL"]),

      .testTarget(name: "ApplicationTests" , dependencies:
[.target(name: "Application"), "Kitura","HeliumLogger" ])
      ]
)
```

2. Create a database for your application after you've started a postgresql service:

```
brew install postgresql
brew services start postgresql
createdb journalbook
```

This makes sure that postgresql is running and a table named journalbook exists on your system. By default, postgresql uses port 5432.

3. Create the `JournalRoutes.swift` file in `/Sources/Application/Routes/`, in the same directory as `HealthRoutes.swift`:

```swift
import Foundation
import Kitura
import KituraStencil
import SwiftKueryORM
import SwiftKueryPostgreSQL
import LoggerAPI

func initializeJournalRoutes(app: App) {
    let mainPage = "/journal/all"
    let title = "My Journal"
    let author = "Angus"

    let poolOptions = ConnectionPoolOptions(initialCapacity: 1,
                                            maxCapacity: 5,
                                            timeout: 10000)
    // Set up database connection
    let psqlPool = PostgreSQLConnection.createPool(host:
"localhost",
                                                   port: 5432,
                                                   options:
[.databaseName("journalbook")],
                                                   poolOptions:
poolOptions)
    Database.default = Database(psqlPool)

    do {
        try JournalItem.createTableSync()
    } catch let error {
        Log.error("Failed to create table in database: \(error)")
    }
}
```

Both the `SwiftKueryORM` and `SwiftKueryPostgreSQL` headers are included before you can call `.createPool()` to set up a database connection.

4. Import both `SwiftKueryORM` and `SwiftKuerySQLite`:

```
import SwiftKueryORM
import SwiftKueryPostgreSQL
```

5. Configure an `poolOptions` object for the PostgreSQL `Connection` instance:

```
let poolOptions = ConnectionPoolOptions(initialCapacity: 1,
                                        maxCapacity: 5,
                                        timeout: 10000)
```

6. Create the instance of the PostgreSQL `Connection` itself:

```
// Set up database connection
let psqlPool = PostgreSQLConnection.createPool(host: "localhost",
                                               port: 5432,
                                               options:
[.databaseName("journalbook")],
                                               poolOptions:
poolOptions)
```

You've specified a PostgreSQL database that is called `journalbook` and runs on localhost at port 5432.

7. Assign the database connection you've just created as the default database connection to use:

```
Database.default = Database(psqlPool)
```

8. Create a table in the database:

```
do {
  try JournalItem.createTableSync()
} catch let error {
  Log.error("Failed to create table in database: \(error)")
}
```

You can create a table synchronously using the `createTableSync()` method, or asynchronously using `createTable()`. The preceding implementation throws an error if a table has been created already. You can either ignore the error or handle it gracefully by printing out a warning message and continue the rest of the operation.

Setting up the SQLite database driver

You may follow the same steps for setting up a PostgreSQL database connection to create a SQLite database. All the setup for the SQLite database goes to the `initializeJournalRoutes(app:)` function in `JournalRoutes.swift`.

1. Create an instance of Swift-Kuery-SQLite by calling the `.createPool` method of `SQLiteConnection`:

```
let pool = SQLiteConnection.createPool(filename: "sqlite.db",
                                       poolOptions:
ConnectionPoolOptions(initialCapacity: 10,
maxCapacity: 30,
timeout: 10000))

 Database.default = Database(pool)
```

`ConnectionPool` allows you to support multiple connections to your SQLite database. If you omit a filename, your database will be in-memory.

2. If you want a single connection, you can create `SQLiteConnection` as follows:

```
let connection = SQLiteConnection(filename: "myjournal.sqlite")
```

That's all for setting up a SQLite database driver in the Kitura project. Read on if you need a MySQL database driver in your project.

Using the MySQL database driver

Following the similar steps as in SQLite and PostgreSQL configuration and add the following code in `initializeJournalRoutes(app:)`:

1. Add appropriate dependencies for Kuery MySQL in `Package.swift`:

```
import PackageDescription

let package = Package(
    name: "myJournal",
    dependencies: [
        ...
        .package(url:
"https://github.com/IBM-Swift/Swift-Kuery-ORM.git", from: "0.3.1"),
        .package(url:
"https://github.com/IBM-Swift/Swift-Kuery-MySQL.git", from:
"1.2.0")
```

```
            ],
            targets: [
               .target(name: "myJournal", dependencies: [...,
       "SwiftKueryORM", "SwiftKueryMySQL"]),
               ...
            ]
       )
```

2. In your Kitura application, import the SwiftKueryORM and SwiftKueryMySQL packages into any files using Kuery methods:

```
import SwiftKueryORM
import SwiftKueryMySQL
```

3. Create a connection to the MySQL database:

```
let connection = MySQLConnection(host: "localhost",
                                 user: "admin",
                                 password: "admin",
                                 database: "myjournal",
                                 port: "1234")
```

All the parameters for MySQLConnection are optional. The port number is used when you want to use non-standard ports for a TCP/IP connection.

Conforming to the Swift-Kuery-ORM Model

Similar to Fluent, Swift-Kuery-ORM provides very convenient high-level features for data persistence using the Model protocol. Once you've designed and built your data structure on Model, you can perform CRUD operations on your data without writing any SQL queries.

Creating a new model

You can design your data structure using either class or struct. In Swift, class is a reference type while struct is a value type. Here, struct is a better choice because using let on a struct turns your data object into a constant. The immutability of struct makes memory-handling easier in multithreaded environment.

1. To create a new model, declare a struct that implements Swift's Codable protocol:

```
struct Entry: Codable {
```

```
    var title: String
    var content: String
}
```

`Codable` simplifies the handling of JSON objects in our RESTful routes.

2. Extend your `struct` to support the `Model` protocol:

```
extension Grade: Model { }
```

The extension adds additional ORM functionalities to your data model. You do not need to include an `id` field to identify each data entry uniquely. Kuery ORM will create the `id` field and increment the value of `id` automatically when you add a new entry to the database.

Implementing the CRUD operations

Once your data `struct` is conforming to `Model`, you can automatically use the data model in the database's CRUD operations.

Displaying all records

The objects in your database can be conveniently retrieved.

1. If you want to get all the instances of your object, call the `finalAll()` function:

```
JournalItem.findAll()
```

2. You can ask Swift-Kuery-ORM to format the retrieved result in a dictionary:

```
JournalItem.findAll { (result: [Int: JournalItem]?, error:
RequestError?) in
  . . .
}
```

3. Alternatively, you can specify the output format as an array of tuples:

```
JournalItem.findAll { (result: [(Int, JournalItem)]?, error:
RequestError?) in
  . . .
}
```

The last two output formats are useful if you need to retrieve the ID for each entry.

4. In the implementation of `initializeJournalRoutes(app:)`, add the implementation of a router to retrieve all data right after the *do-try-catch* block:

```
app.router.get("/journal/all") { _, response, _ in
  JournalItem.findAll { (result: [(Int, JournalItem)]?, error:
RequestError?) in
    guard let items = result else { return }
    var entries: [[String: Any]] = []
    for (index, entry) in items {
      let id = String(index)
      let title : String = entry.title
      let content : String = entry.content
      let map = ["id": id, "title": title, "content": content]
      entries.append(map)
    }
    do {
        try response.render("main", context: ["title": title,
                                              "author": author,
                                              "count":
"\(items.count)",
                                              "entries": entries])
    } catch let error {
        response.send(error.localizedDescription)
    }
  }
}
```

This implementation calls Model's `findAll()` method to retrieve both `ID` and `JournalItem` in a tuple output format. The IDs are needed because you want to embed the Edit and Removal links for each record you are displaying.

Unfortunately, you can't pass the tuple directly as a context to your Stencil template. You'll need to flatten the tuples into a 2D array structure by creating the new array structure, `[[String: Any]]`, mapping the tuple values to a new array object, and appending the mapped array object to the 2D array context.

5. Create the new Stencil template, `main.stencil`, to render the main screen, which takes in the context:

```
{% include "header.stencil" %}
[ <a class="fas fa-plus-square" href="/journal/create"> Add New
Entry</a> ]
<P>
{% for entry in entries %}
<!--Section {{ forloop.counter0 }}-->
<section class="sec{{ forloop.counter0 }}" id="sec{{
forloop.counter0 }}">
```

```
<div class="Container entry">
<h2>{{ entry.title }}</h2>
{{ entry.content }}
<BR> [ ID: {{ entry.id }}
: <a class="fas fa-edit" href="/journal/get/{{ entry.id }}">
Edit</a>
| <a class="fas fa-trash-alt" href="/journal/remove/{{ entry.id
}}"> Remove</a> ]
</div>
</section>
{% endfor %}
Total: {{ count }};
{% include "footer.stencil" %}
```

Here, you can see how the id attribute is used in the URLs for the *Edit* and *Remove* operations for each displayed record.

Displaying a single record

If you want to retrieve only a specified object, use the find() function:

```
JournalItem.find(id: 1) { result, error in
  ...
}
```

The find() function expects the explicit id parameter. Since you do not know each record's ID (IDs are created automatically), you rely on the existing links for each record that are ready populated with the IDs to help retrieve the specific record you are looking for. You can find a similar technique used in the implementation of the *Edit* and *Remove* route handlers.

Creating a new record

With Swift-Kuery-ORM, it is very easy to save a new object to your database, just perform the following steps:

1. Create the object and use the save() function:

```
let item = JournalItem(title: "What a beautiful day!", content:
"Best time for an outing.")
item.save { item, error in
  ...
}
```

2. Swift-Kuery-ORM will automatically add an ID when it saves your object.

3. Add the new stencil file, `new.stencil`, to display a form for the user to fill in a new record:

```
{% include "header.stencil" %}
<!--form-->
<section class="form" id="myForm">
<div class="container">
<div class="row">
<div class="col-lg-12">
<div class="heading">
<h1>Create a Journal Entry</h1>
</div>
</div>
</div>
</div>
<div class="container max-width">
<div class="row">
<div class="done">
<div class="alert alert-success">
<button type="button" class="close" data-dismiss="alert">X</button>
Your message has been submitted.
</div>
</div>
<div class="col-md-12">
<form action="/journal/new" method="post" enctype="application/x-
www-form-urlencoded" target="/journal/all">
<fieldset class="form-group">
<input type="text" class="form-control" name="title"
placeholder="Enter title here">
</fieldset>

<fieldset class="form-group">
<textarea class="form-control" rows="5" name="content"
placeholder="Enter your journal content here..."></textarea>
</fieldset>

<button type="submit" class="entryform submit">Submit</button>
</form>
</div>
</div>
</div>
</section>
{% include "footer.stencil" %}
```

4. This form can be retrieved by this route added to `initializeJournalRoutes(app:)`:

```
app.router.get("/journal/create") { request, response, next in
    response.headers["Content-Type"] = "text/html; charset=utf-8"
    try response.render("new", context: ["title": title, "author":
author])
}
```

5. Add the following HTTP POST route handler to `initializeJournalRoutes(app:)` to process the submitted form data:

```
app.router.post("/journal/new") { request, response, next in
    guard let entry = try? request.read(as: JournalItem.self)
        else { return try
response.status(.unprocessableEntity).end() }
    let item = JournalItem(title: entry.title, content:
entry.content)
    item.save { item, error in
    do {
         try response.redirect(mainPage)
    } catch let error {
        response.send(error.localizedDescription)
    }
    }
}
```

If the saving of a new entry is successful, the user will be redirected to the main page.

Updating an existing record

To modify an existing object in your database, perform the following steps:

1. Use the `update(id:)` function with the object's ID as the parameter:

```
let item = JournalItem(title: "What a beautiful day!", content:
"Best time for an outing.")
item.title = "Nice Weather!"
item.update(id: 1) { item, error in

    ...
}
```

Each record in the main screen has already populated with the Edit link to display a form for editing.

2. Add the following Stencil template, entry.stencil, to the `/Views` directory:

```
{% include "header.stencil" %}
<!--form-->
<section class="form" id="myForm">
<div class="container">
<div class="row">
<div class="col-lg-12">
<div class="heading">
<h1>Edit a Journal Entry</h1>
</div>
</div>
</div>
</div>
<div class="container max-width">
<div class="row">
<div class="done">
<div class="alert alert-success">
<button type="button" class="close" data-dismiss="alert">X</button>
Your message has been submitted.
</div>
</div>
<div class="col-md-12">
<form action="/journal/edit/{{ entry.id }}" method="post"
enctype="application/x-www-form-urlencoded" target="/journal/all">
<fieldset class="form-group">
<input name="id" type="hidden" value="{{ entry.id }}" />
<input name="title" type="text" class="form-control" value="{{
entry.title }}" />
</fieldset>

<fieldset class="form-group">
<textarea class="form-control" rows="5" name="content">
{{ entry.content }}
</textarea>
</fieldset>

<button type="submit" class="entryform submit">Submit</button>
</form>
</div>
</div>
</div>
</section>
{% include "footer.stencil" %}
```

3. The Edit form is retrieved through the following handler in
   `initializeJournalRoutes(app:)`:

```
app.router.get("/journal/get/:index?") { request, response, next in
  guard let index = request.parameters["index"] else {
    return try response.status(.badRequest).send("Missing entry
index").end()
  }
  guard let idx = Int(index) else {
    return try response.status(.badRequest).send("Invalid entry
index").end()
  }

  JournalItem.find(id: idx) { result, error in
    guard let item = result else { return }
    let id = String(idx)
    let title : String = item.title
    let content : String = item.content
    let entry = ["id": id, "title": title, "content": content]
    do {
      try response.render("entry",
                          context: ["title": title,
                                    "author": author,
                                    "entry": entry])
    } catch let error {
       response.send(error.localizedDescription)
    }
  }
}
```

4. The submitted data is processed by an HTTP POST route handler:

```
app.router.post("/journal/edit/:index?") { request, response, next
in
    guard let index = request.parameters["index"] else {
        return try response.status(.badRequest).send("Missing entry
index").end()
    }
    guard let idx = Int(index) else {
        return try response.status(.badRequest).send("Invalid entry
index").end()
    }
    guard let entry = try? request.read(as: JournalItem.self) else
{
        return try response.status(.unprocessableEntity).end()
    }
    let item = JournalItem(title: entry.title, content:
entry.content)
```

```
            item.update(id: index) { item, error in
                do {
                    try response.redirect(mainPage)
                } catch let error {
                    response.send(error.localizedDescription)
                }
            }
        }
    }
```

Updating an existing record is less straightforward because the existing entry's ID must be populated in the *Edit* form so the same entry in the database can be sequentially updated.

Deleting a record

If you want to delete a specific object, perform the following steps:

1. Use `delete(id:)` if you know the object's ID:

    ```
    JournalItem.delete(id: 1) { error in
        . . .
    }
    ```

2. Sometimes, you may want to delete all the entries in the current table of your database. You can use `deleteAll()` to do so:

    ```
    JournalItem.deleteAll { error in
        . . .
    }
    ```

3. The following, shows the route handler for deleting a record in the implementation of `initializeJournalRoutes(app: App)`:

    ```
    app.router.get("/journal/remove/:index?") { request, response, next
    in
     guard let index = request.parameters["index"] else {
     return try response.status(.badRequest).send("Missing entry
    index").end()
     }
     guard let idx = Int(index) else {
     return try response.status(.badRequest).send("Invalid entry
    index").end()
     }

     JournalItem.delete(id: idx) { error in
     do {
     try response.redirect(mainPage)
    ```

```
    } catch let error {
    response.send(error.localizedDescription)
    }
    }
    }
}
```

Generally, it is not recommended for you to use the `deleteAll()` function to wipe out the entire table. A safe way is not to expose a route that implements such a global operation in your application.

Summary

In this chapter, you learned how to set up a database and replaced the temporary storage in `myJournal` applications with more permanent database storage. You learned how to install three SQL databases on your system: SQLite, PostgreSQL, and MySQL. Then, you integrated the PostgreSQL software driver into your Vapor project and came up with a new data model that conforms to the Fluent Model. With Vapor Fluent, you implemented the CRUD operations for PostgreSQL. Next, you integrated database drivers into your Kitura application. Swift-Kuery-ORM is a Fluent-like abstraction for database management and manipulation in Kitura. You took advantage of Swift-Kuery-ORM to implement the CRUD operations for PostgreSQL in the myJournal for Kitura application. In the next chapter, you will add authentication and Admin account management to the codebase you worked on here.

Adding Authentication 9

It is important for your web app to regulate who can access your content and use your services and who can't. In a typical web application, resources are usually placed in either protected or public areas. There are many resources or features you do not want users to get access to, such as administrative features for your app, or subscription-based content, and you want to restrict the access to protected content. For example, in the `myJournal` application, only the application owner, or a small group of users, is allowed to create, edit, or delete a journal entry.

This chapter introduces you to the key features in user-access management: user authentication, cookies, and sessions management. You'll learn how to set up a user model and password-protected content. With the authentication API, you're going to grant and remove access for different users. You'll then learn how to manipulate cookies and manage user login sessions, and implement logic to validate user input.

In this chapter, we will cover the following topics:

- Getting introduced to the Authentication API for Vapor
- Knowing how to set up secured access for protected content
- Getting familiar with HTTP Basic Authentication for Kitura

Introducing the authentication API for Vapor

In Swift web frameworks, there are two authentication approaches: web-based and API-based. For the web-based authentication, a framework takes advantage of web browser's session ability to persist the authenticated access. For API-based authentication, the client to a Swift web framework may not be a web browser. In that case, a token is generated to persist authenticated access for a user. In this chapter, you'll focus on securing your web resources with web-based authentication.

Using web authentication

A Swift web framework uses a web browser's sessions to persist state across multiple HTTP requests. A session is temporary because your session cookie may be deleted sometimes, depending on the policy settings for cookie persistence. The session stores individual data in a browser pertaining to the usage by a unique user who comes to visit your web application. When a session is started, the web application sends a cookie to the web browser. The web browser will store each application's cookie to maintain state throughout a session. The interaction between your web browser and web application is illustrated in this sequence diagram:

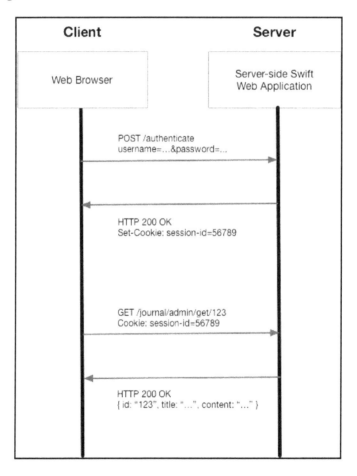

Your Vapor application uses a unique ID to identify a user's session. With the session ID, user-specific information associated with a session can be stored in your web application's cookies and retrieved later. When the next HTTP request comes in, your web application will query for the session data to check whether the user is currently authenticated. If the user is authenticated already, your application won't ask the user to supply the login credentials again.

Setting up AuthenticationProvider

In order to use HTTP authentication, add package dependencies to the Swift Package Manager's manifest file, `Package.swift`:

```
...
.package(url: "https://github.com/vapor/auth.git", from: "2.0.0"),
...
dependencies: ["FluentPostgreSQL",
 "Vapor",
 "Leaf",
 "Authentication"]
```

Like enabling other services in Vapor, you then register `AuthenticationProvider` in `configure.swift`:

```
try services.register(AuthenticationProvider())
```

You then import the authentication package into `configure.swift` and any Swift files that use `Authentication` functions:

```
import Authentication
```

Configuring for SessionMiddleware

While `AuthenticationProvider` allows you to authenticate a user, you'll also need to set up `SessionMiddleware` in Vapor in order to maintain the user's sessions.

Add the following code before `services.register(middlewares)` in `configure.swift`:

```
middlewares.use(SessionsMiddleware.self)
```

The session middleware by default uses in-memory storage for session information. In future Vapor releases, Vapor may add support for Fluent databases, such as SQLite, PostgreSQL, and MySQL, or cache service, such as Redis, to store the session information.

If you want to use key-value storage for sessions, configure your middleware's preference to be the KeyedCache service that is supported in Vapor:

```
config.prefer(MemoryKeyedCache.self, for: KeyedCache.self)
```

Constructing a Model

Now it's time to construct a Model that you can use to hold up the administrator's credentials. Since you may want to manage the administrator accounts in your application, it's better to construct a new model so a new table will be created in the database to store the account information.

First, create a new Swift file, Models/Admin.swift, and import the following packages:

```
import FluentPostgreSQL
import Vapor
import Authentication
```

Next, subclass a new Admin class from one of the Fluent models, PostgreSQLModel:

```
final class Admin: PostgreSQLModel {
    var id: Int?
     var name: String
     var login: String
     var password: String // password is hashed
     init(id: Int? = nil, name: String, login: String, password: String) {
        self.id = id
        self.name = name
        self.login = login
        self.password = password
    }
}
```

The Admin class has a modifier, final, so you don't need to worry anyone who can subclass from your Admin class.

Like any other database model in Fluent, PostgreSQLModel automatically increases the id property and you typically don't need to assign a value to the model's id.

Then, you need to extend your class from the `PasswordAuthenticatable` protocol and specify which properties you want to use for authentication purpose. Here's how it's done:

```
extension Admin: PasswordAuthenticatable {
    static var usernameKey: WritableKeyPath<Admin, String> {
        return \.login
    }
    static var passwordKey: WritableKeyPath<Admin, String> {
        return \.password
    }
}
```

Here, you use the `.login` property as the protocol's `usernameKey` and the `.password` property as the protocol's `passwordKey`.

Finally, add other required protocols to your `Admin` class:

```
extension Admin: SessionAuthenticatable { }
extension Admin: Migration { }
extension Admin: Content { }
extension Admin: Parameter { }
```

The `SessionAuthenticatable` protocol allows you to keep the authenticated state throughout each session once a user has successfully logged in as an administrator. For a review of the `Migration`, `Content`, and `Parameter` protocols, please refer to `Chapter 8`, *Employing Storage Framework*.

Accessing protected content

Since your model can now be authenticated by both password and session, you're ready to separate routes into public and protected content. A clear separation between public and protected content is needed so you don't accidentally expose protected content to unauthenticated users in public routes. The **route grouping** technique in Vapor is useful in organizing public and protected routes into distinct route groups. You can apply an authentication requirement to the route group with routes of protected content.

Any user who wishes to get access to the protected content must first provide login credentials to your Vapor application, and then the application will authenticate the submitted user login and password information using the credential information stored in the database .

Adding public routes

Open the existing `JournalRoutes.swift` and add a new line of code to import the `Authentication` package into the `JournalRoutes` struct:

```
import Authentication
```

Add `loginPage` related constants to the `JournalRoutes` struct:

```
let loginPage = "/journal/login"
let loginPageWithError = "/journal/login?error"
let loginPageNeedLogin = "/journal/login?login"
```

Define a new context, `LoginContext`, to hold the information used in rendering the new template, `login.leaf`:

```
struct LoginContext : Encodable {
  let login: Bool
  let error: Bool
  let title: String
  let author: String
}
```

Group and direct all routes in your web application to the authentication session middleware:

```
func boot(router: Router) throws {
  let authSession = Admin.authSessionsMiddleware()
  let authRouter = router.grouped(authSession)
  ...
}
```

All routes will be processed by the authentication session middleware before reaching you.

You can now separate the routes into public and protected.

Group public routes and add routes to handle login/logout:

```
func boot(router: Router) throws {
  let authSession = Admin.authSessionsMiddleware()
  let authRouter = router.grouped(authSession)
  let publicRouter = authRouter.grouped("journal")
  // public routes
  publicRouter.get("", use: getAll)
  publicRouter.get("all", use: getAll)
  publicRouter.get("login", use: showLogin)
  publicRouter.post("auth", use: checkLogin)
  publicRouter.get("logout", use: logout)
```

```
    . . .
}
```

In addition to the existing routes that are routed to the `getAll()` handler, you are adding three new routes:

- **login**: Renders the `login.leaf` template so a user can use its form to submit login credentials
- **auth**: Handles the HTTP POST request as a result of the submission of the login form
- **logout**: Destroys the current authentication session and reroutes the user to "public" content

The preceding code shows how all public routes are grouped into `publicRouter`. The public routes allow any users to access to the content these routes expose to them. You are exposing two kinds of content to the public users: you allow them to view all journal entries in the database.

Adding the login page

One of the routes you added previously to the public route is to render a Login page for the user to enter credential information.

Add the `showLogin` handler for the "login" route:

```
func showLogin(_ req: Request) throws -> Future<View> {
    let leaf = try req.make(LeafRenderer.self)
    var loginError : Bool = false
    var loginRequired : Bool = false
    if req.query[Bool.self, at: "error"] != nil { loginError = true }
    if req.query[Bool.self, at: "login"] != nil { loginRequired = true }

    let context = LoginContext(login: loginRequired,
                               error: loginError,
                               title: self.title,
                               author: self.author)
        return leaf.render("login", context)
}
```

The `showLogin` handler passes a `LoginContext` instance to render the `login.leaf` template. It checks for the "error" and "login" URL-encoded parameters in the HTTP GET request and puts the information in `LoginContext`. The two Boolean properties in `LoginContext`, `loginError`, and `loginRequired` are used to determine whether there was a previous failed login attempt.

Create the `login.leaf` template for the login page:

```
#embed("header")
<!--form-->
<section class="form" id="myLoginForm">
<div class="container">
    <div class="row">
        <div class="col-lg-12">
            <div class="heading">
                <h1>Login as an Admin</h1>
            </div>
        </div>
    </div>
</div>
<div class="container max-width">
    #if(error) {
        <div class="row">
            <div class="col-md-12">
                <div class="alert alert-danger" role="alert">
                    Incorrect email or password
                </div>
            </div>
        </div>
    }
    #if(login) {
        <div class="row">
            <div class="col-md-12">
                <div class="alert alert-info" role="alert">
                    You need to login as an admin
                </div>
            </div>
        </div>
    }
    <div class="row">
        <div class="col-md-12">
            <form action="/journal/auth" method="post">
                <fieldset class="form-group">
                    <input type="hidden" name="name" value="dontcare"/>
                    <input type="text" class="form-control" name="login"
placeholder="Enter your login (email or username) here.">
                    <input type="password" class="form-control"
name="password" placeholder="Enter your password here.">
                </fieldset>
                <button type="submit" class="entryform
submit">Submit</button>
            </form>
        </div>
    </div>
```

```
    </div>
    </section>
    #embed("footer")
```

This form will send an HTTP POST request to Vapor for user authentication. Since you are not going to use the `name` in authentication, the `name` field is hidden and provided with a dummy string.

Checking login credentials

The login credentials are submitted through the HTTP POST request to the `/journal/auth` route. You can now implement the code to process the submitted login credentials.

Add the `checkLogin` handler to process the login credentials:

```
func checkLogin(_ req: Request) throws -> Future<Response> {
    return try req.content.decode(Admin.self).flatMap { candidate in
        return Admin.authenticate(username: candidate.login,
                                  password: candidate.password,
                                  using: BCryptDigest(),
                                  on: req).map { admin in
                                      guard let admin = admin else {
                                          return req.redirect(to:
self.loginPageWithError)

                                      }
                                      try req.authenticateSession(admin)
                                      return req.redirect(to: self.mainPage)
        }
    }
}
```

Since `Admin` implements the `passwordAuthenticatable` protocol, you can use `Admin.athenticated(username: password: using: on:)` to verify the submitted credentials. For the parameter, specify it to be `BCryptDigest()`. If the login credentials have been authenticated successfully, call `.authenticateSession()` to set up the authentication session and redirect the view to the main page. If the submitted login credentials failed to authenticate successfully, redirect the view to the login page, with the error flag turned on.

Logging out of the current session

For completeness, you can finish the handler for the `logout` route.

Add the following `logout` handler function:

```
func logout(_ req: Request) throws -> Response { // no async call
    try req.unauthenticateSession(Admin.self)
    return req.redirect(to: self.mainPage)
}
```

The logout handler simply calls the `.unauthenticateSession()` provided in the `sessionAuthenticatable` protocol to exit the current session.

Specifying protected routes

Now, you're ready to specify the routes that require secured access. To do that, use `RedirectMiddleware` to reroute any unauthenticated access requests to the `login` template.

Add `secureRouter` in `JournalRoutes.swift`, right after the group of public routes:

```
let securedRouter = authRouter.grouped(RedirectMiddleware<Admin>(path:
"/journal/login"))
```

You can build onto `secureRouter` to specify all protected routes.

Add the following HTTP GET and POST requests to `securedRouter`:

```
// protected routes: entries
let adminRouter = securedRouter.grouped("journal/admin")
adminRouter.get("create", use: createEntry)
adminRouter.post("new", use: newEntry)
adminRouter.get(Int.parameter, "get", use: getEntry)
adminRouter.post(Int.parameter, "edit", use: editEntry)
adminRouter.get(Int.parameter, "remove", use: removeEntry)
```

Using the authenticated state

To display different messages in a template according to the authentication state, you can pass a Boolean value via the `Encodable` context to your Leaf template.

Add the `isAdmin` Boolean to `JournalContext`:

```
struct JournalContext : Encodable {
    let isAdmin: Bool
    let title: String
    let author: String
    let count: String
```

```
    let entries: [JournalEntry]
}
```

In the `header.leaf` template, you use `isAdmin` to display different options for the user. When the user is not authenticated, you want to display a link that allows the user to login; otherwise, display the logout link for an authenticated user to exit the session:

```
<!DOCTYPE html>
<html lang="en">
<head>
<meta charset="utf-8" />
<title>#(title)</title>
<!-- Required meta tags -->
<meta charset="utf-8">
<meta name="viewport" content="width=device-width, initial-scale=1">

<!-- Bootstrap CSS -->
<link rel="stylesheet"
href="https://stackpath.bootstrapcdn.com/bootstrap/4.1.2/css/bootstrap.min.
css" integrity="sha384-
Smlep5jCw/wG7hdkwQ/Z5nLIefveQRIY9nfy6xoR1uRYBtpZgI6339F5dgvm/e9B"
crossorigin="anonymous">

<link rel="stylesheet"
href="https://use.fontawesome.com/releases/v5.2.0/css/all.css"
integrity="sha384-
hWVjflwFxL6sNzntih27bfxkr27PmbbK/iSvJ+a4+0owXq79v+lsFkW54bOGbiDQ"
crossorigin="anonymous">
<!-- Custom CSS -->
<link rel="stylesheet" href="/css/custom.css">

</head>

<body>
<!--wrapper start-->
<div class="wrapper" id="wrapper">

<!--Banner-->
<header>

<!--Navbar-->
<nav class="navbar navbar-expand-lg navbar-dark fixed-top scrolling-
navbar">
    <div class="container">
        <a class="navbar-brand" href="#"><strong>myJournal</strong></a>
        <button class="navbar-toggler" type="button" data-toggle="collapse"
data-target="#myNavbar" aria-controls="myNavbar" aria-expanded="false"
aria-label="Toggle navigation">
```

```
                <span class="navbar-toggler-icon"></span>
        </button>
    <div class="collapse navbar-collapse" id="myNavbar">
        <ul class="navbar-nav mr-auto">
            <li class="nav-item active">
                <a class="nav-link" href="/journal/all">Home <span
class="sr-only">(current)</span></a>
            </li>
            <li class="nav-item">
                #if(isAdmin == true) {
                    <a class="nav-link" href="/journal/logout">Logout</a>
                } else {
                    <a class="nav-link"
href="/journal/login?login">Admin</a>
                }
            </li>
            <li class="nav-item">
                <a class="nav-link" href="#">About</a>
            </li>
        </ul>
    </div>
</div>
</nav>

<!--Jumbotron-->
<div class="jumbotron banner-align-top" id="myBanner">
    <div class="banner-background text-center" style="background-image:
url(/img/pier.png);">
        <div class="container text-center" id="banner-size">
            <h2 class="banner-title">My Journal</h2>
            <h3 class="banner-subtitle">The Path of Heart!</h3>
        </div>
    </div>
</div>

</header>
```

Modify the getAll() handler to add the isAdmin field to JournalContext:

```
func getAll(_ req: Request) throws -> Future<View> {
 return JournalEntry.query(on: req).all().flatMap(to: View.self) { entries
in
 let isAdmin = try req.isAuthenticated(Admin.self)
 let context = JournalContext(isAdmin: isAdmin,
 title: self.title,
 author: self.author,
 count: String(entries.count),
 entries: entries)
```

```
    let leaf = try req.make(LeafRenderer.self)
    return leaf.render("main", context)
  }
}
```

Create a `CreateContext struct` that implements `Encodable`:

```
struct CreateContext : Encodable {
    let isAdmin: Bool
    let title: String
    let author: String
}
```

`CreateContext` contains the `isAdmin` Boolean field to indicate whether the user has administrative rights.

Modify the `createEntry()` handler as well:

```
func createEntry(_ req: Request) throws -> Future<View> {
    let leaf = try req.make(LeafRenderer.self)
    let isAdmin = try req.isAuthenticated(Admin.self)
    let context = CreateContext(isAdmin: isAdmin,
                                title: self.title,
                                author: self.author)
    return leaf.render("new", context)
}
```

Managing accounts

You need to add several new routes to manage your admin account. For that, use `securedRouter` to add another group of routes that handle admin accounts.

Add the following routes right under the protected routes for `adminRouter`:

```
// protected routes: accounts
let accountRouter = securedRouter.grouped("journal/account")
accountRouter.get("all", use: getAccounts)
accountRouter.get("add", use: addAccount)
accountRouter.post("new", use: newAccount)
accountRouter.get(Int.parameter, "remove", use: removeAccount)
```

There are four protected routes in the `securedRouter` route group. They are used to manage the administrative accounts in your `myJournal` application.

Listing all accounts

Define a new path that lists all the accounts:

```
let accountsPage = "/journal/account/all"
```

Create the new `AccountsContext Encodable` context for the `getAccounts()` handler:

```
struct AccountsContext : Encodable {
    let isAdmin: Bool
    let title: String
    let author: String
    let count: String
    let admins: [Admin]
}
```

The context contains all the information required by the `accounts.leaf` template.

Continue to implement the `getAccounts()` handler:

```
func getAccounts(_ req: Request) throws -> Future<View> {
    return Admin.query(on: req).all().flatMap(to: View.self) { admins in
        let isAdmin = try req.isAuthenticated(Admin.self)
        let context = AccountsContext(isAdmin: isAdmin,
                                      title: self.title,
                                      author: self.author,
                                      count: String(admins.count),
                                      admins: admins)
        let leaf = try req.make(LeafRenderer.self)
        return leaf.render("accounts", context)
    }
}
```

The implementation is similar to the `getAll()` handler, which lists all journal entries.

The new `accounts.leaf` template is implemented as follows:

```
#embed("header")
#if(isAdmin == true) {
[ <a class="fas fa-plus-square" href="/journal/all"> Go Home</a>
| <a class="fas fa-user-alt" href="/journal/account/add"> Add New
Account</a>
]
}
<P>
<div class="container">
    <div class="row">
        <div class="col-1"><b>ID</b></div>
```

```
            <div class="col-1"><b>Name</b></div>
            <div class="col-2"><b>Login</b></div>
            <div class="col-7"><b>Hashed Password</b></div>
            <div class="col-1"><b>Action</b></div>
        </div> <!-- row -->
        #for(admin in admins) {
            <div class="row">
                <div class="col-1">#(admin.id)</div>
                <div class="col-1">#(admin.name)</div>
                <div class="col-2">#(admin.login)</div>
                <div class="col-7">#(admin.password)</div>
                <div class="col-1"><a class="fas fa-trash-alt"
  href="/journal/account/#(admin.id)/remove">Remove</a></div>
            </div> <!-- row -->
        }

    </div>
    #if(isAdmin == true) {
        Total: #(count);
    }
    #embed("footer")
```

The template lists all the admin entries in `AccountsContext` and adds new links to add a new account or remove an existing account.

Adding a New Account

The Add New Account feature is based on the `addAccount()` handler. However, in the `addAccount()` function, you don't need to handle the authentication and session directly because Vapor handles all of that for you once your model implements the `passwordAuthenticatable()` and `sessionAuthenticatable()` protocols.

Add the `addAccount()` handler:

```
func addAccount(_ req: Request) throws -> Future<View> {
    let leaf = try req.make(LeafRenderer.self)
    let isAdmin = try req.isAuthenticated(Admin.self)
    let context = CreateContext(isAdmin: isAdmin,
                                title: self.title,
                                author: self.author)
    return leaf.render("add_account", context)
}
```

The handler renders the `add_account.leaf` template, which simply provides a form for the authenticated user to create another admin account.

The submission of the HTTP POST of the `add_account.leaf` template will be then processed by the `newAccount()` handler:

```
func newAccount(_ req: Request) throws -> Future<Response> {
    return try req.content.decode(Admin.self).flatMap(to: Admin.self) {
admin in
        admin.password = try BCrypt.hash(admin.password)
        return admin.save(on: req)
    }.transform(to: req.redirect(to: self.accountsPage))
}
```

It uses `BCrypt` package's `hash()` function to convert the submitted password into its hash value. Then the new admin object will be stored using Fluent's `save(on:)` function to serialize it to the database.

Add the following `add_account.leaf` template:

```
#embed("header")
<!--form-->
<section class="form" id="myForm">
<div class="container">
    <div class="row">
        <div class="col-lg-12">
            <div class="heading">
                <h1>Add an Admin Account</h1>
            </div>
        </div>
    </div>
</div>
<div class="container max-width">
    <div class="row">
        <div class="done">
            <div class="alert alert-success">
                <button type="button" class="close" data-
dismiss="alert">X</button>
                Your message has been submitted.
            </div>
        </div>
        <div class="col-md-12">
            <form action="/journal/account/new/" method="post">
                <fieldset class="form-group">
                    <!input name="id" type="hidden"/>
                    <input type="text" class="form-control" name="name"
placeholder="Enter your name
here">
                    <input type="text" class="form-control" name="login"
placeholder="Enter your email
```

```
address or login here">
                    <input type="password" class="form-control"
name="password" placeholder="Enter your
password here">
                </fieldset>
                <button type="submit" class="entryform
submit">Submit</button>
            </form>
        </div>
    </div>
</div>
</section>
#embed("footer")
```

Removing an account

With Fluent ORM, the removal of an account is straightforward. Simply call the `delete(on:)` function to remove the specific object from the database:

```
func removeAccount(_ req: Request) throws -> Future<Response> {
    let id = try req.parameters.next(Int.self)
    return Admin.find(id, on: req).flatMap { admin in
        guard let admin = admin else { throw Abort(.notFound) }
        return admin.delete(on: req).transform(to: req.redirect(to:
self.accountsPage))
    }
}
```

Seeding databases

You're almost ready to use the new routes to create or remove an admin page. The last thing you need to do is to seed the database so you have at least one known `Admin` account at the beginning. This is very easy with the PostgreSQL frontend utility: **pgadmin4**.

One problem you have right away is that a password must be converted into a hash value before serializing to the database. For a quick workaround, you can use a known password hash for the seed account.

You can check out Vapor's implementation of the **BCrypt** library. BCrypt is a popular hashing algorithm that has configurable complexity and handles salting automatically. Locate the unit tests for the BCrypt library on GitHub: `https://github.com/vapor-community/bcrypt/blob/master/Tests/BCryptTests/BCryptTests.swift`.

You may notice that there is a list of passwords and hash pairs already in the file:

```
let tests = [
    "$2a$04$TI13sbmh3IHnmRepeEFoJOkVZWsn5S1O8QOwm8ZU5gNIpJog9pXZm":
"vapor",
    "$2a$06$DCq7YPn5Rq63x1Lad4cl1.TV4S6ytwfsfvkgY8jIucDrjc8deX1s.": "",
    "$2a$06$m0CrhHm10qJ31XRY.5zDGO3rS2KdeeWLuGmsfG1MfOxih58VYVfxe": "a",
    "$2a$06$If6bvum7DFjUnE9p2uDeDu0YHzrHM6tf.iqN8.yx.jNN1ILEf7h0i": "abc",
    "$2a$06$.rCVZVOThsIa97pEDOxvGuRRgzG64bvtJ0938xuqzv18d3ZpQhstC":
"abcdefghijklmnopqrstuvwxyz",
    "$2a$06$fPIsBO8qRqkjj273rfaOI.HtSV9jLDpTbZn782DC6/t7qT67P6FfO":
"~!@#$%^&*()  ~!@#$%^&*()PNBFRD"
]
```

You can store the "vapor" password's hash value,
"$2a$04$TI13sbmh3IHnmRepeEFoJOkVZWsn5S1O8QOwm8ZU5gNIpJog9pXZm", in the
database.

Using pgAdmin 4, right-click on the **Admin** model and choose **Insert Script** to execute:

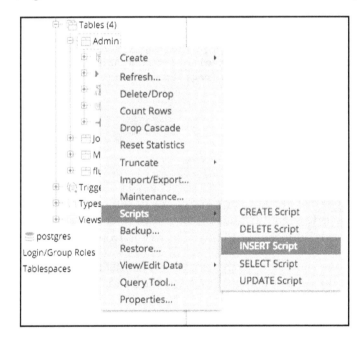

Use the hash code for `vapor` to construct a new `Admin` entry. This is the seed `Admin` object:

```
myjournal on fyeung1@myjournal
1   INSERT INTO public."Admin"(
2       id, name, login, password)
3       VALUES (1, 'Admin', 'admin', '$2a$04$TI13sbrh3IHnmRepeEFoJOkVZWsn5S108QOwm8ZU5gNIpJog9pXZm');
```

If your seed `Admin` object is created correctly, you should be able to verify it using the `BCrypt` library's `verify()` function:

```
let hash = try BCrypt.hash("vapor", cost: 4)
try BCrypt.verify("vapor", created: hash) // true
```

Of course, there are other ways to seed the database. For example, one generic method is to always create a new `Admin` account as part of the first time out-of-box experience for a user. In your Vapor application, you can check whether there is at least one `Admin` user in the database and proceed to prompt the user to create a new `Admin` account if none is found. Using this new `Admin` account, one can then add and manage other `Admin` accounts.

Introducing authentication for Kitura

Credentials is a pluggable framework for validating a user's credentials. One of the credentials plugins Kitura supports is HTTP basic authentication. HTTP authentication uses the credentials in the HTTP authorization request header, which contains user ID and password pairs, to authenticate with a server.

For your server-side Swift application, Kitura provides you with the raw HTTP basic authentication module to process the HTTP credentials.

If you want to authenticate an HTTP request on a `Codable` route, you have an option to choose the TypeSafe HTTP basic authentication method to take advantage of `TypeSafeCredentials`, one of the type-safe middleware introduced in Kitura 2.4.

Setting up HTTP basic authentication

Now, you can add some secured routes based on the code base of the `myJournal` application in *Chapter 8, Employing Storage Framework*.

To set up HTTP basic authentication, add the following package dependencies to the Swift Package Manager's manifest file, `Package.swift`:

```swift
// swift-tools-version:4.0
import PackageDescription

let package = Package(
    name: "myJournal",
    dependencies: [
        .package(url: "https://github.com/IBM-Swift/Kitura.git",
.upToNextMinor(from: "2.5.0")),
        .package(url: "https://github.com/IBM-Swift/HeliumLogger.git",
.upToNextMinor(from: "1.7.1")),
        .package(url: "https://github.com/IBM-Swift/CloudEnvironment.git",
from: "8.0.0"),
        .package(url: "https://github.com/RuntimeTools/SwiftMetrics.git",
from: "2.0.0"),
        .package(url: "https://github.com/IBM-Swift/Health.git", from:
"1.0.0"),
        .package(url:
"https://github.com/IBM-Swift/Kitura-StencilTemplateEngine.git", from:
"1.8.0"),
        .package(url: "https://github.com/IBM-Swift/Swift-Kuery-ORM.git",
.upToNextMinor(from: "0.3.1")),
        .package(url:
"https://github.com/IBM-Swift/Swift-Kuery-PostgreSQL.git", from: "1.2.0"),
        .package(url:
"https://github.com/IBM-Swift/Kitura-CredentialsHTTP.git", from: "2.1.0"),
    ],
    targets: [
        .target(name: "myJournal", dependencies: [ .target(name:
"Application"), "Kitura" , "HeliumLogger", "KituraStencil"]),
        .target(name: "Application", dependencies: [ "CredentialsHTTP",
"Kitura", "CloudEnvironment","SwiftMetrics","Health", "SwiftKueryORM",
"SwiftKueryPostgreSQL"]),

        .testTarget(name: "ApplicationTests" , dependencies: [.target(name:
"Application"), "Kitura","HeliumLogger" ])
    ]
)
```

Import the authentication packages into `JournalRoutes.swift` that use authentication functions:

```swift
import Credentials
import CredentialsHTTP
```

You also need to regenerate the Xcode project so the new `CredentialsHTTP` package is included in a build:

```
swift package generate-xcodeproj
```

Constructing a Model

Now you need a `Model` that can be also authenticated by HTTP basic authentication.

Create a new Swift file, `Admin.swift,` in the `/Sources/Application/Model` directory.

Subclass the `Admin` model from `Model`:

```
import SwiftKueryORM // [1]

struct Admin: Model // [2]
{
  static var idColumnName = "id" // [4]

  public static func checkPassword(username: String,
                                   password: String) -> Bool { // [5]
      var ret = false
      Admin.find(id: username) { user, error in // [6]
          if let user = user { // [7]
              if password == user.password { // [8]
                  ret = true
              }
          }
      }
      return ret
  }

  public var id: String // [3]
  private let password: String
}
```

The new `Admin` model is constructed in the following steps:

1. Import the `SwiftKueryORM` package so you can use the Model protocol
2. Declare the data structure as `Admin`, which conforms to `Model`
3. Add the `String` variable, `id`, as well as the `String` constant, `password`
4. Choose the `id` field as `idColumnName` for database indexing

5. Add the `static` function, `checkPassword()`, which you will use later with credential checking

6. Use the given `username` as the ID for querying the database

7. Unwrap the optional database-querying result into the `user` object

8. Set the return flag to `true` if the given `password` matches that of the `user` object

To link your model to a table in your database, you need to create a new table right after the do-try-catch block where you set up a database connection for `JournalItem` in `JournalRoutes.swift`:

```
do {
    try Admin.createTableSync()
} catch let error {
    Log.error("Failed to create table in database: \(error)")
}
```

Right now, there is no record in the `Admins` table. Run the *INSERT SQL* script in **pgAdmin4** to add a new entry for `Admin`. This sample script adds the 'kitura'/'kitura' pair to the database:

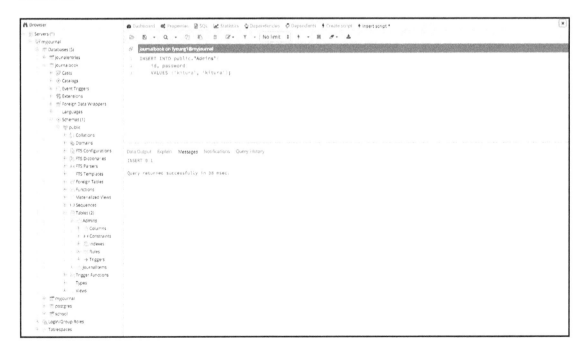

Now you can register a credentials object as a middleware plugin for all the `/journal` paths.

Add the following code right after your `Admin.createTableSync()` code:

```
let cred = Credentials()
cred.register(plugin: app.rawAuth)
app.router.all("/journal", middleware: cred)
```

Any routes that are under the `/journal` root are now protected and require your credential information. Once you're successfully authenticated, the web browser's cookies will persist your authentication status throughout a session.

You can also follow the same steps as in your Vapor application to add new routes for the `Admin` account management. In this way, you don't have to use the pgAdmin tool to add new `Admin` users manually.

The last thing you need to complete the authentication feature is to implement the `app.rawAuth` plugin itself.

Add the `rawAuth` extension to the app after the `initializeJournalRoutes(app:)` function:

```
extension App {
    var rawAuth: CredentialsHTTPBasic {
        let cred = CredentialsHTTPBasic(verifyPassword: { login, password,
callback in
            if Admin.checkPassword(username: login, password: password) {
                callback(UserProfile(id: login, displayName: login,
provider: "HTTPBasic"))
            } else {
                callback(nil)
            }
        })
        cred.realm = "HTTP Basic authentication: Username = username,
Password = password"
        return cred
    }
}
```

As you can see, you use the `Admin.checkPassword()` function you previously created to instantiate a new `CredentialsHTTPBasic` object. The caller function will receive a valid `CredentialsHTTPBasic` object if the user is authenticated successfully, otherwise it will receive `nil`.

Using TypeSafe HTTP authentication

For the TypeSafe HTTP Basic Authentication method, you can add the
`TypeSafeHTTPBasic` protocol to the `Admin` model:

```
public struct Admin: TypeSafeHTTPBasic, Model {
  static var idColumnName = "id" // [1]
  public var id: String
  var name: String
  var login: String
  var password: String // [2]
  public static func verifyPassword(login: String, // [3]
                                    password: String,
                                    callback: @escaping (Admin?) -> Void) {
    Admin.find(id: login) { admin, error in // [4]
      if let admin = admin {
        if password == admin.password { // [5]
          callback(admin) // [6]
          return
        }
      }
      callback(nil) // [7]
    }
  }
}
```

Here are some important points to note:

- The `ID` field is set as the ID column, `idColumnName`, in the database.
- `password` is a String but it can be a hashed value.
- The `verifyPassword` function, required by the `TypeSafeHTTPBasic` protocol, is used to set up HTTP basic authentication. It takes in login and password credentials.
- The login will be used as an `id` for querying the database.
- If the provided password matches the stored password in the database, an `Admin` instance will be returned.
- The database querying is asynchronous, so the callback closure with an instance of `Admin` is used.
- If no matched `Admin` instance is retrieved from the database, a callback closure with `nil` is used.

For any routes that require authentication, you can implement them just like any codable routes using Swift-Kuery-ORM:

```
router.get("/admin") { (user: Admin, respondWith: (Admin?, RequestError?)
-> Void) in
    print("\(user.id) has been authenticated!")
    respondWith(user, nil)
}
```

The preceding code demonstrates how to turn a model into an authenticatable model in Kitura.

Summary

In this chapter, you learned how to use web authentication to secure routes with protected content in your Vapor web application. To do that, you created a new data model for administrative accounts and added routes and templates to manage the accounts. With this account-management feature, you were able to grant administrative rights to some users or provoke the rights later. Now only a specific group of users will be able to create, edit, or delete a journal entry with their credentials. Then, you worked on the same web authentication framework to secure all the routes under the /journal path. This chapter concludes your myJournal web application. In the next chapter, we will look at how to build more advanced web services.

10
Understanding Technologies for Web Services

In this chapter, we'll see the underlying technologies that empower Web Services. You'll learn about the server/client model based on HTTP/HTTPS in more detail, and get introduced to the Model-View-Controller design pattern you've found in most of the Swift web frameworks. For the architecture design of Web Services, it would be better to divide the design into a three-tier architecture consisting of a frontend API gateway, middle business logic, and backend database services. You'll learn how a typical frontend API gateway is designed, how to encapsulate a middle component with business logic into a standalone microservice, and how to design and work with a backend storage framework.

In this chapter, we will cover the following topics:

- Understanding the three-tier architecture for Web Services
- Getting a review of HTTP protocols
- Learning two design patterns for cloud frontend: Backends of Frontends and API Gateway
- Getting introduced to the microservice-oriented architecture
- Getting practical advice on continuous delivery and deploying your software to cloud

Serving clients with web services

In the previous chapters, you have been working on the technologies in building website applications. Website applications refer to the delivery of interactive web content (HTML, CSS, Javascript) to web browsers such as Chrome, Safari, and Firefox. Starting in this chapter, you will work on Web Services intended for a variety of client applications that are customized with their own user interface and user experience. The backend components in Web Services focus on the delivery of data to the client applications and do not use templating engines to render any content.

Designing three-tier architecture for web service

A typical backend architecture for web applications and web services has a three-tier layer of components. The three-tier architecture allows you to conveniently separate features into more manageable modules, offering you an opportunity to extend and reconfigure your web services easily. This is what the architecture looks like:

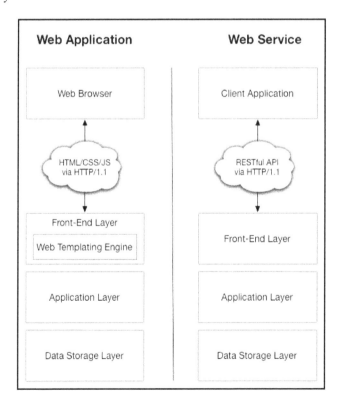

The delivery of resources is typically over HTTP/1.1 protocols, but more and more websites and web infrastructure have been updated to HTTP/2.0 protocols. The three tiers of web backend architecture typically include the **Front-End**, **Application**, and **Data Storage Layers**, which we'll look at in the next sections.

The frontend layer

The frontend layer consists of web content (in the form of HTML/CSS/JS) for website applications or an API for web services. In the case of website applications, the web content could be generated by templating engines, such as Vapor Leaf, Stencil, Mustache, and Markdown, or enhanced by JavaScript frameworks, such as jQuery, Angular, and React. Frontend applications may pull in other resources via the APIs provided by other Web Services. The clients for a website application will be a variety of web browsers on different platforms.

In the case of web services, the clients make HTTP requests to the application server and exchange data in JSON. An application server is not expected to render web content (HTML/JS/CSS), have a concern for **user experience** (**UX**), or handle any presentation of data. Each client decides how to consume and present the data received from a Web Service. Instead, an application server for Web Services organizes all functionalities in terms of the RESTful API, aggregates different services in a single interface (API Gateway), and hides away the details of backend components (the facade for the backend).

The application layer

The application layer of your web service consists of a number of application servers that handle the business logic for the service. For scalability, extensibility, and load-balancing requirements in backend architecture design, each kind of business logic could be implemented in an independent runtime as microservice in modern backend design. The business logic could also be implemented in different programming languages, such as Swift, Java, Javascript/Node.js, C++, C#, or Python. Each microservice is deployed in a Docker container to a hosting cloud location.

The data storage layer

The data storage layer is a database-management system that provides access to your Web Service with stored application data. A database server could be a relational database, such as MySQL, SQLite, or PostgreSQL, or a non-relational database, such as MongoDB or CouchDB. There could be multiple databases serving an application, and it will be up to the application layer to decide which database to use.

Reviewing HTTP protocols

HTTP stands for Hypertext Transfer Protocol. It is the foundation of data communication for the internet. The protocol is developed jointly by the **Internet Engineering Task Force (IETF)** and the **World Wide Web Consortium (W3C)**. There are a series of **Requests for Comments (RFC)** published since 1991. Here is a list of several variants of the HTTP protocol that you may encounter:

Protocol	Year	Spec	Key features
HTTP/0.9	1991		Simple server-server, request-response model; HTTP GET request only; no HTTP headers, no status codes, no URLs, no versioning.
HTTP/1.0	1996	RFC 1945	Web-browser-friendly with HTTP header fields; support of status code, HTTP version number and content type; HTTP GET, HEAD, and POST methods supported.
HTTP/1.1	1997	RFC 2068	Most popular HTTP version in use; support of persistent connection, data compression, chunked transfers, and cache; GET, HEAD, POST, PUT, DELETE, TRACE, OPTIONS methods supported.
HTTPS	2000	RFC 2818	Originally used in Netscape browser in 1994; uses different port (port 443 instead of 80); added encryption layer (SSL/TLS) on the HTTP scheme; same syntax as HTTP.
HTTP/2.0	2015	RFC 7540	Compatible with HTTP/1.1; supports data compression of HTTP headers; server push; pipelining of requests; support for framed and binary data; capable of multiplying multiple requests over a single TCP connection.

HTTP/1.1 evolves from HTTP/0.9 and HTTP/1.0, and becomes the main HTTP protocol used on the internet. There are two other variants you may encounter:

- **HTTPS**: If the server/client communication requires security, for example, for transmitting sensitive personal information or passwords, HTTPS instead of the HTTP protocol will be used. HTTPS refers to HTTP Secure and it ensures all data is encrypted properly. A business or user of HTTPS has to apply for a certificate from one of the Certificate Authority providers in order to use HTTPS properly. As a matter of fact, HTTPS became so popular that more than half of HTTP/1.1 traffic takes place on HTTPS.

- **HTTP/2.0**: This is the major revision of the HTTP protocol in 2015. It is derived from Google's SPDY protocol. HTTP/2.0 supports most of the HTTP/1.1 syntax but also adds support of framed data and binaries. The server implementing HTTP/2.0 no longer operates on passive-only mode. The HTTP/2.0 server can predict whether some data is required by the client and pushes resources to the client ahead of time. Most importantly, HTTP/2.0 improves performance in data delivery by multiplying requests and responses, compressing HTTP headers, and allowing the prioritization of requests. HTTP/2.0 also has a very efficient mechanism for data-streaming. That's the reason for the gRPC framework, a popular open source RPC framework by Google: to choose HTTP/2.0 as the default server/client networking protocol for data-streaming over its data pipeline, called Completion Queue.

Currently, HTTP/1.1 (including HTTPS) is the most popular protocols for websites, taking up more than 70% coverage as compared to HTTP/2.0.

Designing the cloud frontend with pattern

When it comes to the design of the backend architecture for a web service, there are many well-known design patterns that provide a good solution to some of the most common problems you are going to encounter. By taking a preemptive approach to reviewing some of the available design patterns, you will have a more coherent and well-thought-out Web Service design.

The backends for frontends pattern

One of these backend design patterns is the **Backends for Frontends** (**BFF**) pattern. It is useful to avoid having a single backend for multiple interfaces:

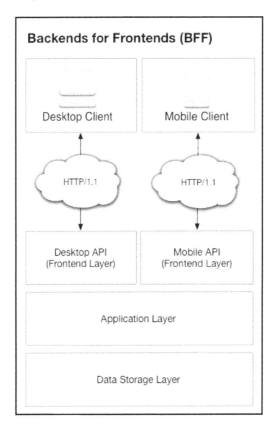

There are many different kinds of client types, such as desktop clients, mobile clients, small device clients, and tablet clients. Each of the client types may have a different optimized user-interface design and preferred user-interaction technologies. To have a single, general-purpose backend service is not only difficult to implement, but also forced to make tradeoffs. A general-purpose frontend layer even becomes a bottleneck in a team-based development process.

BFF provides a way to get around these issues by creating one backend per user interface or client type. This design allows you to customize the behavior and performance of each backend for a specific client type, and creates schedule flexibility in a team-development process so engineers can work on BFFs in parallel.

A potential drawback of BFF is that the handling of shared data, if any, between backends may turn out to be more complicated. However, this issue could be solved with a good concurrent design of a system that handles such shared data.

API gateway

Another useful design pattern is API gateway or API aggregation. In a typical cloud-based enterprise application, there are various sub-services, such as accounting, authentication, user profile, and messaging. In fact, the trend of backend design is that the runtime of each service is getting more lightweight. People use the term **microservice** to refer to such a lightweight runtime. Each microservice performs a small task and many different microservice runtimes work together to deliver a complete solution.

For a client, it means that each may have to make multiple calls to various backend services to complete a fairly complex job. It is obviously not very desirable due to the chattiness between the client and server.

API gateway comes to the rescue for this problem. API gateway not only aggregates multiple services into a centralized endpoint for the client, but also consolidates the steps for a client to get a task done.

Here are the differences between the frontend with and without an API gateway:

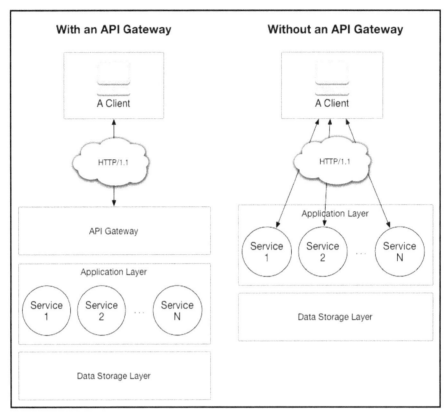

As you can see, an API Gateway acts as a facade for the numerous services running in the Application layer. API Gateway decouples the client-facing API from the implementation of service runtimes, essentially adding extensibility and scalability to the frontend design.

For example, if one of the services needs to be upgraded, you can simply swap in the new server runtime and take the old one away. The API definitions could possibly be kept unchanged if the design is backward-compatible.

API Gateway not only decouples client and backend development, but also serves as a unified interface that streamlines the workflow on the client side.

Encapsulating business logic into microservices

The backend design for web services is usually referred to as distributed architecture because you expect to have service components running on different processes and physical servers. Each service component is accessed remotely through a sort of remote-access protocol. These service components can communicate with each other across different processes, servers, and networks. Similar to **Object-Oriented Design** (OOD) in software architecture, distributed architecture accommodates more loosely-coupled, encapsulated, and modular design for Web Service applications. Such characteristics of distributed architecture are generally advantageous to cloud backend services as they bring better scalability, modularity, and control to the development and deployment of service modules.

Implementing a microservice-oriented architecture

One of the differences between microservices and service-oriented architecture is the granularity of a service. The principle for microservices is to take the modularity of service-oriented architecture further, into smaller and more manageable functional units. The concept of microservice-oriented architecture compared to a componentized application is illustrated as follows:

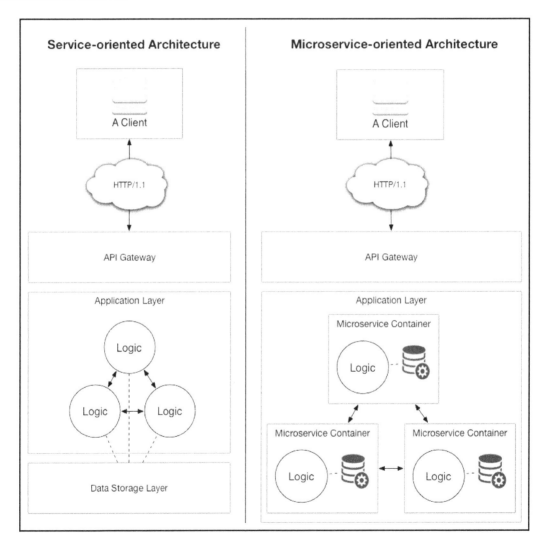

Service components in service-oriented architecture are not designed for reusability; duplicated features may be inadvertently added to the service. A mature service may become bloated and monolithic, making it hard to maintain, debug, and develop. Microservices, however, are designed for tasks at a more granular level and won't become bloated easily.

Designing microservice with key principles

The key principles for the microservice-oriented architecture are as follows:

- **Separation of concerns**: Each microservice is modular and is held for a single responsibility
- **Loosely coupled**: Each microservice is isolated from other microservices and components as much as possible
- **Independently deployable**: Each microservice is an entity that can be individually deployed as needed
- **Cross-platform and cross-language**: Each microservice can be developed independently in a different programming language and communicate with each other across platform boundaries
- **Scalability**: The same type of a microservice can be added to deployment as many as needed
- **Automation**: The deployment of the microservice is automated
- **Build for failure**: A microservice will gracefully exit during catastrophic failure and get a chance to be relaunched if required

Even though these principles are not mandatory, you may want to observe them to reap the maximum benefit from the microservice-oriented architecture.

Cloud deployment

After you've designed your application for Web Services, you will start pondering over the deployment of your application to a hosted cloud location. While you have many choices of hosting solutions, there are an array of technologies that make your deployment.

Containing microservices with Docker

Most of the microservice components are deployed using containers. Container technology, such as Docker, provides a granular virtualized infrastructure to microservices, making it extremely easy to partition finer-grained execution environments:

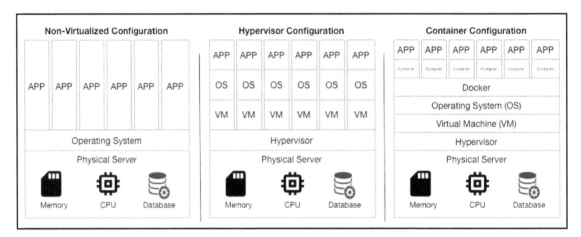

Containers allow multiple execution environments to run on a single operating system instance. Unlike a hypervisor configuration, where each application sits on an individualized operation system, container configuration enables the sharing of operating-system-level resources across different applications. A containerized application works in the same way as that in the hypervisor configuration, except that the container for each application accounts for any modification or provision specific to the application itself.

Using container technology to perform execution isolation at the operating-system level offers the following advantages for microservice deployment:

- **Better component cohabitation**: Each microservice has a private environment and won't affect other microservices.
- **More efficient utilization of resource**: All containerized microservices on a single operating system instance share the same resource; only changes to the underlying operating system are captured in each container.
- **Faster initialization and execution**: The container is generally lightweight and doesn't require the typical operating system spin-up time required in a virtual machine, making it faster to initialize and run.
- **Better scalability for workload**: Better isolation nature of containerized microservice helps addition and removal of a microservice when workload changes.

- **More reusability opportunities**: A low deployment cost, simplicity, and the lightweight nature of a containerized microservice mean that the microservice is more likely to be reused in another application.

Container technology offers such great benefits that Docker is becoming the default method for deploying microservices to the cloud.

Continuously deploying to the cloud

The runtime of a new version of web services packaged in Docker container is deployed to a cloud hosting server continuously. There are two types of deployment methods: continuous delivery and continuous deployment.

In both deployment methods, new code changes get pushed from your local source code repository to the remote source repository. This often triggers a post-hook notification to a continuous-integration server, triggering all of your unit tests to run with the new code changes you have made. If all tests are passed, you'll receive a notification. At a later time, a new version of the software will be deployed to your cloud hosting account. Continuous delivery means that the deployment to cloud hosting is done manually, while continuous deployment means that the deployment is done automatically.

Working with a sample workflow

The workflow for continuous delivery/continuous deployment to the cloud is illustrated in the following diagram:

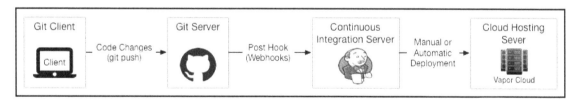

When you have committed new changes in your local git repository, you use git push to push all committed changes to the remote repository on GitHub. GitHub provides the webhook API function so that a git push will notify external server, your Jerkins (or alternatives such as Bitrise, CircleCI, or BuddyBuild) **continuous-integration** (**CI**) server. This notification triggers all unit tests to run. If all test cases pass, you'll receive a notification in the case of Continuous Delivery, or a script will trigger the upload of a containerized new package automatically in the case of Continuous Deployment.

Summary

While you didn't do any coding in this chapter, you learned quite a lot of technical terms that will help you navigate the technologies you are going to work on in the next few chapters. First, you learned how to divide the backend into a three-tier architecture for Web Services. Next, you learned the nuts and bolts of HTTP protocols. Then, you were introduced to two design patterns for cloud frontend: BFFand API Gateway. After that, you learned some key design principles for microservice-oriented architectures. Finally, you were given practical advice on continuously integrating your server-side Swift projects for delivery and deployment to the cloud. In the next chapter, you'll roll up your sleeves again to design and implement an API Gateway.

11
Designing for API Gateway

Representational State Transfer (**REST**) is the most popular architecture for creating HTTP/HTTPS-based APIs to represent web services that a site has to offer to end users. The REST architecture builds upon the GET/POST/PUT/DELETE requests offered in the HTTP/HTTPS standards. In this chapter, you'll learn how to build a RESTful API, get introduced to the basic rules for API design, create endpoints for requests that a client sends to a server, and define response status codes. You'll then learn how the design of the REST API can be extended to the idea of building an API Gateway, which is the single entry point for all clients and routes client's requests to different MVC components or microservices.

After finishing this chapter, you'll have the following knowledge:

- Understanding the basic server/client model based on HTTP
- Gaining an insight into designing RESTful API
- Knowing how to assign HTTP methods for the API endpoints
- Acquiring the skill set to implement the endpoints and HTTP responses

Serving clients with the RESTful API

The RESTful API refers to an interface that is based on the REST architectural style and separates the implementation of web services on a server from the user interface implemented by a client. This separation provides good portability for a web service so it can serve different clients across multiple platforms, and offers great user experience for the client so it can keep the native design of the client platform and provides a uniform look and feel to the users.

In general, the REST architecture assumes a stateless server, hence the session state is kept entirely on the client side. Each HTTP request the client makes must contain all information the server needs to understand the request and provide an expected response. In `Chapter 9`, *Adding Authentication*, you've already learned how to maintain the session of a successful login via session cookies. The session cookies can be used by the web browser and other clients.

For speed optimization, the client can cache some responses and reuse the response data from the server for other requests. In fact, a server may not know about such requests even though it may appear that new requests are made to the server. The response data must be labeled implicitly or explicitly to be cacheable. Only if a response is cacheable would a client be given the right to store and reuse the response for later requests.

Understanding the server/client model based on HTTP

Once a TCP connect has been established between a client and a server, the client can start communicating with the server using the higher-level HTTP protocol built on top of TCP. Common HTTP requests include GET, POST, PUT and DELETE. In HTTP/1.1, the connection needs to be established only once, and additional requests and the retrieval of resources (HTML pages, JSON data, images) will be executed using the same connection.

A typical HTTP GET request works as follows:

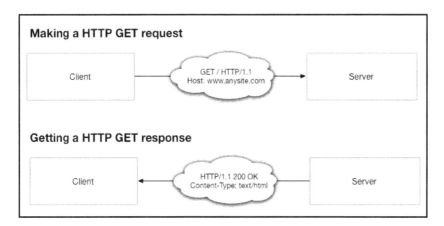

First, the client knows the IP address of the server. It establishes an HTTP connection to the IP address and makes an HTTP GET request by sending the type of HTTP request, GET, followed by the version of HTTP protocol, HTTP/1.1, and the path on the server, `www.anysite.com`.

Next, the server responds with the same version of the HTTP protocol, HTTP/1.1, and the HTTP status code, 200 OK, to confirm that everything seems to be OK and it is going to send the resource per the client's request. The type of resource is on the second line: **Content-Type: text/html**.

Designing the RESTful API

You can perform the following three easy-to-follow steps to design a RESTful API using HTTP protocols:

1. Identify an object model to represent one kind of resource.
2. Define resource endpoints for different levels of resources.
3. Assign HTTP methods to operations for the resources.

Identifying object models

The resources that are offered to the client are represented as objects on a server. You've already modeled for the content, that is, `JournalEntry`, and the administrators who have the permission to create, edit, and delete journal entries, that is, `Admin`. You can identify other objects to represent the resources in your application, such as preferences, user profiles, blogs, and pictures.

The `JournalEntry` you've created in previous chapters is shown again here:

```
final class JournalEntry: PostgreSQLModel {
    var id: Int?
    var title: String
    var content: String
    init(id: Int? = nil, title: String, content: String) {
        self.id = id
        self.title = title
        self.content = content
    }
}
```

```
extension JournalEntry: Migration { }
extension JournalEntry: Content { }
extension JournalEntry: Parameter { }
```

For any objects/resources in your model, you'll need to have a unique identifier. In the `JournalEntry` model, this is the `id` integer property.

In server-side Swift frameworks, the model can implement `Codable` (`Content` in Vapor) for object encoding and decoding for external representations, such as JSON, as well as other useful protocols for handling object models, such as `Authenticatable`, `Migration`, database model, and `Parameters`.

Defining resource endpoints

With the object models defined, you can decide the resource URIs. In this step, you will focus on the relationship between resources and their sub-resources, and create resource URIs as endpoints for RESTful services.

Defining endpoints for top-level resources

In this chapter's `myJournal` application, all resources are under `/api`, which indicates that the resources are available through an API. Each endpoint in the API represents one kind of resource. If you intend to provide both web applications that render web pages (similar to what you have done in previous chapters) and web services with the RESTful API, the top-level `/api` path in the URIs is used to distinguish your RESTful APIs from the rest of the web applications.

After that, the top-level resource is the journal itself, as in `/api/journal`.

It is recommended to start the top-level resource with the application because you may want to have other sub-applications at the top-level URI.

For example, you may have `/api/journal` for the journal's blogging sub-application, `/api/news` for the news-aggregation sub-application, or `/api/guestbook` for the visitor-guest-book-signing sub-application.

Your top-level resources for top-level URIs may look like this:

```
/api/journal
/api/news
/api/guestbook
```

The design of top-level URIs not only allows you to extend the features of your web services without affecting any existing features, but also adds extensibility to the implementation so each top-level resource could be served by services on different systems. It is also a convention that URIs use only nouns and do not use any verb or operation. This convention makes perfect sense because each endpoint of a URI literally represents one type of resource.

For resources that are shared across different sub-applications, you can also leave them to the top level:

```
/api/account
/api/configuration
/api/profile
```

In the preceding examples, you have the `account` resource, which manages the administrative rights of a registered user, the `configuration` resource, which sets the global configuration that affect all sub-applications, as well as the `profile` resource, which maintains the profile for a registered user.

Defining Endpoints for Sub-resources

Within each sub-application, the URIs for all the main sub-resources can be mapped out. For any operations applicable to *all* resources at an endpoint, you can simply use the top-level endpoint itself. For example, to retrieve all journal entries, your endpoint could be simply `/api/journal`. If an operation is applicable to a specific resource, an ID is often used to indicate the specific sub-resource, as in `/api/journal/{id}`.

The URIs for top-level resources and sub-resources in the `myJournal` application are listed as the following:

```
/api/journal
/api/journal/{id}
```

The `/api/journal/{id}` sub-resource is applicable to a specific journal entry.

Assigning HTTP methods

With properly-defined URIs and representations of resources, you can define all the operations in the application on resource URIs. Let's look at how each operation is mapped, come on, let's go.

Browsing all journal entries

To get the collection of all journal entries, use the HTTP GET operation on the top-level `/api/journal` URI:

```
HTTP GET /api/journal
```

The preceding request will fetch all records from the collection. If the collection size is too large, you can add paging and filtering capabilities to the request. This can be accomplished using URI-encoded parameters by specifying the desired starting index and number of records:

```
HTTP GET /api/journal?start=40&size=20
```

Of course, the handler of this request needs to implement necessary logic to enable pagination and filtering features.

Creating a new journal entry

To post a new journal entry, use the HTTP POST request on the top-level URI:

```
HTTP POST /api/journal
```

You do not need to assign an `id` for the new entry because the `id` for an entry will be automatically assigned by the `JournalEntry` model when it is created.

Getting a specific journal entry

To get an existing journal entry, use the HTTP GET request and provide the `id` for the existing entry:

```
HTTP GET /api/journal/{id}
```

The user is not aware of the `id` and you won't expect the user to provide the `id`. Instead, your application needs to find a way to populate an entry's `id` in the URI.

Editing a specific journal entry

To edit the content of an existing journal entry, you use HTTP PUT request and provide the `id` of the existing data:

```
HTTP PUT /api/journal/{id}
```

Similar to the HTTP GET operation, your application populates the existing entry's `id` in its URI.

Deleting a specific journal entry

To delete an existing record of journal entries, you make a HTTP DELETE request and provide the `id` of the record in the URI:

```
HTTP DELETE /journal/api/{id}
```

Implementing the endpoints and responses

In the Vapor framework, you can create a `struct` for API Routes that implements the `RouteCollection` protocol:

```
struct ApiRoutes : RouteCollection {
    func boot(router: Router) throws {
        let apiRouter = router.grouped("/api")
    //...
    }
//...
}
```

In the `boot(route:)` function, set up a router that starts with the top-level `/api` URI and append each route corresponding to each of your HTTP methods to the `boot(route:)` function:

```
// public routes
let publicRouter = apiRouter.grouped("/journal")
publicRouter.get("", use: getAll)

// admin routes
let adminRouter = apiRouter.grouped("/admin")
adminRouter.post(use: newEntry)
adminRouter.get(Int.parameter, use: getEntry)
adminRouter.put(Int.parameter, use: editEntry)
adminRouter.delete(Int.parameter, use: removeEntry)
```

Take note that you haven't specified any authentication methods to the protected routes, such as `admin` routes. The design is structured in such a way that it is easier to add authentication methods directly to these two route groups. In this chapter, you can focus on the nuts and bolts of API design.

After all handlers have been specified in the `boot(router:)` function, you can proceed to implement handler for each route.

Implementing Handlers for Public Routes

Thanks to the powerful database data-modeling offered in Vapor, the handler implementation for the HTTP GET `/journal/api/` turns out to be straightforward:

```
func getAll(_ req: Request) throws -> Future<[JournalEntry]> {
  return JournalEntry.query(on: req).all()
}
```

The operation for retrieving all existing journal entries is simply a call to the model's `query(on:).all()` methods.

Since the querying for entries in the database takes a finite amount of time, the transaction is asynchronous and the function returns the `Future` type.

For the `myJournal` web service, you do not use Leaf to generate any templates. Instead of testing your API with the web browser, it may be more convenient if you use the command-line *curl* tool or the *Postman* utility application to verify the result.

Run the following curl command to retrieve all records in your database:

```
$ curl http://localhost:8080/api/journal
```

The JSON object retrieved from the PostgreSQL database will appear on the screen.

Implementing handlers for admin routes

Next, let's move on to implementing all handlers for the `Admin` routes.

Creating a new item

The handler for creating a new journal entry decodes the JSON content received from the HTTP POST request on `/journal/api/admin` and saves it directly to the database:

```
func newEntry(_ req: Request) throws -> Future<JournalEntry> {
  return try req.content.decode(JournalEntry.self)
      .flatMap(to: JournalEntry.self) { entry in
         return entry.save(on: req)
      }
```

```
}
```

It's a matter of making two calls, `req.content.decode()` and `entry.save(on:)`, for the `JournalEntry` data model to decode and then save the new content into the database.

Check the handler for creating a new journal entry with the following `curl` command:

```
$ curl --header "Content-Type: application/json" \
--request POST \
--data '{"title":"New Entry","content":"This is a brand new entry."}' \
http://localhost:8080/api/admin
```

Then retrieve all records in the database to verify that a new entry is created:

```
$ curl http://localhost:8080/api/journal
```

You'll see the new entry appears as one of the items in the JSON object printed out on the screen.

Retrieving an item by ID

The handler for getting a record of an existing journal entry makes use of `parameters` to get the `id` for the entry and retrieve the `JournalEntry` object automatically using the `next(JournalEntry.self)` method call:

```
func getEntry(_ req: Request) throws -> Future<JournalEntry> {
    return try req.parameters.next(JournalEntry.self)
}
```

You can try to retrieve a journal entry with `curl` and provide an ID for the item:

```
$ curl http://localhost:8080/api/admin/1
```

With the `/api/admin/<id>` endpoint, `curl` will ask your handler to retrieve the specified item and print out the journal entry wrapped in a JSON object if the item is found.

Updating an item

The handler for editing a record follows the similar workflow as in the handler for entry retrieval, but takes an additional step to update the record with the intended changes:

```
func editEntry(_ req: Request) throws -> Future<JournalEntry> {
    let id = try req.parameters.next(Int.self)
    return try req.content.decode(JournalEntry.self).flatMap { updated in
        return JournalEntry.find(id, on: req)
```

```
                        .flatMap(to: JournalEntry.self) { original in
                            guard let original = original else { throw Abort(.notFound)
    }

                            original.title = updated.title
                            original.content = updated.content
                            return original.save(on: req)
                    }
                }
    }
```

In the preceding code, the id is retrieved first using parameters.next(Int.self), and then a query using find(on:) is issued to retrieve the record. The record is updated with the changes and then put back into the database using save(on:).

You can use the curl command to check this handler:

```
curl --header "Content-Type: application/json" \
--request PUT \
--data '{"title":"New Update","content":"This is an update."}' \
http://localhost:8080/api/admin/1
```

Then use curl to check the effect:

```
$ curl http://localhost:8080/api/admin/1
```

If the update handler works properly, you should expect the JSON object printed on the screen to reflect the changes you've just made.

Deleting an Item

The handler for deleting a record is not so different from the HTTP PUT operation. After retrieving the record, you simply call the delete(on:) method:

```
func removeEntry(_ req: Request) throws -> Future<HTTPStatus> {
    let id = try req.parameters.next(Int.self)
    return JournalEntry.find(id, on: req).flatMap { entry in
        guard let entry = entry else { throw Abort(.notFound) }
        return entry.delete(on: req).transform(to: HTTPStatus.noContent)
    }
}
```

The return type for the preceding function is Future. After the record has been deleted, you issue HTTPStatus.noContent to the client.

Now, use `curl` again to test the delete handler:

```
$ curl --request DELETE http://localhost:8080/api/admin/1
```

The preceding command should have erased the record of the specified `journal` entry from the database.

Run curl to verify that this record doesn't exist anymore:

```
$ curl http://localhost:8080/api/admin/1
```

As expected, nothing should be printed on the screen if you try to retrieve the record you've just deleted.

Next, you will move on to implementing similar API endpoints for Kitura.

Implementing API endpoints for Kitura

Kitura takes full advantage of the `Codable` protocol introduced in Swift 4.0. For `Codable` routes, you can create router an endpoint method that accepts a `Codable` object for the request and uses a completion closure to pass a `Codable` object as the response.

As you'll see in the following source code, Kitura's `Codable` routers can simplify the creation of a CRUD API and the handling of JSON objects.

Creating a new project for the Kitura web service application

Create a new Kitura project using the CLI command in a new directory:

```
$ kitura init
```

Add the dependencies for the Kuery ORM framework and PostgreSQL driver:

```
// swift-tools-version:4.0
import PackageDescription

let package = Package(
    name: "myJournal",
    dependencies: [
        .package(url: "https://github.com/IBM-Swift/Kitura.git",
.upToNextMinor(from: "2.5.0")),
```

```
        .package(url: "https://github.com/IBM-Swift/HeliumLogger.git",
    .upToNextMinor(from: "1.7.1")),
        .package(url: "https://github.com/IBM-Swift/CloudEnvironment.git",
    from: "8.0.0"),
        .package(url: "https://github.com/RuntimeTools/SwiftMetrics.git",
    from: "2.0.0"),
        .package(url: "https://github.com/IBM-Swift/Health.git", from:
    "1.0.0"),
        .package(url: "https://github.com/IBM-Swift/Swift-Kuery-ORM.git",
    .upToNextMinor(from: "0.3.1")),
        .package(url:
    "https://github.com/IBM-Swift/Swift-Kuery-PostgreSQL.git", from: "1.2.0"),
    ],
    targets: [
        .target(name: "myJournal", dependencies: [ .target(name:
    "Application"), "Kitura" , "HeliumLogger"]),
        .target(name: "Application", dependencies: [ "Kitura",
    "CloudEnvironment","SwiftMetrics","Health", "SwiftKueryORM",
    "SwiftKueryPostgreSQL"]),

        .testTarget(name: "ApplicationTests" , dependencies: [.target(name:
    "Application"), "Kitura","HeliumLogger" ])
    ]
)
```

Build and run your project to make sure the template project works as expected:

```
$ swift run
```

Working with the Kitural model

Create a new file, `JournalItem.swift`, for
the `/Application/Routes/ApiRoutes.swift` directory.

In `JournalItem.swift`, create a struct that implements `Model`:

```
import SwiftKueryORM

struct JournalItem: Model {
    var title: String
    var content: String
}
```

Since `Model` itself implements `Codable`, the `JournalItem` struct you've defined here will work in the same way as other `Codable` objects, in addition to its conformance to Kitura-Kuery-ORM.

Setting up a database

In `Application.swift`, create an instance of PostgreSQL data in the `postInit()` method:

```
func postInit() throws {
    //...
    let poolOptions = ConnectionPoolOptions(initialCapacity: 1,
                                            maxCapacity: 5,
                                            timeout: 10000)
    // Set up database connection
    let psqlPool = PostgreSQLConnection.createPool(host: "localhost",
                                                   port: 5432,
                                                   options:
[.databaseName("journalbook")],
                                                   poolOptions: poolOptions)

    Database.default = Database(psqlPool)

    do {
        try JournalItem.createTableSync()
    } catch let error {
        Log.error("Failed to create table in database: \(error)")
    }
}
```

You've used the same database code before, in `Chapter 8`, *Employing Storage Framework*. The preceding code will attempt to create a table for `JournalItem`. If there is an existing table already, it will log an error. You can simply ignore the log message if this is the case.

Adding route handlers

For CRUD operations, add the following router endpoints. The URLs are kept the same as those you used in your Vapor project. This allows the iOS client application you're going to build in `Chapter 13`, *Developing an iPhone Client*, to work with both Vapor and Kitura web applications:

```
func postInit() throws {
    //...
    router.get("/api/journal/", handler: getAllHandler)
    router.get("/api/admin", handler: getItemHandler)
    router.post("/api/admin", handler: createItemHandler)
    router.put("/api/admin", handler: updateItemHandler)
    router.delete("/api/admin", handler: deleteItemHandler)
    router.delete("/api/admin", handler: deleteItemHandler)
}
```

Each router endpoint method also specifies a handler that accepts a request and gives out a response.

Create a new `/Sources/Application/Routes/ApiRoutes.swift` file to implement all router endpoint handlers in an extension of `App`:

```
import Foundation
import Kitura
import SwiftKueryORM
import SwiftKueryPostgreSQL
import LoggerAPI

extension App
{

 // Add all handlers here
}
```

Retrieving all items

Add the `getAllHandler(completion:)` method to handle the request for retrieving all items in the database:

```
// retrieve all items
func getAllHandler(completion: @escaping([JournalItem]?, RequestError?) ->
Void) {
  JournalItem.findAll() { items, error in
    guard let items = items else {
      return completion(nil, error)
    }
    completion(items, nil)
  }
}
```

In the closure for the `findAll()` method, the retrieved array optional items is unwrapped. If the `items` array is a valid object, a completion closure with unwrapped items will be invoked; otherwise, a completion closure with an error will be called.

Since you do not need to render Stencil web pages for API-based web functions, it is convenient to use the `curl` command-line tool or a web analysis tool, such as Postman, to verify the result:

```
$ curl http://localhost:8080/api/journal
```

The JSON object retrieved from the PostgreSQL database will be dumped out on the screen.

You may notice the preceding command is the same *curl* command you used in testing the "retrieve all" endpoint in the API of your Vapor web service. That's right! Since you use the same API design in both Vapor and Kitura web services, you should expect them to work similarly. In the rest of your Kitura code here, you're going to use the same set of `curl` commands you've used before.

Creating a new item

To create a new item, call the `save()` method to save the `JournalItem` object to the database:

```
func createItemHandler(item: JournalItem,
                       completion: @escaping(JournalItem?, RequestError?) ->
Void) {
  item.save(completion)
}
```

Similar to the `updateItemHandler(item, completion)` method, `createItemHandler(item, completion)` expects a new `JournalItem` object submitted by user.

Check the `createItemHandler(item:completion:)` function with the following `curl` command:

```
$ curl --header "Content-Type: application/json" \
--request POST \
--data '{"title":"New Entry","content":"This is a brand new entry."}' \
http://localhost:8080/api/admin
```

After posting the request to create a new journal entry, check all of your records in the database again:

```
$ curl http://localhost:8080/api/journal
```

You'll see the new journal entry now appears as one of the items in the retrieved JSON object.

Retrieving an item by ID

Unlike the website application, which does not have any need to retrieve an individual journal entry, your web service is required to add such method to the API. This is because in some clients, such as the iOS mobile app, it is difficult to fit the title and content of all journal entries on a small screen. The user is expected to select one item at a time from a list of entries and then view the content of the selected item on a separate screen.

To retrieve a specific item, use the `find()` method to search for the item by its ID:

```
// retrieve an item by ID and return it
func getItemHandler(id: Int,
                    completion: @escaping(JournalItem?, RequestError?) ->
Void) {
  JournalItem.find(id: id) { item, error in
    guard let item = item else {
      return completion(nil, error)
    }
    completion(item, nil)
  }
}
```

Kitura will parse the ID encoded as the URL parameter in a request. If the item is found with the `find(id:)` method, a `completion` closure will respond the request with the retrieved item.

You can check the handler with `curl`:

```
$ curl http://localhost:8080/api/admin/1
```

The `/api/admin/<id>` endpoint is used here. The preceding command prints out a JSON object with the requested journal entry, if found.

Updating an item

To update an existing item, you simply call the `update()` method:

```
// find an item by ID and replace it
func updateItemHandler(id: Int,
                       item: JournalItem,
                       completion: @escaping(JournalItem?, RequestError?)
-> Void) {
  item.update(id: id, completion)
}
```

The `updateItemHandler(item, completion)` method expects both the ID of an existing item (decoded from the URL parameter) and a new `JournalItem` object (decoded from the request's JSON object).

You can also check the handler with the `curl` command:

```
curl --header "Content-Type: application/json" \
--request PUT \
--data '{"title":"New Update","content":"This is an update."}' \
http://localhost:8080/api/admin/1
```

The item with ID 1 should have been updated by the `updateItemHandler(id:item:completion:)` handler. Use `curl` to check the result again:

```
$ curl http://localhost:8080/api/admin/1
```

The JSON object printed on the screen should reflect the changes to the specified journal entry.

Deleting an item

To delete a specific item, you just need to provide the item's ID and call the `delete()` method of the model:

```
// delete an item by ID
func deleteItemHandler(id: Int,
                       completion: @escaping(RequestError?) -> Void) {
  JournalItem.delete(id: id, completion)
}
```

Use *curl* to delete one of the existing items:

```
$ curl --request DELETE http://localhost:8080/api/admin/1
```

Then run the *curl* command again to retrieve the specific item:

```
$ curl http://localhost:8080/api/admin/1
```

Nothing is printed on the screen. The `deleteItemHandler(id:completion:)` handler works as expected!

Deleting All items

You can delete all records with the `deleteAll()` method:

```
// delete all items
func deleteAllHandler(completion: @escaping(RequestError?) -> Void) {
  JournalItem.deleteAll(completion)
}
```

The preceding handler will erase all `JournalItem` entries in the database. It is recommended not to implement this handler as one of your actual API methods.

Summary

You learned how to build web services in this chapter. First, you were introduced to the REST architecture for the server/client model based on HTTP. Then you learned the basic rules for the RESTful API's design; you modified the `myJournal` website application from previous chapters and implemented a RESTful API that contains the endpoints for all the routes in `myJournal`. You essentially turned your website application into a web service. Instead of rendering web pages for the clients, your `myJournal` application now offers web services to clients via the RESTful API. In the next chapters, you're going to learn how to deploy your Vapor and Kitura applications to the cloud and write an iOS client application that works with API Gateway.

12
Deploying to the Cloud

In this chapter, you'll learn how to deploy your web services to the cloud. You'll get introduced to four hosted cloud solutions: **Vapor Cloud** and **IBM Cloud** (**Bluemix**). Vapor Cloud is the official hosting service for Vapor and there is built-in support in Vapor CLI to let you deploy and manage your Vapor instance easily without installing additional libraries and tools. Similarly, IBM Cloud is a natural choice for a hosted solution for Kitura web service since both of them are part of IBM cloud solutions.

You'll have the following knowledge after finishing this chapter:

- Getting familiar with the features offered in Vapor Cloud
- Having hands-on experience with deploying a sample project to Vapor Cloud
- Knowing how to monitor and manage your deployed applications on Vapor Cloud
- Getting familiar with IBM Cloud and its offered features for Kitura applications
- Using developer tools to deploy a Kitura sample project to IBM Cloud

Deploying Vapor web service to Vapor Cloud

Vapor Cloud is a cloud service integrated into Vapor Toolbox CLI, making the deployment of your Vapor application to the cloud straightforward. If you are looking for a seamless experience in launching your Vapor application, consider hosting your application in Vapor Cloud.

Vapor Cloud itself is built on top of **Amazon Web Services** (**AWS**). You can easily scale your application to meet higher demand after you have fully launched your cloud application. You need to pay extra for those hours that have high demand.

Checking out Vapor Cloud features

Here are some of the major cloud-hosting features for Vapor Cloud:

- Database and Cache Support
- Application Monitoring
- Recurrent Job Scheduling
- Accessible to File Storage and CDN Services
- Zero-Downtime Deployment

Database and Cache Support

Vapor Cloud supports several databases, such as MySQL, PostgreSQL, MongoDB, and AWS Aurora. The database credentials are automatically made available to your application upon deployment. The database support makes data persistence in your Vapor application very easy. In addition, Vapor Cloud offers the Redis cache to speed up your cloud applications.

Application Monitoring

With the Vapor Cloud **Dashboard** application, you can easily track network traffic to your application. Useful statistics, such as average response time and memory usage of your application, will be available for you to monitor the status of application in real time and make sure that everything is running smoothly.

Recurrent Job Scheduling

Sometimes you may want to offload and schedule recurring tasks, hoping that they do not slow down your hosted web application deployed to Vapor Cloud. Recurrent jobs are often called **Cronjobs**. You specify a job to be executed at a specified time, whether it is every 10 minutes, every 12 hours, or every Saturday morning at 9:00 AM. Vapor Cloud will spin up a new replica when a cronjob is started and run the cronjob inside the replica.

Accessible to File Storage and CDN Services

Since Vapor Cloud is built on top of **Amazon AWS**, all Vapor Cloud applications have access to file-storage services, such as S3 bucket, for uploading and storing files, and the CDN API for doing things such as cropping an image on the fly, at the edge locations all around the world.

Zero-Downtime Deployment

When you deploy your Vapor application to Vapor Cloud, the new deployment is rolled out with zero downtime. This ensures that your application is always available at any given time, even when you are rolling out a new version of the application.

Signing up Vapor Cloud

To sign up for a free Vapor Cloud account, visit `https://dashboard.vapor.cloud/signup`.

After the signup, you'll be taken to the **Vapor Cloud Dashboard**. The dashboard looks like the following:

The Dashboard is where you can see your profile, account information, organization, pricing information, statistics, logs, and much more.

By default, your payment plan includes up to 20,000 requests a month, free of charge. This is enough for you to test your application during development. After the successful launch of your application, you can consider upgrading to one of the paid plans.

Deploying to Vapor Cloud

After you have signed up for a Vapor Cloud account, you can log in and deploy your existing Vapor application using the Vapor Toolbox CLI.

Using the Vapor Cloud commands

All the Vapor Cloud commands are integrated into the Vapor Toolbox CLI under the cloud command group.

For example, you can list all Vapor Cloud commands using the following command:

```
$ vapor cloud --help
```

The output looks like the following:

```
Usage: vapor cloud command

Commands for interacting with Vapor Cloud.

Commands:
login Logs you into Vapor Cloud.
logout Logs you out of Vapor Cloud.
signup Creates a new Vapor Cloud user.
refresh Refreshes vapor token.
me Shows info about the currently logged in user.
token Cached token metadata for debugging.
dump Dump info for current user.
logs Displays logs from remote Vapor application.
list List various owned items of user
deploy Deploy a project to Vapor Cloud
create Create new instances of Vapor Cloud objects like
applications, environments, databases, etc.
run Runs commands on your application
git-hash Get the Git has deployed live
config View, create, modify, and delete environment configs
db Manage database servers, and databases, warning: this feature is still
in beta, use with caution.
database Opens a database editor for the selected environment in your web
browser

Use `vapor cloud command --help` for more information on a command.
```

Creating Your First Deployment

To get start with your first deployment to Vapor Cloud, use the following command to log in:

```
$ vapor cloud login
```

It will prompt you for your email and password credentials. If you haven't signed up for an account using the URL provided to you previously, you can also sign up using the Vapor Clouds command:

```
$ vapor cloud signup
```

If you don't have an existing project to deploy, you can create a new one using Vapor's template:

```
$ vapor new myNewApp
$ cd myNewApp
```

Make sure that you are in the root directory of your application.

If you have an existing application, change to the root directory where you can find the Package.swift file.

Once you are in the root directory, the deployment of your application to the cloud takes only one Vapor Cloud command:

```
$ vapor cloud deploy
```

You can follow the prompts from this command to complete the rest of deployment steps. The output of the vapor cloud deploy comment looks something like the following:

```
$ vapor cloud deploy
app: FirstVapor
git: https://github.com/AngusY/myNewApp.git
env: beta
db: none
replicas: 1
replica size: free
branch: master
build: clean
Creating deployment [Done]
Connecting to build logs ...
Waiting in Queue [Done]
Starting deployment: 'firstvapor-angus' [Done]
Getting project from Git 'https://github.com/AngusY/myNewApp.git' [Done]
Checkout branch 'master' [Done]
```

```
Verifying base folder [Done]
Selected swift version: 4.2.0 [Done]
Building vapor (release) [Done]
Trying to find executable [Done]
Found executable: Run [Done]
Creating container registry [Done]
Building container [Done]
Updating replicas [Done]
Deployment succeeded: https://firstvapor-angus-beta.vapor.cloud [Done]
Successfully deployed.
```

When the deployment succeeds, you may try the `https://firstvapor-angus-beta.vapor.cloud/hello` URL to verify that your web application is operational. You will see the **Hello, world!** output in your web browser:

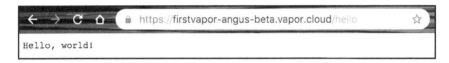

Next, you'll learn various options that are available in each of the preceding deployment steps.

Creating an Application from Git Remote

Vapor Cloud allows you to pull your source code from a remote Git repository. Creating a public remote Git repository will make deploying your code very easy.

You should consider taking advantage of this built-in Git Remote feature. For example, if your source code is hosted on GitHub, copy the SSH (not HTTP) URL into the prompt when the vapor cloud tool asks you to do so.

Working with Slug and Environment

When you are asked to create an application, you'll be prompted for a name and a slug. The slug for an application is the identifier used to access your Vapor application. For example, if your slug is `firstvapor-angus`, the URL for your application becomes `https://firstvapor-angus.vapor.cloud`.

Vapor Cloud's hosting service also allows you to configure different environments. You can create different environments for different stages of development, such as alpha, beta, testing, staging, and development. The URL for your application will add a suffix to the slug. For example, the beta development environment for your application will have the following URL for your application: `https://firstvapor-angus-beta.vapor.cloud`. The `beta` suffix, preceded by "-", is appended to the `firstvapor-angus` slug.

The production environment is treated in a special way. When you specify `production` as the environment, Vapor Cloud won't append the suffix to your slug. So your URL for the production environment looks like `https://firstvapor-angus.vapor.cloud`, instead of `https://firstvapor-angus-production.vapor.cloud`.

Since you have your code hosted on a remote Git repository, you are able to specify a specific branch to the environment you have just created. For the `production` environment, you usually associate it with the `master` branch of your Git remote repository.

Choosing a Replica Size and Database

Normally, you choose the Free size replicas to host your project for free when you are actively developing your application. Each free size replica has a monthly request limit. You can choose other paid replicas when the traffic to your application grows substantially.

Vapor cloud allows you to deploy your application to multiple replicas. However, you're allowed to deploy your application only to one replica if you choose to use the free size replicas.

If your application uses a database, you can also choose to add a hosting database. In the Vapor Cloud deployment, hosting database services always cost a small monthly fee. If you are not ready, you can ignore the prompt to add a database right way.

If you do need to add a database later on, you can use the following Vapor Cloud command:

```
$ vapor cloud create db
```

Choosing a Build Type

The last option you're prompted to configure is the Build Type. There are three different ways you can do so: incremental, update, and clean.

For the **incremental** build type, Vapor Cloud simply runs the Swift build command on your application. This is the fastest way to build since it doesn't update any dependencies.

For the **update** build type, Vapor Cloud runs the Swift package update before running the Swift build. This allows Swift Package Manager to check the modifications of your `Package.swift` file and update dependencies only when needed.

For the **clean** build type, Vapor Cloud deletes the `.build` folder before running Swift build. It is the slowest build option, but makes sure that everything, including the dependencies, is updated.

Managing Your Cloud application

There are a bunch of Vapor Cloud toolbox features you can leverage to manage your Cloud application. Several of them are discussed here.

Getting live log output

You can get the live log output using the vapor cloud `logs` toolbox command. This command, similar to the tail command in Linux, lists the latest events in a log file. It has the following syntax:

```
$ vapor cloud logs --app=[name] --env=[environment] --since=[time]
```

- The [name] is the application name in your slug, such as firstvapor-angus
- The [environment] is the hosting environment for your development stage, such as production or beta
- The [time] is the time you want to track back from the last logging event time, such as 2h for 2 hours, 5m for 5 minutes, or 30s for 30 seconds

Consider the following as an example:

```
$ vapor cloud logs --app=firstvapor-angus --env=beta --since=2d
```

The command in the preceding code instructs vapor cloud to print out the log file for all the entries in two days for the beta environment of the firstvapor-angus application.

The output looks as follows:

```
app: FirstVapor
env: beta
tail 1 logs...
firstvapor-angus-beta-deployment-6874c7f469-4kjqq
```

The Vapor cloud `logs` command keeps watching for the arrival of new logging events. Use *Ctrl* + *C* to get out of this wait loop.

Working with environment variables

In many cases, you'd like to set some environment variables for your Vapor application. The vapor cloud toolbox provides vapor cloud config just for that.

To create or modify configuration variables, use the modify in the following syntax:

```
$ vapor cloud config modify --app=my-app --env=staging VAR1=KEY1 VAR2=KEY2
```

For example, you create a USERNAME environment variable and set its initial value to ANGUS in the following way:

```
$ vapor cloud config modify --app=firstvapor-angus --env=beta
USERNAME=ANGUS
```

The output of this command confirms that the USERNAME environment variable has been created and it is assigned with the ANGUS value:

```
app: FirstVapor
env: beta
USERNAME: ANGUS
Updating configs [Done]
```

Use the `vapor cloud config dump` command to list all the existing environment variables:

```
$ vapor cloud config dump --app=firstvapor-angus --env=beta
```

This lists USERNAME as one of the environment variables for your application:

```
app: FirstVapor
env: beta
USERNAME: ANGUS
```

Adding a custom domain

Instead of using the `vapor.cloud` domain, you may want to have your own custom domain. So, you want to replace `https://firstvapor-angus.vapor.cloud` with a custom domain, such as `https://firstvapor-angus.com`. The Vapor Cloud toolbox provides a feature for you to create your custom domain.

First, you'll need to tell Vapor Cloud to direct the network traffic to your custom domain using the Vapor Cloud command:

```
$ vapor cloud create domain
```

Second, you need to configure a CNAME record configuration to have your DNS provider point `firstvapor-angus.com` to `firstvapor-angus.vapor.cloud`. Since Vapor Cloud assigns a fixed IP address to you, you can set up your redirect by creating an ALIAS record for that. Many DNS providers support the ALIAS record. One of these DNS providers is `dnsimple.com`.

Scheduling a New cronjob

If you want to run a `cronjob`, you specify it in the `cloud.yml` optional file in the root directory of your application. Add the following to `cloud.yml`:

```
cronjobs:
    production:
        ping:
            time: "* * * */24 *"
            command: "ping http://www.vapor.com"
```

The preceding script specifies the **environment** to be "production" and the **name** to be "ping".

The **time** is specified to be `* * * */24 *`, per the following format:

```
* * * * * command to be executed
- - - - -
| | | | |
| | | | ----- Day of week (0 - 7) (Sunday=0 or 7)
| | | ------- Month (1 - 12)
| | --------- Day of month (1 - 31)
| ----------- Hour (0 - 23)
------------- Minute (0 - 59)
```

This means that the command will be executed once every 24 hours.

The **command** specifies the full command to be executed. In this case, it simply pings a website.

To run `crobjobs`, issue the following Vapor Toolbox CLI command:

```
$ vapor run ping
```

It typically takes 5 to 30 seconds to spin up a new replica. Then your `cronjob` will be executed after this initial delay.

Deploying the Kitura web service to IBM Cloud

It takes several simple steps for you to install the tools you need to build your app, run the app locally, and then deploy it to IBM Cloud. IBM provides you with a development environment that gives you a seamless workflow to do all of this together.

Working with an IBM Cloud Account

First of all, you must have an account with IBM Cloud before your can deploy your application to the cloud. By default, you're offered to start with the Lite (Free) account type. It is free of charge for you and comes with 256 MB of free memory each month. There are several types of account upgrades when you are ready to use more resources.

Registering for an Account on IBM Cloud

To start, use your web browser to visit IBM Cloud's official site at `https://console.bluemix.net`. You will see IBM Cloud's login page after successful email verification:

After that, you'll be given a chance to review the privacy disclosure associated with your newly-created account.

Working with the IBM Cloud Dashboard

The Dashboard is a starting page for all resources available in your cloud account. As you grow the features of your application, you can leverage resources such as Watson artificial intelligence platform, mobile services, and security services.

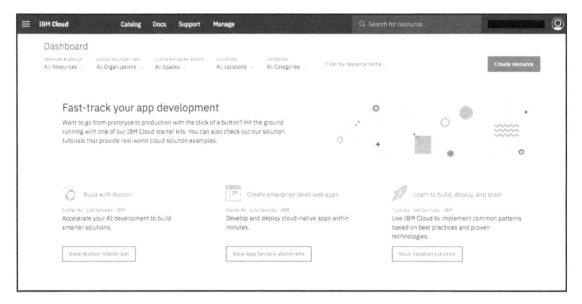

You will come back to this **Dashboard** page again to create a starter web app after you've made your local system ready for IBM Cloud deployment.

Readying the Local System for IBM Cloud Deployment

You need to install IBM Cloud Developer Tools on your local system, which we'll cover here.

Installing IBM Cloud Developer Tools

In order to install IBM Cloud Developer Tools, run the following command in a Terminal application on your system:

```
$ curl -sL http://ibm.biz/idt-installer | bash
```

The output looks like the following after executing the preceding command:

```
[main] --==[ IBM Cloud Developer Tools for Linux/MacOS - Installer, v1.2.3 ]==--
[install] Starting Update...
[install] Note: You may be prompted for your 'sudo' password during install.
[install_deps] Checking for external dependency: brew
[install_deps] Installing/updating external dependency: git
[install_deps] Installing/updating external dependency: docker
[install_deps] Installing/updating external dependency: kubectl
################################################################## 100.0%
Password:
[install_deps] Please review any setup requirements for 'kubectl' from:
https://kubernetes.io/docs/tasks/tools/install-kubectl/
[install_deps] Installing/updating external dependency: helm
 Updating Homebrew...

 ...
[Deleted]

 ...
[install] Install finished.
[main] --==[ Total time: 74 seconds ]==--
```

Container technology, such as Docker, is installed as part of the IBM developer tool chain. In fact, you have to create a Docker account and install Docker runtime on your local machine in order to use the build tools to deploy your app to IBM Cloud.

If you haven't installed Docker on your system before, go to `www.docker.com` to download and install Docker Desktop for your system.

After proper installation, Docker Desktop will be running in the background:

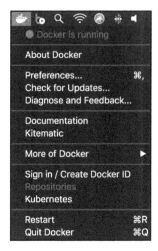

Create a new Docker ID or sign in with an existing Docker ID. You'll need to use the Docker credential locally when deploying your Kitura application to IBM Cloud.

Alternatively, you can install Docker on your Mac with `brew`:

```
$ brew install docker
```

You can run `docker info` to learn more about your docker installation:

```
$ docker info
```

For installing Docker on Ubuntu or getting more help with the Docker installation, you can find more useful information on Docker's website: `https://docs.docker.com/install/`.

Using IBM Cloud Developer Tools

To verify that IBM Cloud Developer Tools have been properly installed, execute the following main command:

```
$ idt
```

The execution of the `idt` command prints the following message on the screen:

```
NAME:
 bx dev - A CLI plugin to create, manage, and run applications on IBM Cloud
USAGE:
 bx dev command [arguments...] [command options]
VERSION:
 2.1.4
COMMANDS:
 build Build the application in a local container
 code Download the code from an application
 console Opens the IBM Cloud console for an application
 create Creates a new application and gives you the option to add services
 diag This command displays version information about installed
dependencies
 debug Debug your application in a local container
 delete Deletes an application from your space
 deploy Deploy an application to IBM Cloud
 edit Add or remove services for your application
 enable Add IBM Cloud files to an existing application.
 get-credentials Gets credentials required by the application to enable use
of connected services.
 list List all IBM Cloud applications in a space
 run Run your application in a local container
 shell Open a shell into a local container
 status Check the status of the containers used by the CLI
 stop Stop a container
 test Test your application in a local container
 view View the URL of your application
 help Show help
Enter 'bx dev help [command]' for more information about a command.
GLOBAL OPTIONS:
 --version, -v Print the version
 --help, -h Show help
```

The `idt` command is actually a shortcut for the `bx dev` command, which is used to create, manage, and run applications on IBM Cloud.

Besides the `idt` shortcut, there is also `idt update` and `idt uninstall` to help you update the IBM Cloud developer tools to the latest version and uninstall the tools from your local system, respectively:

```
$ idt update
$ idt uninstall
```

Creating a Kitura app that is deployable to IBM Cloud

You can create a Kitura application easily using the starter Kitura Kitura web application template.

From the dashboard for your IBM Cloud account, click on the icon for **App Service Starter Kits**. Different starter kits are listed for you to choose from. Navigate down the list and click on the **Swift Web App with Kitura** icon to start generating a Starter Kitura web application:

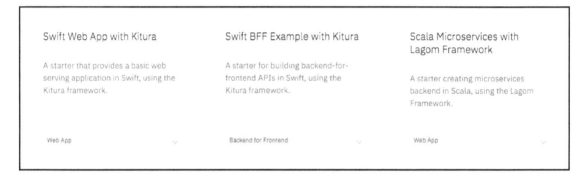

Generating a Starter Kitura Web Application

Once you are on the main page for the Starter Kitura Web Application, review how the starter kit will help you. Click on the **Create App** button on the top-right corner:

Swift Web App with Kitura

Create app

Web App

Overview

This starter kit comes pre-configured as a Web App with Kitura, a high performance and simple to use web framework for building modern Swift applications. Add services, generate and download the code, use the IBM Cloud Developer Tools CLI to run and debug locally, then deploy to Kubernetes, Cloud Foundry with a DevOps Toolchain.

This starter kit will help you

* Create a Web App according to the IBM Cloud Garage Method's web app architecture pattern

* Generate an application with Kitura

* Generate an application files for deploying to Kubernetes, Cloud Foundry with a DevOps Toolchain

* Generate an application with files for monitoring and distributed trace using Swift Metrics

* Connect to provisioned services

For your Kitura app deployable to IBM Cloud, enter the name "My New Kitura App" at the prompt. IBM Cloud will populate the app's name to the starter kit source code.

Take note that your application name has to be unique because all applications share the same domain as in `my-new-kitura-app.mybluemix.net`. You can add a suffix of your organization name, such as abc-org in `my-app-abc-org.mybluemix.net`, to ensure that the URL is unique and acceptable to IBM Cloud.

Next, you'll be taken to the **App Details** page where you can manage the deployment of the web app IBM Cloud has just created for you. Click on the **Download Code** button to download the starter source code to your system so you can build locally first:

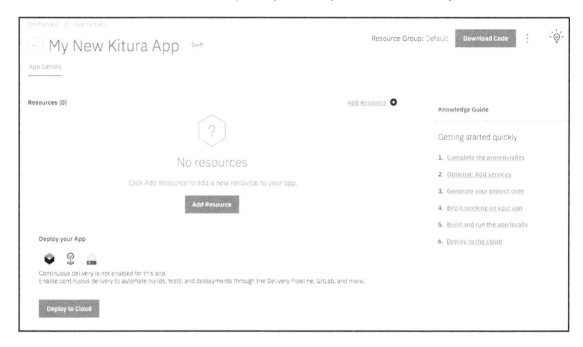

After unzipping the zipped package you've just downloaded, check out the files this starter kit created for you:

In addition to what you can see in File Manager, the starter kit has the `.bluemix` hidden directory to store scripts for the configuration of the toolchain, deployment, container, and orchestration services. This directory is hidden from you because you are not expected to modify the scripts in this directory directly.

The source code for your Kitura application is in the `/my-new-kitura-app/Sources` directory. You can work with the starter code to try out the deployment to IBM Cloud before you add your Kitura app to this project.

Logging into IBM Cloud

Assuming you have created an account on IBM Cloud already, you can now log in using the following command:

```
$ ibmcloud login -a https://api.ng.bluemix.net
```

In the preceding code, it specifies the US South API endpoint location with the `-a` command flag, followed by the `https://api.ng.bluemix.net` URL for the location. If you have specified a location already, you can ignore the `-a` flag.

The login command will prompt you for your credentials and print out your account information:

```
API endpoint: https://api.ng.bluemix.net
Email> [deleted]
Password> [deleted]
 Authenticating...
 OK
Targeted account Angus's Account
Targeted resource group Default
 API endpoint: https://api.ng.bluemix.net
 Region: us-south
 User: [deleted]
 Account: Angus's Account
 Resource group: Default
 CF API endpoint:
 Org:
 Space:
Tip: If you are managing Cloud Foundry applications and services
 - Use 'ibmcloud target --cf' to target Cloud Foundry org/space
interactively, or use 'ibmcloud target --cf-api ENDPOINT -o ORG -s SPACE'
to target the org/space.
 - Use 'ibmcloud cf' if you want to run the Cloud Foundry CLI with current
IBM Cloud CLI context.
```

Building Your App with the IBM Cloud Tool

Now you can build your source code and deploy it in a Docker container.

Since you need to build a Docker image in order to build your application, use the following Docker command to log in to your Docker account first:

```
$ docker login --username=angus
```

You are now ready to build your application locally using the `dev build` command:

```
$ ibmcloud dev build
```

The command will proceed to get your service credential and do the Docker image build:

```
Getting service credentials for the application.
 OK
 Validating Docker image name
 OK
 Checking if Docker container mynewkituraapp-swift-tools is running
 OK
 Checking Docker image history to see if image already exists
```

```
OK
 Creating image mynewkituraapp-swift-tools based on Dockerfile-tools ...
  Image will have user fyeung1 with id 502 added
Executing docker image build --file Dockerfile-tools --tag mynewkituraapp-
swift-tools --rm --pull --build-arg bx_dev_userid=502 --build-arg
bx_dev_user=fyeung1 .
OK
 Creating a container named 'mynewkituraapp-swift-tools' from that image...
 OK
 Starting the 'mynewkituraapp-swift-tools' container...
 OK
 OK
 Stopping the 'mynewkituraapp-swift-tools' container...
 OK
```

Running the Kitura App in the Local Container

Before you start the deployment of your Kitura application to IBM Cloud, you want to run it in the local environment first. Execute the following command to run your application:

```
$ ibmcloud dev run
```

The output of this command looks like the following:

The run-cmd option was not specified
Stopping the 'mynewkituraapp-swift-run' container...
The 'mynewkituraapp-swift-run' container was not found
Validating Docker image name
Binding IP and ports for Docker image.
OK
Checking if Docker container mynewkituraapp-swift-run is running
OK
Checking Docker image history to see if image already exists
OK
Creating image mynewkituraapp-swift-run based on Dockerfile ...

Executing docker image build --file Dockerfile --tag mynewkituraapp-swift-run --rm --pull .

OK
Creating a container named 'mynewkituraapp-swift-run' from that image...
OK
Starting the 'mynewkituraapp-swift-run' container...
OK
Logs for the mynewkituraapp-swift-run container:
[2018-10-10T18:48:51.208Z] [WARNING] [ConfigurationManager.swift:261
load(url:deserializerName:)] Unable to load data from URL /swift-project/config/mappings.json
[Wed Oct 10 18:48:51 2018] com.ibm.diagnostics.healthcenter.loader INFO: Swift Application
Metrics

[2018-10-10T18:48:51.583Z] [INFO] [Metrics.swift:20 initializeMetrics(router:)] Initialized metrics.
[2018-10-10T18:48:51.588Z] [INFO] [HTTPServer.swift:195 listen(on:)] Listening on port 8080

The application is running on your local system.

Open your browser to `http://localhost:8080` and you will see the following startup screen:

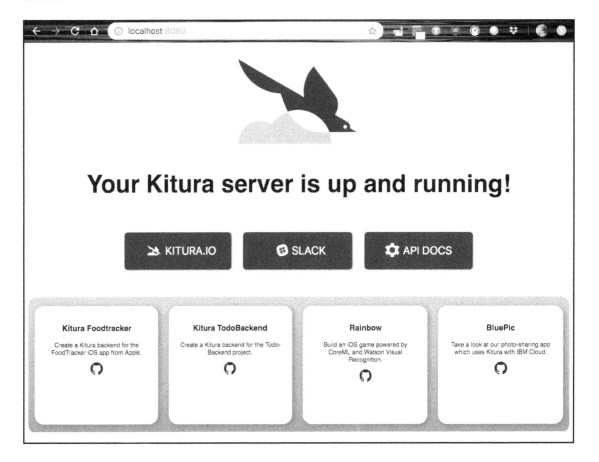

Deploying Your app

The IBM Cloud CLI provides you with a shortcut to deploy your application to IBM Cloud. After you have tested and executed your local container successfully, you can run the following command to deploy it to the cloud:

```
$ ibmcloud dev deploy
```

If it complains about an authorization failure to access the IBM Cloud, log out and then log in again to access IBM Cloud:

```
$ ibmcloud logout
$ ibmcloud login
$ ibmcloud target --cf
$ ibmcloud dev get-credentials
```

The deployment takes some time when the dependencies of your application are being fetched and compiled on the remote server.

If you visit `https://console.bluemix.net`, you can click on **Runtime** on the left navigation panel and check the current status of the running instance of your application:

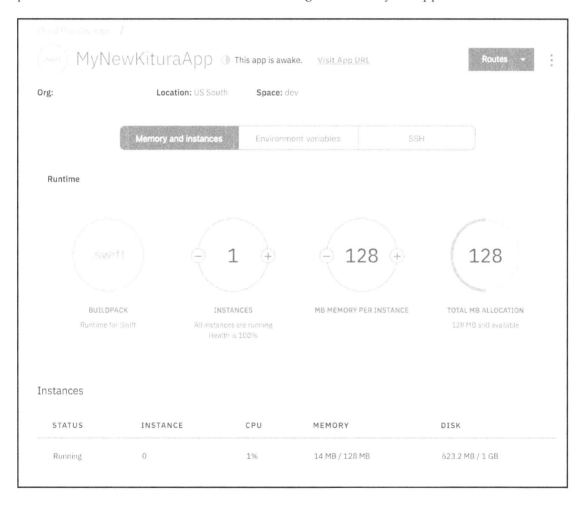

Since you have a Free account type, only one instance is allowed. Make sure that your runtime is awake and running.

Now take your web browser to `http://my-new-kitura-app.mybluemix.net/`, you will see the same default web page as the one you see when running your Kitura app on a local system. The difference, of course, is that your application is now active and running on IBM Cloud.

Summary

Deploying your applications to the cloud is part of the development process for Vapor and Kitura projects. In this chapter, you were introduced to the features offered in both Vapor Cloud and IBM Cloud, learned how to register for new accounts, and then followed the instructions to deploy starter Vapor and Kitura applications to your cloud accounts. In the next chapter, you'll be working on another side of the end-to-end Swift development workflow: developing iOS client applications.

Developing an iPhone Client 13

This chapter puts everything you've learned so far about server-side Swift together and uses an iOS app to show how a client "travel journal" app can leverage the login, database, and other cloud services you built with a Swift web framework. You'll first get started with building a travel journal iOS app, adding logic and UI components to the app design. You'll create a model for journal data and add the support of CRUD operations for the PostgreSQL database on the server. At the end of this chapter, you'll have a functional travel journal app that works seamlessly with your web services.

You're going to have learned about the following topics after finishing this chapter:

- Creating a table view controller in an iOS application
- Constructing a data model using the `Codable` protocol
- Adding content to the table view controller using the prototype cell
- Getting familiar with Storyboard and using it to add controls to the user interface
- Building additional screens to view and edit a journal entry
- Making HTTP requests to Vapor or Kitura web services
- Leveraging the Codable protocol to perform the encoding and decoding of JSON objects

Developing an iOS App for a server-side Swift application

In this section, you're going to start building an iOS application with the table view controller. You'll use this skeleton application to populate the table view with all the journal entries retrieved with the RESTful API you built in Chapter 11, *Designing for API Gateway*. The iOS application you're going to build here will work for both Vapor and Kitura web services, since they share the same API.

Creating a new project

Now you can go ahead and your Xcode IDE. If you have an existing installation of Xcode, remember to check its version and upgrade it to the latest version if it's an older version. I recommend you use Xcode 10.0 or better for the project in this chapter.

After launching Xcode, you're going to create a new project from one of the provided templates and then configure the project setting appropriately.

To create a new project for your iOS application, choose the **Single View App** template:

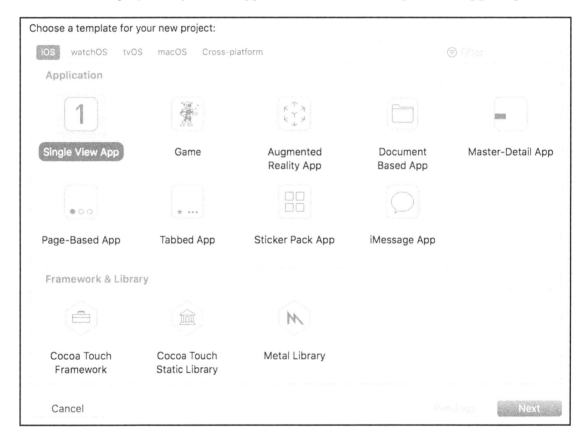

Fill in the options. Use `myJournal` as the **Product Name** and specify the **Organization Name**:

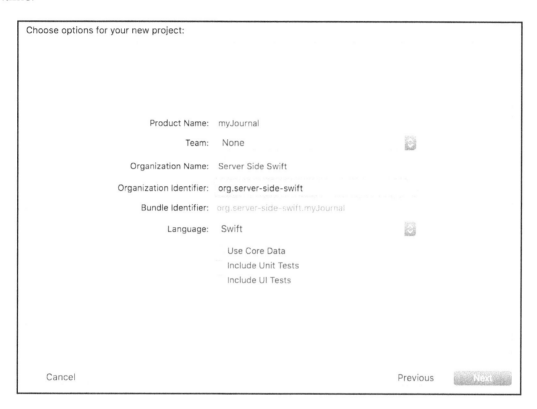

Next, go to **Project Navigator** on the left panel and select the first `myJournal` item. This brings you to the project settings page. The last section of this page is Deployment Info.

Uncheck both the **Landscape Left** and **Landscape Right** device orientation option and support **Portrait** mode only:

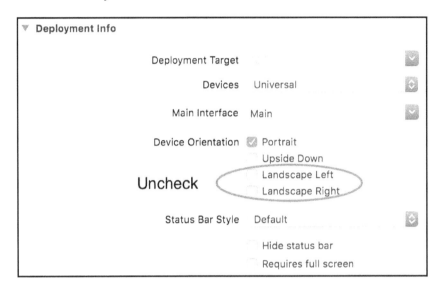

That's all the configuration you'll need for your project. Next, you can add a new `TableViewController` to your project.

Creating a new TableViewController

In this section, instead of the default `ViewController`, you're going to use a new `TableViewController` for the main screen:

1. Remove the `ViewController.swift` file XCode created for you.
2. Add a new `MainScreenViewController.swift` file to your project:

```
// File: MainScreenViewController.swift
import UIKit

class MainScreenViewController: UITableViewController {

    override func viewDidLoad() {
        super.viewDidLoad()
    }
}
```

3. In storyboard, delete the **View Controller** item from **View Controller Scene**:

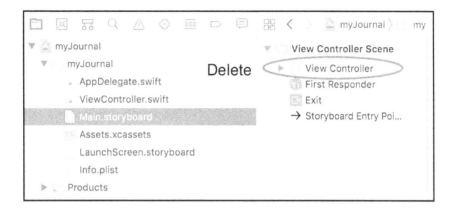

4. Go **View** | **Libraries** | **Show Library** or *Ctrl + command + L* to reveal the Library tray:

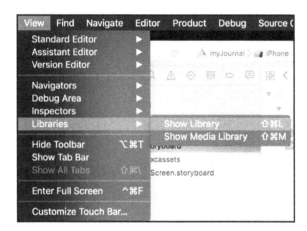

5. Alternatively, you can click on the **Libraries** button, the leftmost button on the top-right tray:

6. Drag the **Table View Controller** from the Library tray and drop it into the
    Storyboard:

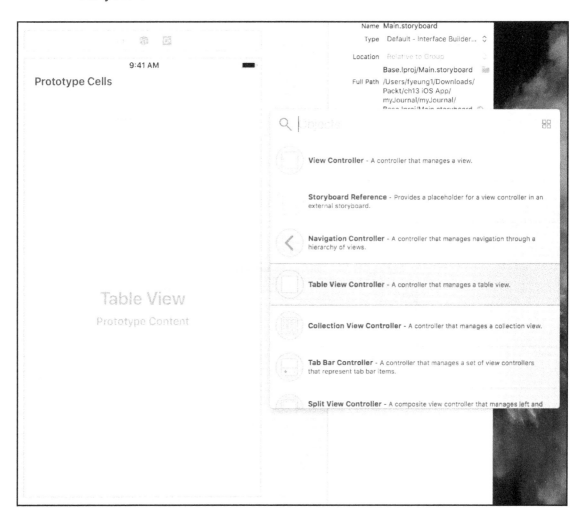

7. Click on **Attribute Inspector** and check the **Is Initial ViewController** option in the **View Controller** panel on the right:

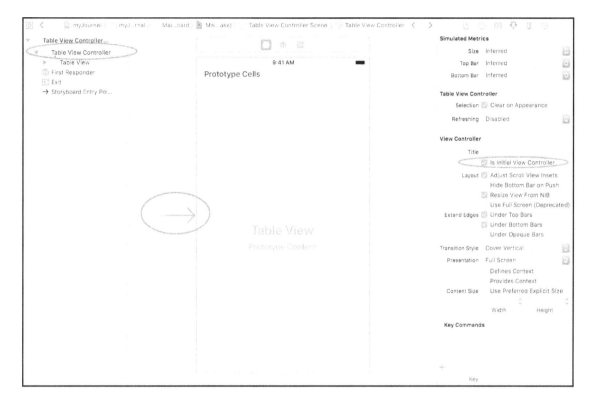

8. On the left panel of Storyboard, select the **Main Screen View Controller** item and click on Identity Inspector—that's the third icon from the left in the Inspectors panel.

10. From the pulldown menu of the **Class** option, choose to link to the `MainScreenViewController` class:

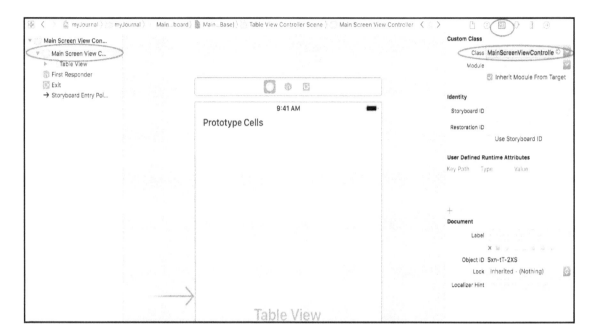

10. Run the app. After choosing the `myJournal` scheme and selecting one of the iOS device emulators from the top-left menu, you can run the app by either pressing on the "Run" button or using the *command + R* shortcut. The start screen shows a table view but it has no content:

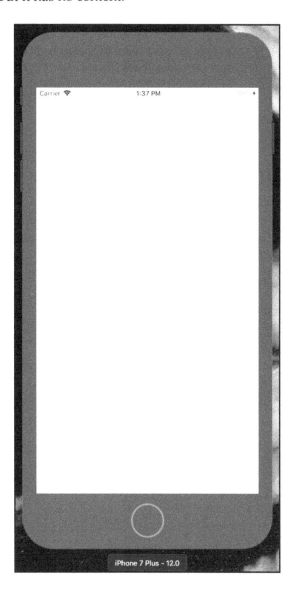

Now you have a skeleton table view application to work with. Next, you'll learn how to add some content to `TableViewController`.

Adding content to TableViewController

Before you can display all journal entries, you need to make an HTTP request to your server-side Swift application to retrieve data in the JSON object. The `Codable` protocol allows you to quickly create a data model that supports decoding and de-serializing JSON objects automatically. With the JSON objects, you can display each entry by appending a new item to the table list.

Preparing your data model

The first step is to create a new final class, called `JournalEntry`, that implements the `Codable` protocol. There are three fields, `id`, `title`, and `content`, in this model. As shown in the following code, all fields are optional because there is a chance that a field may miss from an `JournalEntry` object when you retrieve the object from the cloud application:

```
final class JournalEntry: Codable {
    let id: Int?
    var title: String?
    var content: String?

    public init(title: String?, content: String?) {
    self.id = nil
    self.title = title
    self.content = content
    }
}
```

The initializer only accepts `title` and `content` parameters. Since the value of the `id` field is automatically generated by the database-handling process, you can set an instance's `id` to `nil` for the time being.

Configuring table properties

Now you can bring your attention to the table component itself in `MainScreenViewController.swift`. You need to construct an `Array` object to hold local copies of all `JournalEntry` objects, then tell iOS about the number of sections in `UITableView` as well as the number of rows in the section.

Create an instance of the `JournalEntry` array object in `MainScreenViewController`:

```
var journalEntries = [JournalEntry]()
```

iOS allows you to group cells in `UITableView` into sections. However, for this iOS application, you simply specify the number of sections to be `1`:

```
override func numberOfSections(in tableView: UITableView) -> Int {
    return 1
}
```

The number of rows in the section corresponds to the total number of elements in your `JournalEntry` array object:

```
override func tableView(_ tableView: UITableView,
 numberOfRowsInSection section: Int) -> Int {
    return journalEntries.count
}
```

You're ready to configure the user interface component to display each `JournalEntry` object. For `UITableView`, the reusable cell prototype allows you to do exactly that.

Adding a label to the prototype cell

Before adding a label to the table view cell, you need to assign a reuse identifier for the table view cell. In the storyboard, select the **Table View Cell** item in the Storyboard's left navigation panel and choose **Identify Inspector** on the right panel—you will see the **Identifier** field. Enter **TitleCell** in the field:

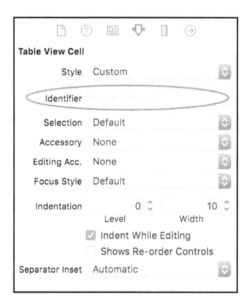

To add a label to **Prototype Cells**, drag a `Label` object from the Library tray and drop it into the area right below **Prototype Cells**. The same design of a prototype cell will be used to apply to all concrete instances of the table cell:

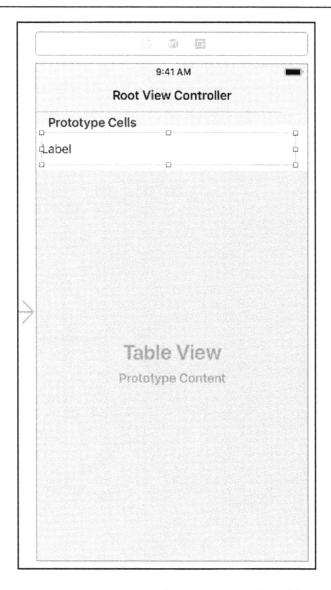

Adjust the size of `Label` so it covers most of the prototype cell and leaves small margins for all the four sides.

While selecting the **Label** item of **Prototype Cells**, click on the Constraint menu and set 10 pixels as the constraint to each border. The constraints will help ensure the proper layout of the **Label** with different iOS screen's devices:

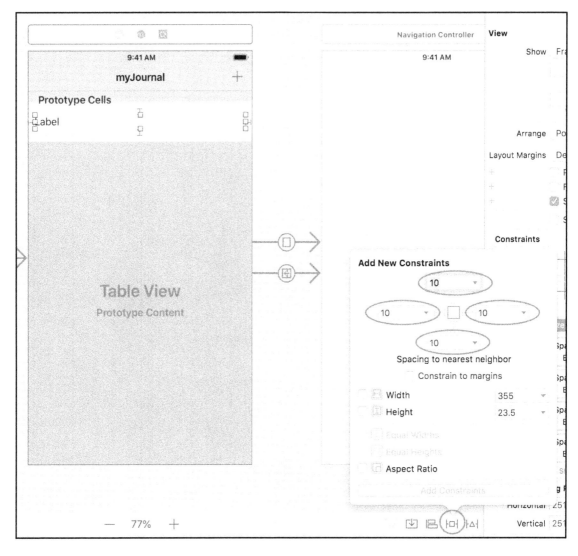

Next, select the `Label` object and use the Attributes Inspector to inspect the configuration of the object's attributes. Change the **View | Tag** field to `1000`. The tag will be used to reference to this `Label` object in your Swift code:

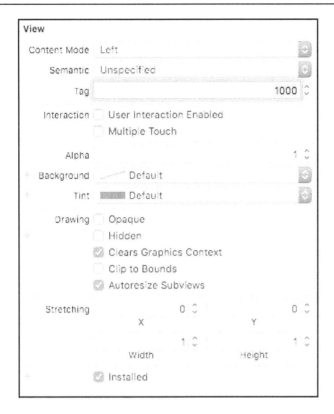

In the `MainScreenViewController` class, override this `UITableView` function to tell iOS what to display for each cell:

```
override func tableView(_ tableView: UITableView,
cellForRowAt indexPath: IndexPath) -> UITableViewCell {
    let cell = tableView.dequeueReusableCell(withIdentifier: "TitleCell",
for: indexPath)
    if let title = journalEntries[indexPath.row].title {
        let label = cell.viewWithTag(1000) as! UILabel
        label.text = title
    }
    return cell
}
```

Developing an iPhone Client

The implementation calls the `dequeueReusableCell(withIdentifier: for:)` function of `UITableView` to get a reference to the Prototype Cell you worked on. You can use the row of the current cell to retrieve the corresponding `JournalEntry` object from the local array. Now all you need to do is to apply the unwrapped value of the `JournalEntry` object's title (which is optional) to the Prototype Cell's Label. You use the `viewWithTag()` function to retrieve the view object with the "1000" tag and then cast it back the `UILabel` object type.

Constructing route handlers for web services

The data for your Prototype Cell to display is fetched from the web service API endpoints. You use a `URLSession` instance to send your request to an endpoint. Add the `getAll()` function by adding an extension to `MainScreenViewController` in a new `RouteHandlers.swift` file:

```
extension MainScreenViewController {
    // Read all entries
    func getAll() {
        guard let journalUrl = URL(string: apiURL + "/all") else { return }
        URLSession.shared.dataTask(with: journalUrl) { (data, response, error) in
        // Handle your retrieved data here
        }.resume()
    }
}
```

`journalUrl` holds the endpoint you are requesting the data from. The `apiURL` constant is defined in the original `MainScreenViewController` class:

```
let apiURL : String = "http://localhost:8080/api"
```

For testing purposes, we are running the `myJournal` web API application on the same local machine. You can deploy and run cloud-hosted applications after the development phase is complete.

Using `URLSession`, you can invoke the shared instance of a data task (`dataTask`) with `journalUrl` to start a data-downloading task. The task is created in a suspended state, so you call the `resume()` function to start the task.

The data-fetching request takes a finite amount of time to complete because it involves the client app making HTTP requests across the internet and the server making calls to a database to retrieve stored data in the backend. You're required to implement a completion handler, which is a closure that handles the return data after an asynchronous data-fetching task is successfully complete.

Several return objects are available to you: `data`, `response`, and `error`. The `data` object contains the data you've requested if you have a success. The `response` object contains any data result returned from the web API application, and the `error` object holds the error messages if an error occurs in this transaction.

After unwrapping the return data, you can take advantage of the `Codable` protocol to decode the JSON object into memory:

```swift
URLSession.shared.dataTask(with: journalUrl) { (data, response, error) in
    guard let jsonData = data else { return }
    do {
        let entries = try JSONDecoder().decode([JournalEntry].self, from:
jsonData)
        // Add more here later
    } catch {
        print("Error", error)
    }
}
```

The `entries` array object contains all the journal entries you have retrieved. Append the entire `entries` sequence to your `journalEntries` local store:

```swift
self.journalEntries.append(contentsOf: entries)
```

Since the content of `journalEntries` has been updated, you need to tell `tableView` to reload its data. Unfortunately, this is not straightforward because you'll be trying to post the result to the UI thread (which is also the main thread) from another worker thread owned by `URLSession`. You'll get an exception if you call the `tableView` object directly:

```swift
self.tableView.reloadData()
```

You need to resort to Swift's inter-thread communication in order to solve this issue.

Wrap the preceding call into `DispatchQueue` in the following way:

```swift
DispatchQueue.main.async { self.tableView.reloadData() }
```

Then the asynchronous call can successfully be made across threads.

The following is the general workflow for data-fetching and posting the result back to the table view object:

```
extension MainScreenViewController {
    func getAll() {
        guard let journalUrl = URL(string: apiURL + "/journal") else {
return }
        URLSession.shared.dataTask(with: journalUrl) { (data, response,
error) in
            guard let jsonData = data else { return }
            do {
                let entries = try JSONDecoder().decode([JournalEntry].self,
from: jsonData)
                self.journalEntries.append(contentsOf: entries)
                DispatchQueue.main.async { self.tableView.reloadData() }
            } catch {
                print("Error", error)
            }
        }.resume()
    }
}
```

Now, you can call the `getAll()` function in the `viewDidLoad()` function in `MainScreenViewController.swift`:

```
override func viewDidLoad() {
    super.viewDidLoad()
    getAll()
}
```

You're almost done here. You still need to handle the security setting issues with your project before you can take your iOS app for a spin.

Adding domain exceptions for App Transport Security

Even after you have all code implementation in place, you'll still be unable to fetch the data from a local web application successfully. This is because Apple requires **App Transport Security** (**ATS**) by default and blocks your calls. Proper configuration of ATS is required because of the HTTPS and security enforcement on iOS.

Even though you can explicitly opt out of ATS by adding the following option to `Info.plist`, it is not recommended to opt out of ATS entirely:

```
<key>NSAppTransportSecurity</key>
    <dict>
        <key>NSAllowsArbitraryLoads</key>
        <true/>
    </dict>
```

The recommended way is to get the domains you are working with exempt from the rules. You can specify which domains are exempt from the rules you define for ATS.

Open the `Info.plist` file in XCode and add a new entry for **App Transport Security Settings** under **Information Property List**:

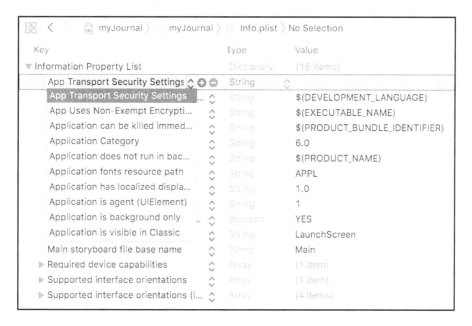

Add the **Allow Arbitrary Loads** subitem to **App Transport Security Settings**, and set its type to **Boolean** and value to **Yes**:

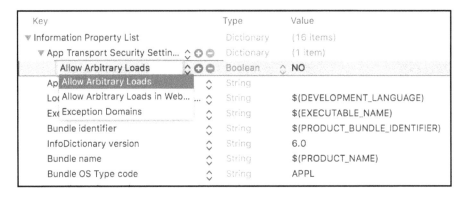

Also add the **Exception Domains** subitem to **App Transport Security Settings**:

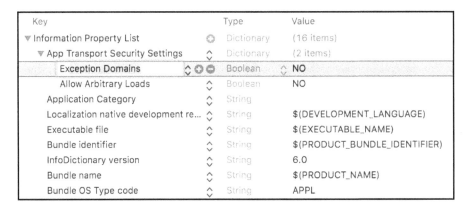

Under the **Exception Domains** item, add **localhost** as the **Dictionary** type; then add two **Boolean** values for **NSIncludesSubdomains** and **NSExceptionAllowsInsecureHTTPLoads**, and set both to **Yes**:

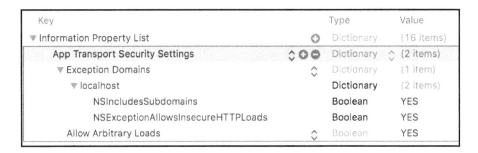

You should follow the preceding steps to add any host domain for your Vapor or Kitura web services to the **Exception Domains** list.

Testing the Vapor Server app

It's also a good idea to test whether the web app is working properly by using a third-party HTTP client tool. Use `curl` to create a HTTP GET request at the same endpoint:

```
$ curl http://localhost:8080/api/journal
```

If the web app is working, you should be able to retrieve the JSON objects as a result.

Running the iOS app

The following screen shows you how your table view should look like if your `getAll()` function successfully fetches the requested data from your web application:

Next, you can complete the rest of the features for the **myJournal** iOS application.

Adding a new entry to journal

To add a new entry to the **myJournal** iOS application, you're going to add another screen for a user to enter a new entry. After the user fills in the title and content of the new entry, this screen gives such data back to the main table view screen.

Designing the user interface for a new entry

You need to add a toolbar button item on the main screen to navigate to the new screen you are about to add. Drag a **Bar Button Item** from the Library tray and drop it into the right side of the main screen toolbar:

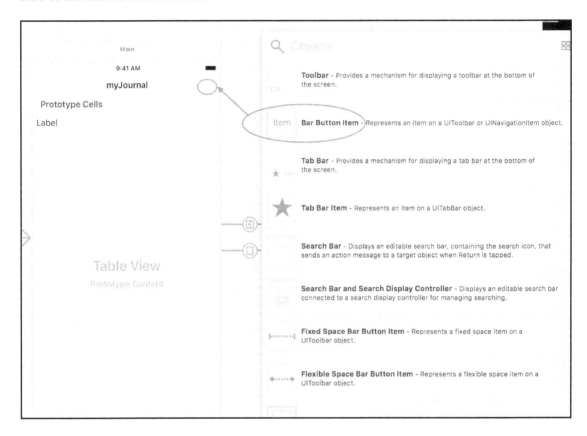

From **Attributes Inspector**, specify the **Bar Button Item** as the **Add** System Item:

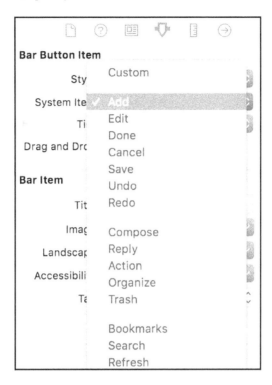

For the new screen, choose **Navigation Controller** and **View Controller** from the Library tray and add them to Storyboard.

While holding down the *Ctrl* key, drag from the **Add** toolbar button in the main screen to the new **Navigation Controller** you've just created. The **Action Segue** pop-up menu appears. Select the **Present Modally** segue type:

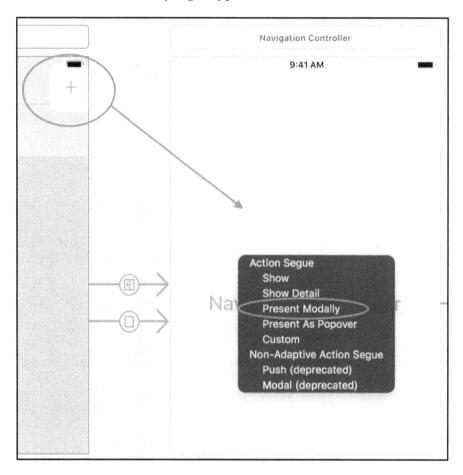

In the **Attributes Inspector**, set the segue's Identifier to **NewEntry**. With this new Action Segue, the new screen will appear **modally** when the **Add** toolbar button is clicked on.

Now, you can proceed to add a couple of UI items to the new screen.

Add a **Text Field** item from Library and place it near the top of screen. From the **Attributes Inspector**, change the attributes to according to the following diagram:

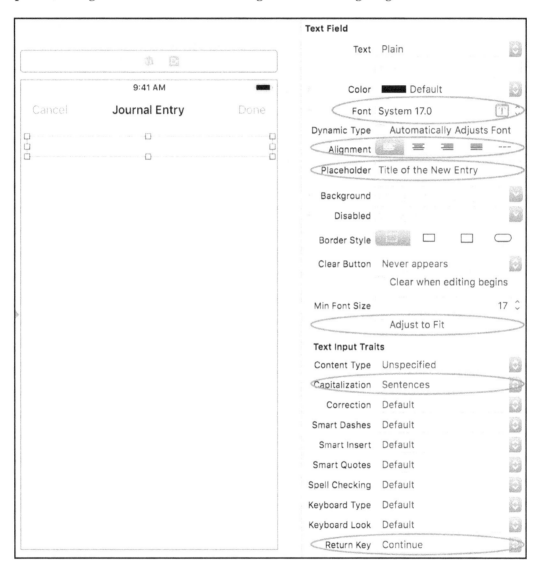

Add two Bar Button Items to the toolbar. Specify the left bar button as the **Cancel** system item in the Attributes Inspector and the right bar button as the **Done** system item. The **Title** text field should look something like this:

Add the constraints for the four borders of the **Title** text field in the same way as you've just done for the **Label** text field in **Prototype Cells**:

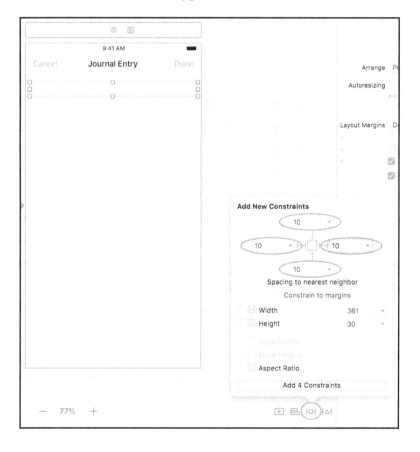

Continue to add a new **Text View** item under the Title text field. This **Text View** item holds the multiline text of an entry's content:

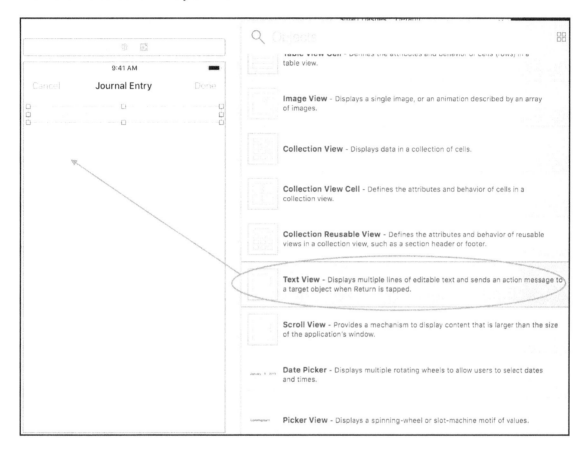

For the **Content Text View** item, remember to add constraints to its border as well.

The attributes of the Content text view are configured as follows:

Next, add a new `EntryDetailsViewController.swift` file and add the following code:

```
import UIKit

class EntryDetailsViewController : UIViewController {

    override func viewDidLoad() {
        super.viewDidLoad()
    }
}
```

In **Storyboard**, use the **Identify Inspector** to link your new view controller to the `EntryDetailsViewController` class:

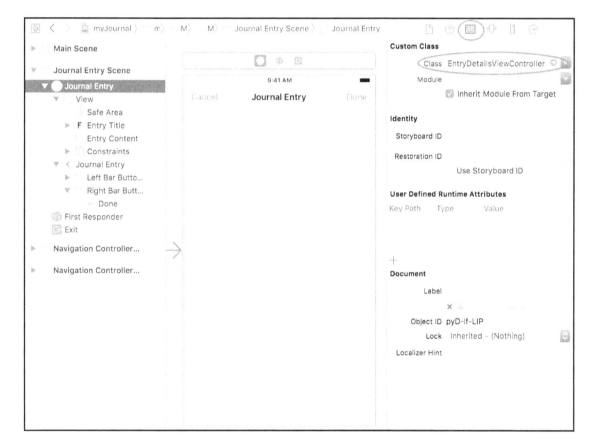

Before you keep going, you still need to do something with the `NewEntry` segue you've created; you need to add code to tell `EntryDetailsViewController` about the `NewEntry` segue.

In the `MainScreenViewController` class, add the following function:

```
override func prepare(for segue: UIStoryboardSegue, sender: Any?) {
    if segue.identifier == "NewEntry" {
        let navigationController = segue.destination as!
UINavigationController
        let controller = navigationController.topViewController as!
EntryDetailsViewController
        controller.delegate = self
    }
}
```

The preceding code basically assigns `MainScreenViewController` to be the delegate for `EntryDetailsViewController`.

Now you are ready to add functionalities for the user interface you've just created.

Using the Delegate Pattern

In iOS programming, it is common to use the **delegate** pattern for one component to pass information to another. The **delegator** component defines a delegate protocol with functions that it can use to pass out information. The **delegatee** component implements the provided delegate protocol by overriding the protocol's functions and handles the received information.

In your case, the new screen for adding a new entry is the delegator, while the main screen with table view is the delegatee to whom the information is passed.

Create the following delegate protocol in the same Swift file as the `EntryDetailsViewController` class (delegator) so it can inform `MainScreenViewController` (delegatee) when user is done creating the new entry:

```
protocol EntryDetailsViewControllerDelegate: class {
    // Delegate Cancel Event
    func entryDetailsViewControllerDidCancel(_ controller:
EntryDetailsViewController)

    // Delegate Done Adding Event
    func entryDetailsViewController(_ controller:
EntryDetailsViewController,
    didFinishAdding entry: JournalEntry)
}
```

Two functions are defined in the delegate protocol. The
`entryDetailsViewControllerDidCancel(_ controller:)` function delegates the
`DidCancel` event when the user clicks on the **Cancel** button. The
`entryDetailsViewController(_ controller:, didFinishAdding entry:)`
function delegates `didFinishAdding` when the user finishes adding a new entry and clicks
on the **Done** button.

In the `MainScreenViewController` class (delegatee),
add `EntryDetailsViewControllerDelegate` as one of the protocols the class
implements:

```
class MainScreenViewController: UITableViewController,
    EntryDetailsViewControllerDelegate {
    // ....
}
```

Now you need to override the two functions defined in the delegate protocol and provide
the implementation.

Add the implementation for the `entryDetailsViewControllerDidCancel(_ controller:)` function:

```
func entryDetailsViewControllerDidCancel(_ controller:
EntryDetailsViewController) {
    dismiss(animated: true, completion: nil)
}
```

The function simply dismisses the `EntryDetailsViewController` screen in **modally
present** mode so the focus of the user interface goes back to the original main screen.

Add the implementation for the `entryDetailsViewController(_ controller:,
didFinishAdding entry:)` function in a similar way:

```
func entryDetailsViewController(_ controller: EntryDetailsViewController,
didFinishAdding entry: JournalEntry) {
    createEntry(entry: entry)
    dismiss(animated: true, completion: nil)
}
```

The function calls the `createEntry(entry:)` helper function and then dismisses the
`EntryDetailsViewController` screen.

The `createEntry()` helper function appends a new entry to the `journalEntries` array and calls `newEntry(entry:)` in the extension to make an HTTP request to the web application. Then a new row is inserted into the table view:

```
func createEntry(entry: JournalEntry) {
    let newRowIndex = journalEntries.count
    journalEntries.append(entry)
    newEntry(entry: entry)

    let indexPath = IndexPath(row: newRowIndex, section: 0)
    let indexPaths = [indexPath]
    tableView.insertRows(at: indexPaths, with: .automatic)
}
```

Before implementing the `newEntry(entry:)` function, you can step aside and finish up the user interface for `EntryDetailsViewController`.

Hooking up new functionalities for UI items

Select the **Assistant Editor** from the top-right menu tray to lay out the storyboard and the `EntryDetailsViewController.swift` file side by side.

While holding down the *Ctrl* key, click on the **Done** button and drag it to the line under the declaration of the `EntryDetailsViewController` class. A **Connection** context menu appears. Create an `IBOutlet` and specify the name to be `entryTitle`:

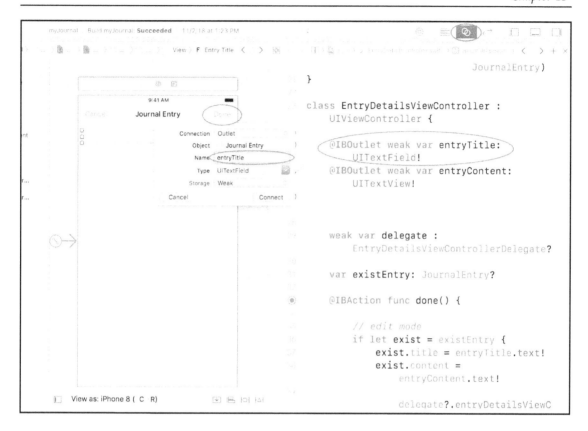

Follow the same steps to create an IBOutlet for entryContent.

The two IBOutlet fields should be created and connected to the corresponding bar button items:

```
class EntryDetailsViewController : UIViewController {
    @IBOutlet weak var entryTitle: UITextField!
    @IBOutlet weak var entryContent: UITextView!
}
```

In the same EntryDetailsViewController class, add a reference to EntryDetailsViewControllerDelegate:

```
weak var delegate : EntryDetailsViewControllerDelegate?
```

Create the done() function for IBAction:

```
@IBAction func done() {
    let entry = JournalEntry(title: entryTitle.text!, content:
```

```
    entryContent.text!)
        delegate?.entryDetailsViewController(self, didFinishAdding: entry)
    }
```

This basically creates a new instance of `JournalEntry` from the text of `entryTitle` and `entryContent`, and then passes the object to the main screen via one of the delegate protocol functions.

Also create the `cancel()` function for `IBAction`, which simply calls the `entryDetailsViewControllerDidCancel()` function of the delegate protocol:

```
    @IBAction func cancel() {
        delegate?.entryDetailsViewControllerDidCancel(self)
    }
```

Both the IBAction functions need to be connected to the corresponding UI items. *Ctrl* + drag the **Done** button to the `done()` function for `IBAction` in Assistant Editor to make a connection between them. Do the same for the **Cancel** button and the `cancel()` function for `IBAction`.

There are two more minor features to add to the `EntryDetailsViewController` user interface. First, make the `title` text field the first responder so the `title` will be in focus when the screen first appears:

```
    override func viewWillAppear(_ animated: Bool) {
        super.viewWillAppear(animated)
        entryTitle.becomeFirstResponder()
    }
```

Next, add a default title to the screen in the `viewDidLoad()` function:

```
    override func viewDidLoad() {
        super.viewDidLoad()
        title = "Create an Entry"
    }
```

That's all you need to do to get things going for the user interface. Next, you can finish implementing the `newEntry(entry:)` function.

Steps to Make Requests to the server

You can follow these simple steps to make requests to a server with the resource you want:

1. Prepare for encoded JSON data for your data model conforming to Codable
2. Configure an upload request with HTTP methods and your JSON object
3. Start a new `URLSession` task with the request you've configured
4. Call the `URLSession`'s `resume()` method to start uploading

Preparing for Encoded JSON Data

Since your data model has already been conforming to `Codable`, you can use the `JSONEncoder` class to encode the data into a JSON object easily for upload:

```
guard let jsonData = try? JSONEncoder().encode(entry) else { return }
```

Configuring an Upload Request

You can use a `URLRequest` instance to start an upload task:

```
var request = URLRequest(url: journalUrl)
request.httpMethod = "POST"
request.setValue("application/json", forHTTPHeaderField: "Content-Type")
```

`URLRequest` allows you to set the HTTP method (POST, PUT, GET, DELETE) using the `httpMethod` property of the request, as well as to set the values of any HTTP headers using the `setValue(_:forHTTPHeaderField:)` method.

Starting an Upload Task

To start uploading, use a shared `URLSession` instance to create an uploading `URLSessionTask` instance with the passing in `URLRquest` and the JSON data you have:

```
// Start an URLSession Task
URLSession.shared.uploadTask(with: request, from: jsonData) { (data,
response, error) in
    if let error = error {
        print("Error", error)
    return
    }
}.resume()
```

Since all tasks start in a suspended state, `.resume()` will be called to start the task after the `.uploadTask(with: from:)` method is called. Upon the completion of task upload, the results are received in a completion handler that checks for any transport or server errors and returns the requested data.

Putting Everything Together for the upload task

After learning the basics for creating an uploading task, you can assemble the `newEntry(entry:)` function:

```swift
// Create a new entry
func newEntry(entry: JournalEntry) {

    // prepare JSON data to upload
    guard let jsonData = try? JSONEncoder().encode(entry) else { return }

    // configure URL request
    let journalUrl = URL(string: apiURL + "/admin")!
    var request = URLRequest(url: journalUrl)
    request.httpMethod = "POST"
    request.setValue("application/json", forHTTPHeaderField: "Content-Type")

    // Start an URLSession Task
    URLSession.shared.uploadTask(with: request, from: jsonData) { (data,
    response, error) in
        if let error = error {
            print("Error", error)
            return
            }
        }.resume()
}
```

Try to edit a journal entry now. The corresponding entry in the database should reflect all the changes you've made in your iOS application. If you encounter any problems, refer to this chapter's source code to figure out the issue with your code.

Finishing the CRUD operations

You still need to finish the rest of the CRUD operations for your iOS application: editing an existing entry and deleting an existing entry.

Editing an existing entry

Most of the code used in creating a new entry can be reused here to edit an existing journal entry.

Creating the EditEntry segue

First of all, create a new segue by *Ctrl* + dragging from the table view component to the Navigation Controller. Name the segue `EditEntry` and specify the kind of attribute to be **Show**:

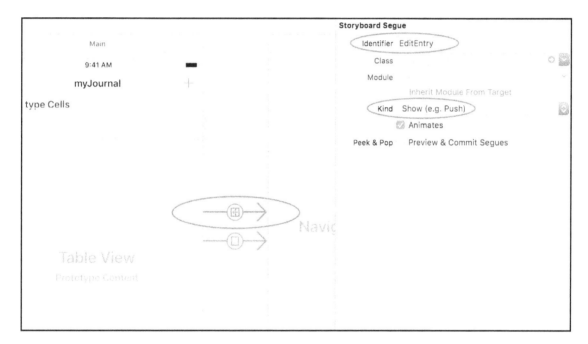

In the `MainScreenViewController` class, add the following code to the `prepare(for segue: sender:)` function to tell `EntryDetailsViewController` about the `EditEntry` segue:

```
override func prepare(for segue: UIStoryboardSegue, sender: Any?) {
    if segue.identifier == "NewEntry" {
        let navigationController = segue.destination as!
UINavigationController
        let controller = navigationController.topViewController as!
EntryDetailsViewController
        controller.delegate = self
```

```
    } else if segue.identifier == "EditEntry" {
        let navigationController = segue.destination as!
UINavigationController
        let controller = navigationController.topViewController as!
EntryDetailsViewController
        controller.delegate = self
        if let indexPath = tableView.indexPath(for: sender as!
UITableViewCell) {
            controller.existEntry = journalEntries[indexPath.row]
        }
    }
}
```

The handling of EditEntry is implemented in the else-if block. The code states that MainScreenViewController is the delegate for EntryDetailsViewController and assigns the current item of the journalEntries array as the existEntry object in EntryDetailsViewController.

Adding a new function to the delegate protocol

Next, add a new function to the delegate protocol to support editing an existing entry.

Add an additional function to delegate the **Done Editing** event to MainScreenViewController:

```
// Define the delegate protocol to inform Main Screen View Controller
protocol EntryDetailsViewControllerDelegate: class {
    //... previously defined functions

    // Delegate Done Editing Event
    func entryDetailsViewController(_ controller:
EntryDetailsViewController, didFinishEditing entry: JournalEntry)
}
```

Implement the corresponding function in the MainScreenViewController class:

```
func entryDetailsViewController(_ controller: EntryDetailsViewController,
didFinishEditing entry: JournalEntry) {
    updateEntry(entry: entry)
    dismiss(animated: true, completion: nil)
}
```

This function calls the `updateEntry(entry:)` function and then dismisses the `EntryDetailsViewController` screen:

```swift
func updateEntry(entry: JournalEntry) {
    if let index = journalEntries.index(of: entry) {
        journalEntries[index] = entry
        editEntry(entry: entry)
        let indexPath = IndexPath(row: index, section: 0)
        if let cell = tableView.cellForRow(at: indexPath) {
            let label = cell.viewWithTag(1000) as! UILabel
            label.text = entry.title
        }
    }
}
```

In order to use the `JournalEntry.index(of:)` function to retrieve the matched object, you need to subclass the `JournalEntry` class model from `NSObject`:

```swift
final class JournalEntry: NSObject, Codable {
    let id: Int?
    var title: String?
    var content: String?

    public init(title: String?, content: String?) {
        self.id = nil
        self.title = title
        self.content = content
    }
}
```

The subclassing of the `NSObject` class gives a `JournalEntry` instance the ability to compare against all other instances and check for equality. So it is very convenient for you to extend `JournalEntry` from the `NSObject` class here.

Making an HTTP PUT request

The `editEntry(entry:)` function creates a new `URLSession` task to upload the JSON object of the newly-updated `JournalEntry` object to the web application:

```
// Edit an existing entry
func editEntry(entry: JournalEntry) {
    print("INFO: Receiving modified entry: \(entry)")
    guard let jsonData = try? JSONEncoder().encode(entry) else { return }
    guard let id = entry.id else {
        print("Error: Invalid ID")
        return
    }
    let idString : String = "/admin/\(id)"
    let journalUrl = URL(string: apiURL + idString)!
    var request = URLRequest(url: journalUrl)
    request.httpMethod = "PUT"
    request.setValue("application/json", forHTTPHeaderField: "Content-
Type")

    URLSession.shared.uploadTask(with: request, from: jsonData) { (data,
response, error) in
        if let error = error {
            print("Error", error)
            return
        }
    }.resume()
}
```

`URLRequest` is configured as an HTTP PUT request. After the `URLSession` task is configured, the `resume()` call will start the uploading process.

Configuring the user interface to edit an entry

Now, go back to the `EntryDetailsViewController` class. Add the following reference to the `JournalEntry` object passed from the `MainScreenViewController` delegate:

```
var existEntry: JournalEntry?
```

Modify the `done()` function to check whether there is a valid `existEntry` object. If there is, it means this is the **Edit Entry** mode for `EntryDetailsViewController`. The `title` and `content` values of the existing Journal Entry object will be replaced by the text of `entryTitle` and `entryContent`:

```
@IBAction func done() {
    // edit mode
    if let exist = existEntry {
        exist.title = entryTitle.text!
        exist.content = entryContent.text!
    delegate?.entryDetailsViewController(self, didFinishEditing: exist)
    }
    // create mode
    else {
        let entry = JournalEntry(title: entryTitle.text!,
        content: entryContent.text!)
        delegate?.entryDetailsViewController(self, didFinishAdding: entry)
    }
}
```

For the **Edit Entry** mode, the screen's title is also updated accordingly:

```
override func viewDidLoad() {
    super.viewDidLoad()

    if let entry = existEntry {
        entryTitle.text = entry.title
        entryContent.text = entry.content
    } else {
        title = "Create an Entry"
    }
}
```

The final result of editing the entry operation should look like the following:

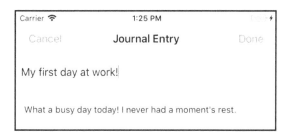

Deleting an existing entry

The last thing to do is to add the **DELETE** operation. If the user swipes a table item to the left, a **DELETE** button will appear. An entry will be deleted if the user continues to press on the button:

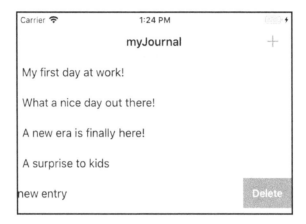

Override the tableView(_ tableView: commit editingStyle: forRowAt indexPath:) function:

```
override func tableView(_ tableView: UITableView, commit editingStyle:
UITableViewCell.EditingStyle, forRowAt indexPath: IndexPath) {
    // remove from database first before deleting it locally
    removeEntry(entry: journalEntries[indexPath.row]) // [1]
    journalEntries.remove(at: indexPath.row) // [2]
    let indexPaths = [indexPath]
    tableView.deleteRows(at: indexPaths, with: .automatic) // [3]
}
```

The function does several things:

1. It calls the removeEntry(entry:) function to tell the web application to remove the remote record of this entry
2. It remove the corresponding entry from the journalEntries local store
3. It deletes the corresponding row from the table view

The `removeEntry(entry:)` function performs a similar `URLSession` task to issue an HTTP DELETE request to the web application:

```
// Remove an existing entry
func removeEntry(entry: JournalEntry) {
 print("INFO: Receiving the entry to be deleted: \(entry)")

 // prepare JSON data to upload
 guard let jsonData = try? JSONEncoder().encode(entry) else { return }
 print("INFO: Packing int JSON object: \(jsonData)")

 // configure URL request
 guard let id = entry.id else {
     print("Error: Invalid ID")
     return
 }
 let idString : String = "/admin/\(id)"
 let journalUrl = URL(string: apiURL + idString)!
 var request = URLRequest(url: journalUrl)
 request.httpMethod = "DELETE"
 print("INFO: Requesting Server to delete: \(request)")

 // Start an URLSession Task
 URLSession.shared.uploadTask(with: request, from: jsonData) { (data,
response, error) in
     if let error = error {
         print("Error", error)
         return
     }
 }.resume()
}
```

Congratulations! Now you have a fully-functional iOS client application that works with your Vapor or Kitura web applications on the cloud.

Summary

You are now equipped with the knowledge to be a full-stack developer who knows how to write Swift code to perform both server and client development. In this chapter, you learned basic iOS development skills to develop a table-view-controller-based application that interacts with the `myJournal` web service you developed previously. Building on the skeleton table view controller, you learned how to establish a `URLSession` that makes a HTTP GET request to the RESTful API you developed in `Chapter 11`, *Designing for API Gateway*, and retrieve all journal entries to populate the table view. Then, you moved on to implement other CRUD operations on the client side: creating, editing, and deleting a journal entry. The topics you covered in this chapter give you good basis for building more professional and feature-rich iOS client applications that work with your Vapor and Kitura web services.

14
Developing Microservices

In contrast to a monolithic server-side application that contains all business logic, a Swift web framework may employ microservices in the business logic layer. Microservices are standalone logical components that handle different functional areas of a backend application.

You'll learn about container technology, such as Docker, that is used to deploy and run a Swift package artifact as a microservice. You'll learn how to deploy a Docker container and use a container-orchestration tool to manage and scale the deployment of containerized applications in a cluster. Orchestration software, such as Kubernetes, contains deployment and management tools that automate the processes and workflows of your containerized applications. Finally, you'll deploy microservices of containerized applications to deliver a coherent and scalable web service by collaborating among themselves.

Let's take a look at the topics covered in this chapter:

- Leveraging Microservices in Backend Applications
- Deploying a Containerized Application to a Cluster

Leveraging Microservices in Backend Applications

When we are designing backend services for a server-side Swift application, we are generally talking about designing for a distributed architecture. This means that service components are accessed remotely through some sort of remote-access protocol, so these components can communicate across different processes, servers, and networks. Similar to **Object-Oriented Design (OOD)** in software architecture, distributed architectures lend themselves to more loosely-coupled, encapsulated, and modular applications. This, in turn, promotes better scalability, modularity, and control over the development, testing, and deployment of backend service modules.

The microservice-oriented architecture

In the **service-oriented architecture (SOA)**, the reusability of functions hasn't been fully exploited. For example, the logging feature in one service may be duplicated as we find a similar logging feature in another service. Since a service is not designed for reusability, duplicated features are inadvertently added to a service. The concept of component-sharing is not explicitly integrated and promoted in SOA. A mature service may become bloated and monolithic, making it hard to maintain, debug, and develop.

Microservices, however, are designed for tasks at a more granular level and won't become bloated easily. For example, there could be a logger microservice that handles string formatting, filtering, converting and reporting. Multiple microservices can use the same instance of logger microservice for logging information.

Design Principles of the Microservice Framework

The key design principles for the Microservice Framework are as follows:

- **Separation of Concerns**: Each microservice is modular and is held for single responsibility

- **Loose Coupling**: Each microservice shall be isolated from other microservices and components as much as possible

- **Independently Deployable**: Each microservice is an entity that can be individually deployed as needed

- **Scalable Architecture**: We shall be able to add as many of the same type of microservices as needed

- **Automation**: The deployment of microservices is automated

- **Built for Failure**: A microservice shall gracefully exit during catastrophic failure and then get relaunched

Deploying a Containerized Application to a Cluster

Even though microservices can be deployed and managed via different means, we recommend you deploy each microservice in a Docker container. In a virtualized environment provided by a container, the logic and I/O for each microservice instance are completely separated even if they reside on the same physical server. This container-based approach lets us scale our deployment with maximum flexibility. For example, we can deploy 10 containerized microservices on a physical service. When the workload is increased, we can add more containers to the same server or a different server, depending on the resource utilization of a physical server. The deployment and load-balancing of microservices are managed by orchestration tools such as Kubernetes. Moreover, if one of the deployed microservices encounters a catastrophic failure, the orchestration tool will attempt to let the instance of the microservice gracefully exit and then relaunch a new instance.

Working with Containers and Orchestrations

Once you have a containerized application, you are going to plan deploying your container to a cluster. A cluster refers to a set of resources, networks, working nodes, and storage services in the backend that your containerized application needs to work with. Connected computing units, resources, and services in a cluster work as a single unit.

When working with a cluster, you usually choose a container-orchestration tool to automate deployment, scale your containerized applications, and manage your containers in the cluster. Kubernetes is a production-ready open source container-orchestration platform that was originally developed by Google and is now maintained by the Cloud Native Computing Foundation.

Kubernetes does the following tasks very well:

- Manages containerized applications to run where and when you want.
- Finds the resources required for containers to work properly.
- Abstracts out the deployment of containerized applications so each is not tied to an individual machine.
- Automates the distribution and scheduling of application containers across a cluster.

- Monitors the status of deployed applications periodically.
- Instantiates a new instance of a containerized application in case of the failure of an instance.

There are two types of resources in a Kubernetes cluster:

- **Master:** Each cluster has a Master that coordinates the cluster. Master schedules the deployment of a containerized application, maintains the application's states, and rolls out new updates to the application. When there is a change in usage, Master can also scale the application appropriately to meet new demand.
- **Worker nodes:** There are a number of working nodes in a typical cluster. Nodes are the workers that host the running containerized applications. Each node could be a virtual machine or a physical computer. The kubelet agent in each node communicates with Master via the Kubernetes API and manages the node itself.

In the following sections, you'll learn how to create your own container for your server-side Swift application and deploy it to a cluster. The workflow for creating a containerized application using Docker and deploying to a Kubernetes cluster is similar for the Vapor and Kitura frameworks. As such, you'll learn how to deploy a Kitura application to your IBM Cloud account. It is easier for you to follow along with the implementation of containers and orchestrations for Kitura applications on IBM Cloud because these technologies are well integrated into the infrastructure in IBM Cloud and you can find all relevant documentation and resources within your developer account.

Understanding the Container Deployment workflow

The following diagram illustrates the workflow for deploying a containerized application to a cluster on the cloud:

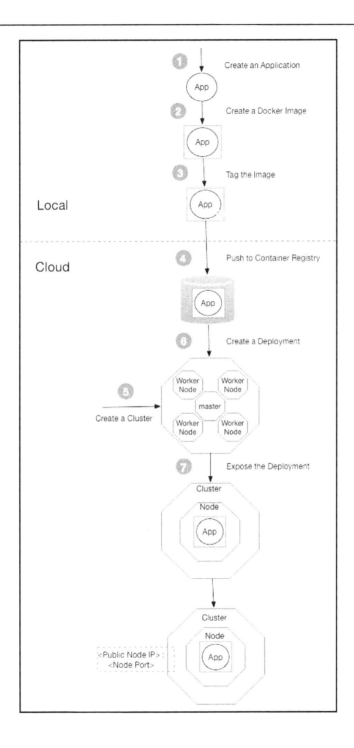

The workflow consists of the following steps:

1. Create an Application. Start a server-side Swift application from a boilerplate project that comes with the sample Dockerfile configuration.
2. Create a Docker Image. Modify the Dockerfile and build a new Docker container image.
3. Tag the Image. Tag the new container image with the repository name and version info.
4. Push to the Container Registry. Create a namespace to use in Container Registry and push your image to the registry.
5. Create a Cluster. Create a new cluster with a master and at least one worker node.
6. Create a Deployment. Pull your image from the Container Registry to create a new deployment in a worker node.
7. Expose the Deployment. Create a NodePort service to expose the deployment at the node's public IP and static port.

With this overview of the container-deployment workflow, you can dive into the details of each step.

Publishing a Docker image to IBM Cloud Registry

If you want to let the container-orchestration tool manage the instances of your Swift applications, you'll find it easy to work with **Container Registry**. By registering your container images in IBM Container Registry, you allow the orchestration tool to deploy new instances when required.

In case you haven't installed the Container Registry plugin, use the following command to add the plugin to the IBM Cloud CLI:

```
$ ibmcloud plugin install container-registry -r Bluemix
```

If you haven't installed IBM Cloud CLI on your system, refer back to `Chapter 12`, *Deploying to Cloud*, for the details.

Logging into IBM Cloud

Now you are going to register your container image to Container Registry.

On your local computer, perform the following steps:

1. Log into your IBM Cloud account using the IBM Cloud CLI:

```
$ ibmcloud login -a https://api.ng.bluemix.net
```

2. In case you haven't set the region, you may want to set the region-set environment to where you are located, for example, us-south. Refer to the IBM Cloud documentation to identify the right region for your location:

```
$ ibmcloud cs region-set us-south
```

3. If you don't already have an existing **namespace** to work with, you're required to create one for the rest of the setup. The namespace used in the following example is angus but you should choose whatever name best represents your project:

```
$ ibmcloud cr namespace-add angus
```

4. The output shows the angus namespace has been successfully added to the environment:

```
Adding namespace 'angus'...
Successfully added namespace 'angus'
OK
```

You'll also find the new namespace on the Dashboard application if you use the web browser to log into your IBM Cloud account. Sometimes you may need to log into Registry Services on IBM Cloud before you can create a container image and push the image to Container Registry.

Log into registry.ng.bluemix.net using the following CLI command:

```
ibmcloud cr login
```

Now, you're ready to create a new Docker container image and deploy it to Container Registry.

Working with the Docker CLI

You set up the Docker environment in Chapter 12, *Deploying to Cloud*. In case you haven't installed Docker CLI on your local system, refer back to Chapter 12, *Deploying to Cloud,* for instructions on how to install the Docker CLI and create a Docker-enabled Kitura application from a boilerplate project.

If you are using Docker Desktop for Mac, the Docker daemon should be running in the background already. For Ubuntu, you may need to start the Docker daemon manually using the `systemctl` command:

```
$ sudo systemctl start docker
```

Assuming that you have docker running properly, perform the following steps to build a container image for your Kitura application:

1. Change the directory to the root path of your Docker-enabled Kitura application and use the following Docker CLI command to build an image:

   ```
   $ docker image build .
   ```

   Docker will process `Dockerfile` to build an image.

2. Use the Docker Image command to list the image you've just created:

   ```
   $ docker image ls
   ```

3. The output shows that a new image with the `dc056e17b52a` ID was just created about a minute ago:

   ```
   REPOSITORY TAG IMAGE ID CREATED SIZE
   <none> <none> dc056e17b52a About a minute ago 674MB
   mynewkituraapp-swift-run latest 3a2a59c534e4 28 hours ago 674MB
   mynewkituraapp-swift-tools latest 2fb4a17c3c57 29 hours ago 1.67GB
   ibmcom/swift-ubuntu-runtime 4.1.1 23bd1a58b015 4 months ago 318MB
   ibmcom/swift-ubuntu 4.1.1 9d6e9b75db3d 4 months ago 1.41GB
   ```

Once your container image has been successfully registered, you can start to get the container image ready for deployment.

Tagging Your Docker Image

Your new image doesn't yet have a repository and tag assigned to it. Both are needed to deploy to Container Registry on IBM Cloud. Perform the following steps to set this up:

1. Use the following Docker command to tag your image:

   ```
   $ docker tag dc056e17b52a mynewkituraapp
   ```

   The source image is `dc056e17b52a` and the target image is `mynewkituraapp`.

2. List the images again using the following:

```
$ docker image ls
```

You'll see the image now has assigned values for Repository and Tag:

```
REPOSITORY TAG IMAGE ID CREATED SIZE
mynewkituraapp latest dc056e17b52a 11 minutes ago 674MB
mynewkituraapp-swift-run latest 3a2a59c534e4 29 hours ago 674MB
mynewkituraapp-swift-tools latest 2fb4a17c3c57 29 hours ago 1.67GB
ibmcom/swift-ubuntu-runtime 4.1.1 23bd1a58b015 4 months ago 318MB
ibmcom/swift-ubuntu 4.1.1 9d6e9b75db3d 4 months ago 1.41GB
```

By default, Docker assigns `latest` to your image if you don't specify a version to tag. Tagging is useful for the version management of your container images, so it is always a good idea to tag a version for each container image.

To tag a specific version, for example, `1.0.0`, add the tag right behind the target image:

```
$ docker tag dc056e17b52a mynewkituraapp:1.0.0
```

In practice, you may want to put a tag that matches your application version on the Git repository.

Deploying a Docker Image to IBM Cloud Registry

With a namespace and newly-tagged Docker image, you can now push the image to Container Registry:

1. Add another tag to your image:

```
$ docker tag mynewkituraapp
registry.ng.bluemix.net/angus/mynewkituraapp
```

This time, the target image has a prefix of the destination path on Container Registry, which is `registry.ng.bluemix.net` followed by your namespace, `/angus`.

2. List all of your Docker images again:

```
$ docker image ls
```

You'll see a new repository is created under
the `registry.ng.bluemix.net/angus/` path:

```
REPOSITORY TAG IMAGE ID CREATED SIZE
mynewkituraapp latest dc056e17b52a 15 minutes ago 674MB
registry.ng.bluemix.net/angus/mynewkituraapp latest dc056e17b52a 15
minutes ago 674MB
mynewkituraapp-swift-run latest 3a2a59c534e4 29 hours ago 674MB
mynewkituraapp-swift-tools latest 2fb4a17c3c57 29 hours ago 1.67GB
ibmcom/swift-ubuntu-runtime 4.1.1 23bd1a58b015 4 months ago 318MB
ibmcom/swift-ubuntu 4.1.1 9d6e9b75db3d 4 months ago 1.41GB
```

3. Push this new image to IBM Cloud:

```
$ docker push registry.ng.bluemix.net/angus/mynewkituraapp:latest
```

The entire image is partitioned into several segments when uploading to
Container Registry:

```
The push refers to repository
[registry.ng.bluemix.net/angus/mynewkituraapp]
6fb9392393bf: Pushed
cd9c92ad770c: Pushed
5e51fc2d02fb: Pushed
a48c7e6e2611: Pushed
44d26f7a9e5a: Pushed
2a915ee685f5: Pushed
4622c8e1bdc0: Pushed
b33859b66bfd: Pushed
14fa4a9494bf: Pushed
0c3819952093: Pushed
05b0f7f2a817: Pushed
latest: digest:
sha256:a4c3c83b4b29588faeaea18f1313a3c5728fdda093763cbb9510b8b5339c
ab7d size: 2615
```

4. If you use the IBM Cloud CLI command to list all the available images on
   Container Registry, you'll see that the image has been just pushed to the cloud:

```
$ ibmcloud cr image-list
```

The images are listed here:

```
Listing images...
REPOSITORY TAG DIGEST NAMESPACE CREATED SIZE SECURITY STATUS
registry.ng.bluemix.net/angus/mynewkituraapp latest a4c3c83b4b29 angus 32
minutes ago 277 MB 19 Issues
OK
```

There may be some security issues that require your attention. Follow the documentation on IBM Cloud to see how to configure your application's security settings.

If you take your web browser to Dashboard, you can find the same image under the /Containers/Registry/Private Repositories:

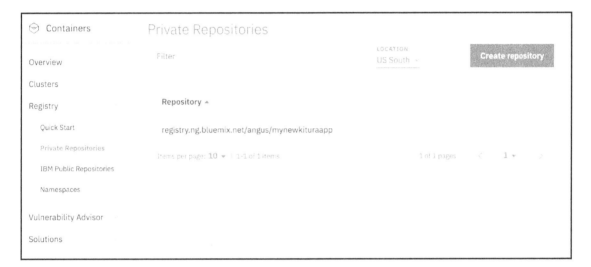

Creating a Cluster on IBM Cloud

You can create a new cluster directly from your IBM Cloud account's Dashboard application. A standard cluster is limited to **Pay-As-You-Go** or **Subscription** account types only. If you have a **Trial** account, you are limited to one free cluster, which expires in 30 days. You cannot create a cluster if your account type is **Lite**. Upgrade to either a Pay-As-You-Go or Subscription account to proceed.

Assuming you have a Trial account, you can choose the **Free** cluster type after selecting **IBM Cloud Kubernetes Service** from Dashboard:

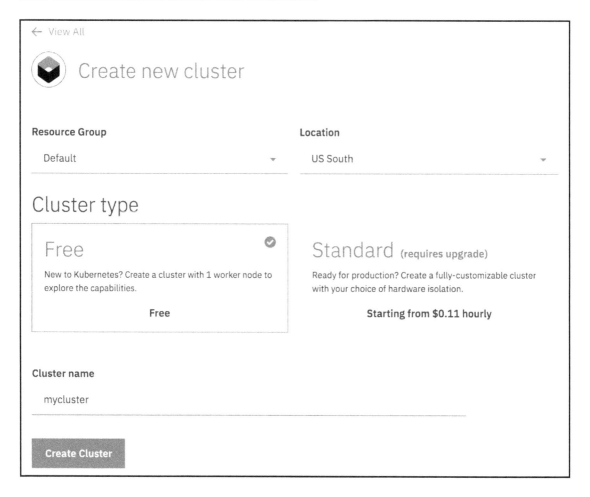

Enter the cluster name as `mycluster` and hit the **Create Cluster** button to proceed.

The deployment of a new cluster may take some time. Wait until the cluster has been fully deployed. You'd expect to see an overview screen similar to the following if the cluster becomes online:

The **Access** tab lists the steps required for you to get access to the cluster.

Setting up the Kubernetes CLI

You need to install a couple of CLIs and plugins in order to manage clusters from your system:

- IBM Cloud CLI
- IBM Cloud Kubernetes Service Plug-in
- Kubernetes CLI
- IBM Cloud Container Registry Plug-in

Note that you have installed the IBM Cloud CLI on your system already. The best way to install the rest of the CLIs and plugins is to use the IBM Cloud Developer Tools for Linux/MacOS Installer (`idt-installer`):

```
curl -sL https://ibm.biz/idt-installer | bash
```

The installer then proceeds to update your current toolset and install tools/plugins not found on your system:

```
[main] --==[ IBM Cloud Developer Tools for Linux/MacOS - Installer, v1.2.3
]==--
[install] Starting Installation...
[install] Note: You may be prompted for your 'sudo' password during
install.
[install_deps] Checking for external dependency: brew
[install_deps] Installing/updating external dependency: git
[install_deps] Installing/updating external dependency: docker
[install_deps] Installing/updating external dependency: kubectl
[install_deps] Installing/updating external dependency: helm
[install_bx] Updating existing IBM Cloud 'bx' CLI...
Checking for updates...
...
[Deleted]
...
Listing installed plug-ins...


Plugin Name Version
container-service/kubernetes-service 0.1.593
dev 2.1.4
sdk-gen 0.1.12
cloud-functions/wsk/functions/fn 1.0.22
container-registry 0.1.339

[install_plugins] Finished installing/updating plugins
[install] Install finished.
[main] --==[ Total time: 11 seconds ]==--
```

Before trying out the Kubernetes tools you've just installed, you may need to log in again:

```
$ ibmcloud login -a https://api.ng.bluemix.net
```

When your login is successful, you can try out the following command of the Kubernetes CLI:

```
$ kubectl version
```

The preceding command will print out the version information for your installed Kubernetes.

Downloading the Cluster Configuration

In order to work with the `mycluster` active cluster you have just created, perform the following steps:

1. Download the cluster configuration files to your local system:

   ```
   $ ibmcloud cs cluster-config mycluster
   ```

   The output of the preceding command reminds you that you'll need to set up environment variables properly to start using Kubernetes:

   ```
   OK
   The configuration for mycluster was downloaded successfully. Export
   environment variables to start using Kubernetes.
   export KUBECONFIG=/Users/fyeung1/.bluemix/plugins/container-
   service/clusters/mycluster/kube-config-hou02-mycluster.yml
   ```

2. Export the `KUBECONFIG` environment variable by copying the last line from the preceding code and paste it into a Terminal:

   ```
   $ export KUBECONFIG=/Users/fyeung1/.bluemix/plugins/container-
   service/clusters/mycluster/kube-config-hou02-mycluster.yml
   ```

   The `KUBECONFIG` environment variable specifies which current cluster you are working with. If you have more than one cluster and want to switch to another cluster, you need to follow the preceding steps to download the cluster configuration and export the `KUBECONFIG` environment variable that is pointed to in the other cluster.

Don't copy the `KUBECONFIG` environment variable from the book text here. It uses my personalized settings. You should copy from your own output screen from the last IBM Cloud CLI command and export the `KUBECONFIG` environment variable.

3. If everything works out as expected, you are able to use the following `kubectrl` command to list all the worker nodes in your cluster.

   ```
   $ kubectl get nodes
   ```

   A list of active worker nodes in your cluster is listed in the output:

   ```
   NAME STATUS ROLES AGE VERSION
   10.77.174.186 Ready <none> 2h v1.10.8+IKS
   ```

You should expect one active worker node in the cluster. Since you are using the free kubernetes feature, it limits you to only one worker node.

4. If you point your web browser to your IBM Cloud account, you can check out the status of the active worker node in your cluster page as well:

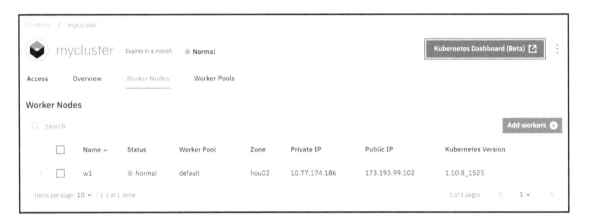

Creating a Deployment Using Container Registry

Once you have an active Kubernetes cluster, you can deploy your containerized application to it. To do so, you can use `kubectl` to create a deployment. The deployment tells Kubernetes how to create and update instances of your application. The Kubernetes Deployment Controller will monitor these instances and provide a self-healing mechanism. If an instance in your worker node goes down, the Kubernetes Deployment controller will attempt to replace it. Even if the hosting machine of your worker node goes down, the Deployment controller can still detect the machine failure and address the recovery.

1. Use the following `kubectl` command to create a new deployment from your image in the container registry:

```
$ kubectl create deployment my-new-kitura-app-deployment --
image=registry.ng.bluemix.net/angus/mynewkituraapp
```

2. If you forget your namelist, use this command to list the existing namespaces:

```
$ ibmcloud cr namespace-list
```

The command outputs something like the following:

```
Listing namespaces...
Namespace
angus
OK
```

3. Assuming that you have created a container registry, you can use Kubernetes Dashboard to access your cluster information.
4. Click on the button to open Kubernetes Dashboard:

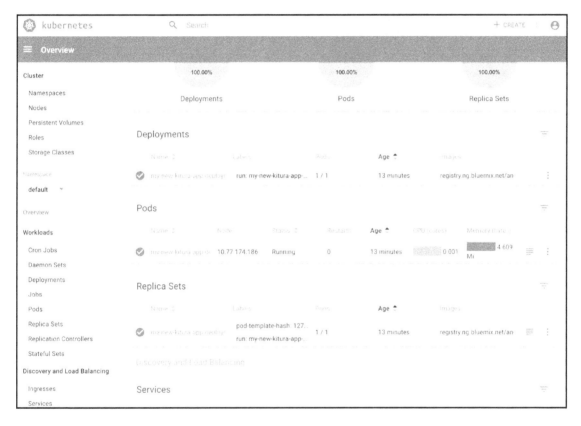

The dashboard gives you more detailed information, such as **Deployments**, **Pods**, and **Replica Sets**. Check out https://kubernetes.io to learn the basics of this terminology.

Exposing the deployment and launching the app

End users won't be able to get access to your application instances in the cluster unless you explicitly create a service object that exposes an external IP address for your application deployment. To do so, perform the following steps:

1. Use the `kubectl expose` command to change the access of your newly-created deployment to public:

   ```
   $ kubectl expose deployment/my-new-kitura-app-deployment --
   type=NodePort --port=8080 --name=my-new-kitura-app-service --
   target-port=8080
   ```

   Here, you instruct Kubernetes to expose your deployment service through the `NodePort` service, `my-new-kitura-app-service`, which serves on port `8080` and connects to the containers that are also on the `8080` target port.

2. Run the following command to check out the deployment resource that has been exposed:

   ```
   $ kubectl describe service my-new-kitura-app-service
   ```

   The `NodePort` object now exposes the services on each Node's IP at the `32663` static port (`NodePort`):

   ```
   Name: my-new-kitura-app-service
   Namespace: default
   Labels: run=my-new-kitura-app-deployment
   Annotations: <none>
   Selector: run=my-new-kitura-app-deployment
   Type: NodePort
   IP: 172.21.76.242
   Port: <unset> 8080/TCP
   TargetPort: 8080/TCP
   NodePort: <unset> 32663/TCP
   Endpoints: 172.30.77.71:8080
   Session Affinity: None
   External Traffic Policy: Cluster
   Events: <none>
   ```

Since your service runs on an internal IP, the service is reachable from within the cluster only. In order to expose your service to the outside, Kubernetes automatically creates a default service called ClusterIP. Your service can be exposed in different ways as specified by the type, such as the NodePort type. NodePort uses NAT to expose the service on the same port of each selected node in the cluster. For example, the 32663 static port will be mapped to port 8080 internally so your deployment service at 8080 will be exposed to 32663.

3. Run the following command to find out the public IP address for your worker node:

```
$ ibmcloud ks workers mycluster
```

The public IP address assigned to your node is 173.193.99.102:

```
OK
ID Public IP Private IP Machine Type State Status Zone Version
kube-hou02-pa1542b64383f4463a84fc4bf6fa57ea6d-w1 173.193.99.102
10.77.174.186 free normal Ready hou02 1.10.8_1525

Your deployment running on this worker node is available to outside
as [Public Node IP] : [ Node Port]. That is [173.193.99.102] :
[32663].
```

4. Point your web browser to `173.193.99.102:32663`, and you can see your Kitura application deployment online:

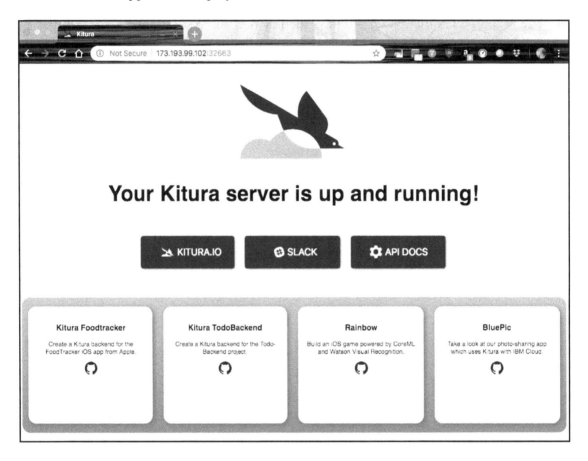

That's all it takes to deploy a containerized application to a working node in a cluster.

In the future, you can follow the steps here to deploy more applications that work together as microservices. Each microservice is hosted independently on a working node and all microservices in clusters collaborate with each other to offer unified service to clients.

Summary

This chapter introduced to you the concept of breaking your Vapor or Kitura applications into smaller, self-contained components called microservices. You learned the advantages of using the microservice-oriented architecture. Then you gained a working knowledge of containers and orchestrations. Specifically, you learned how to put your application into a container using Docker as well as how to register and deploy a containized application to a Kubernetes cluster on IBM Cloud. This chapter concludes the book. But for you, this marks the beginning of an exciting new journey with server-side Swift!

Vapor Boilerplate Project

This topic in the appendix will give you a clear understanding the boilerplate code in Vapor. Carrying forward from where we left off in `Chapter 3`, *Building Your First Web App,* here is a summary of the steps that you've used in creating a `helloWorld` boilerplate project using Vapor's default template:

```
$ vapor new helloWorld
$ cd helloWorld
$ vapor build
$ vapor xcode
$ open hellowWorld.xcodeproj
```

After executing the preceding commands in the Terminal, you changed Xcode project's *scheme* to *Run* and *device* to *My Mac*. The `helloWorld` server will be running at `http://localhost:8080` when you use command + *R* to run your project.

The following sections will provide you with a better idea regarding the same:

- Reviewing Vapor-generated files
- Understanding the source code files
- Configuring Swift Package Manager
- Starting with entry point
- Instantiating an application object
- Configuring before instantiating application
- Adding initialization code after application instantiation
- Registering the application's routes
- Implementing endpoint logic in controllers
- Using a data model

Reviewing Vapor-generated files

After using the preceding steps to create a boilerplate `helloWorld` project, use the `ls -a` command in the `helloWorld` project directory to list all files and child directories:

```
# List all files and directories, including the hidden ones
ls -a
```

The **-a** flag is used here so you can view all files, including hidden files and directories:

```
.           .build      .gitignore          Package.swift     README.md       Tests
cloud.yml
..          .git        Package.resolved    Public Sources    circle.yml
```

Vapor generates some hidden directories, such as `.build` and `.git`.

The `.build` directory contains all the dependencies and temporary files when you build your project. If you execute the vapor clean Vapor CLI command, the `.build` directory will be removed. Then you have to use vapor build to fetch the dependencies and build the project again. This usually takes a long time. If you simply want to update few dependencies, you can use vapor update to fetch those dependencies that you don't have already.

The `.git` directory is used by the *git* source code version control. It is classified as a distributed version-control system. The `.git` is the directory it used to keep a local copy of the source code repository. The `.gitignore` hidden file is the place where you can specify the kinds of files you want to exclude from source control.

Installing tree to view the file structure

Perhaps a better tool than **ls** is the **tree** Terminal command. Install **tree** on your system if you don't have it installed already:

To install it on macOS, perform the following:

```
# Install the tool tree if needed
brew install tree
```

To install it on Ubuntu, use the following code:

```
# Install the tool tree if needed
sudo apt install tree
```

Reviewing a Vapor project's file structure

With *tree* properly installed on your system, you can use the following command to display the entire file structure in the helloWorld app:

```
# Display the file structure in the helloWorld app
tree
```

Your output should be something similar to the following:

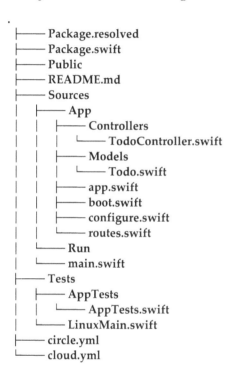

```
.
├── Package.resolved
├── Package.swift
├── Public
├── README.md
├── Sources
│   ├── App
│   │   ├── Controllers
│   │   │   └── TodoController.swift
│   │   ├── Models
│   │   │   └── Todo.swift
│   │   ├── app.swift
│   │   ├── boot.swift
│   │   ├── configure.swift
│   │   └── routes.swift
│   └── Run
│       └── main.swift
├── Tests
│   ├── AppTests
│   │   └── AppTests.swift
│   └── LinuxMain.swift
├── circle.yml
└── cloud.yml
```

If you use the **-a** flag in your tree command, you will see a lot of dependency files in the .build directory and git working files in the .git directory. You may want to check out the dependency files fetched to the .build directory after you build the project.

Understanding the file structure in a Vapor project

The usages for high-level files and directories in your project are described in the following table:

File/directory	Usage
`Package.resolved`	Registry for resolved dependencies and packages
`Package.swift`	Configuration for **Swift Package Manager** (**SPM**)
`/Public`	Directory for publicly-accessible files such as images, JavaScript scripts, and CSS style sheets
`README.md`	README file in Markdown format
`/Sources`	Directory for source files
`/Tests`	Directory for all tests
`circle.yml`	Configuration for continuous integration and continuous deployment using `CircleCI`
`cloud.ml`	Custom configurations for deploying your project to Vapor Cloud

You'll become more familiar with the file structure of a Vapor project as you work on the project. For now, you just need to pay attention to the `/Sources` directory, which contains all the source files in your project.

The `/Sources` directory has two sub directories, `/App` and `/Run`, as shown in the following table:

File/directory	Usage
`/App`	Directory for the App module containing all of the application logic
`/App/Controllers/TodoController.swift`	Adds controllers to perform application logic to requests
`/App/Models/Todo.swift`	Adds model to help retrieve/store your content
`/App/app.swift`	Creates an instance of your Vapor app
`/App/boot.swift`	Performs initialization before your Vapor app has started running
`/App/configure.swift`	Makes changes to your config and environment, or registers services to your app
`/App/routes.swift`	Adds routes to your router
`/Run`	Directory for the Run module
`/Run/main.swift`	Adds an entry point for Vapor runtime

There is only one function in `/Run/main.swift` and it serves as the entry point for Vapor framework. Usually you won't need to modify the `/Run/main.swift` file at all. You will mostly work on the files in the `/App` directory.

Like any other popular framework, Vapor uses the **Inversion of Control** (**IoC**) technique to allow you to receive the flow of control from the framework. If you want to change the behavior of the framework, you simply add the specific function that will be called upon by the framework.

The functions in the `/App/configure.swift` and `/App/boot.swift` files are good examples of IoC. In `/App/configure.swift`, you'll configure the required components for your project before your application initializes. In `/App/boot.swift`, you'll perform initialization before your app has started running the rest of the code.

Since the Vapor framework implements the **Model-View-Controller** (**MVC**) model, you'll take note of the `Controllers` and `Models` sub directories in `/App`.

The `Controllers` directory contains each controller that implements application logic to handle a client request routed to an endpoint. The routing function is added in the `/App/routes.swift` file. In order to handle a new client request, you'll add a new route to forward the request to a controller. How to set up routes and controllers will be covered in `Chapter 5`, *Setting Up Routes and Controllers*.

The `Models` directory contains the implementation of object models for your data. By leveraging Swift's `Codable` class in data models and abstracting out the database-specific command using Swift's **fluent** storage framework, Vapor makes it very easy for you to handle data objects and perform basic **Create, Retrieve, Update, and Delete** (**CRUD**) database operations.

We'll now dive into a detailed discussion of each file in the boilerplate source code.

Configuring Swift Package Manager

`Package.swift` is the project's manifest file that describes all the packages your project relies on. It is always located in the root directory of a Vapor project:

```swift
// File: Package.swift
// swift-tools-version:4.0
import PackageDescription

let package = Package(
    name: "helloWorld",    // [1]
```

```
        dependencies: [    // [2]
            //  A server-side Swift web framework.
            .package(url: "https://github.com/vapor/vapor.git", from: "3.0.0"),
// [3]

            //  Swift ORM (queries, models, relations, etc) built on SQLite 3.
            .package(url: "https://github.com/vapor/fluent-sqlite.git", from:
"3.0.0-rc.2") // [4]
        ],
        targets: [    // [5]
            .target(name: "App", dependencies: ["FluentSQLite", "Vapor"]),
            .target(name: "Run", dependencies: ["App"]),
            .testTarget(name: "AppTests", dependencies: ["App"])
        ]
)
```

The preceding package is configured as follows:

1. The "helloWorld" string is used as the application name
2. The project's dependencies array contains all other packages this project depends on
3. This project requires Vapor 3.0 or later
4. The project also requires Fluent SQLite 3 or later
5. The targets array allows you to add build targets

Package dependencies

Vapor Toolbox adds two package dependencies, Vapor and Fluent SQLite, automatically into the project created with the default template.

You can add as many package dependencies as you need by appending the new package to the dependencies array. However, you have to use the Vapor update command to fetch the package and effect the changes if you have modified a package or added a new package to the dependency list.

If you run the swift package show-dependencies command on your Terminal, you can see that *Vapor* and Fluent SQLite have a long list of dependencies:

Here is # List of package dependencies in a Vapor boilerplate project:

```
.
├── Vapor<https://github.com/vapor/vapor.git@3.0.1>
│   ├── Console<https://github.com/vapor/console.git@3.0.2>
│   │   ├── Core<https://github.com/vapor/core.git@3.1.6>
│   │   │   └── swift-nio<https://github.com/apple/swift-nio.git@1.6.1>
│   │   │   └── swift-nio-zlib-support<https://github.com/apple/swift-nio-zlib-support.git@1.0.0>
│   │   └── Service<https://github.com/vapor/service.git@1.0.0>
│   │   └── Core<https://github.com/vapor/core.git@3.1.6>
│   │   └── swift-nio<https://github.com/apple/swift-nio.git@1.6.1>
│   │   └── swift-nio-zlib-support<https://github.com/apple/swift-nio-zlib-support.git@1.0.0>
│   ├── Core<https://github.com/vapor/core.git@3.1.6>
│   │   └── swift-nio<https://github.com/apple/swift-nio.git@1.6.1>
│   │   └── swift-nio-zlib-support<https://github.com/apple/swift-nio-zlib-support.git@1.0.0>
│   ├── Crypto<https://github.com/vapor/crypto.git@3.1.1>
│   │   ├── Core<https://github.com/vapor/core.git@3.1.6>
│   │   │   └── swift-nio<https://github.com/apple/swift-nio.git@1.6.1>
│   │   │   └── swift-nio-zlib-support<https://github.com/apple/swift-nio-zlib-support.git@1.0.0>
│   │   └── swift-nio-ssl<https://github.com/apple/swift-nio-ssl.git@1.1.0>
│   │   ├── swift-nio<https://github.com/apple/swift-nio.git@1.6.1>
│   │   │   └── swift-nio-zlib-support<https://github.com/apple/swift-nio-zlib-support.git@1.0.0>
│   │   └── swift-nio-ssl-support<https://github.com/apple/swift-nio-ssl-support.git@1.0.0>
│   ├── DatabaseKit<https://github.com/vapor/database-kit.git@1.0.1>
│   │   ├── Core<https://github.com/vapor/core.git@3.1.6>
│   │   │   └── swift-nio<https://github.com/apple/swift-nio.git@1.6.1>
│   │   │   └── swift-nio-zlib-support<https://github.com/apple/swift-nio-zlib-support.git@1.0.0>
│   │   └── Service<https://github.com/vapor/service.git@1.0.0>
│   │   └── Core<https://github.com/vapor/core.git@3.1.6>
│   │   └── swift-nio<https://github.com/apple/swift-nio.git@1.6.1>
│   │   └── swift-nio-zlib-support<https://github.com/apple/swift-nio-zlib-support.git@1.0.0>
│   ├── HTTP<https://github.com/vapor/http.git@3.0.4>
│   │   ├── Core<https://github.com/vapor/core.git@3.1.6>
│   │   │   └── swift-nio<https://github.com/apple/swift-nio.git@1.6.1>
│   │   │   └── swift-nio-zlib-support<https://github.com/apple/swift-nio-zlib-support.git@1.0.0>
│   │   ├── swift-nio<https://github.com/apple/swift-nio.git@1.6.1>
│   │   │   └── swift-nio-zlib-support<https://github.com/apple/swift-nio-zlib-support.git@1.0.0>
│   │   └── swift-nio-ssl<https://github.com/apple/swift-nio-ssl.git@1.1.0>
│   │   ├── swift-nio<https://github.com/apple/swift-nio.git@1.6.1>
│   │   │   └── swift-nio-zlib-support<https://github.com/apple/swift-nio-zlib-support.git@1.0.0>
```

```
| | └── swift-nio-ssl-support<https://github.com/apple/swift-nio-ssl-support.git@1.0.0>
| ├── Multipart<https://github.com/vapor/multipart.git@3.0.1>
| | └── Core<https://github.com/vapor/core.git@3.1.6>
| | └── swift-nio<https://github.com/apple/swift-nio.git@1.6.1>
| | └── swift-nio-zlib-support<https://github.com/apple/swift-nio-zlib-support.git@1.0.0>
| ├── Routing<https://github.com/vapor/routing.git@3.0.1>
| | ├── Core<https://github.com/vapor/core.git@3.1.6>
| | | └── swift-nio<https://github.com/apple/swift-nio.git@1.6.1>
| | | └── swift-nio-zlib-support<https://github.com/apple/swift-nio-zlib-support.git@1.0.0>
| | └── Service<https://github.com/vapor/service.git@1.0.0>
| | └── Core<https://github.com/vapor/core.git@3.1.6>
| | └── swift-nio<https://github.com/apple/swift-nio.git@1.6.1>
| | └── swift-nio-zlib-support<https://github.com/apple/swift-nio-zlib-support.git@1.0.0>
| ├── Service<https://github.com/vapor/service.git@1.0.0>
| | └── Core<https://github.com/vapor/core.git@3.1.6>
| | └── swift-nio<https://github.com/apple/swift-nio.git@1.6.1>
| | └── swift-nio-zlib-support<https://github.com/apple/swift-nio-zlib-support.git@1.0.0>
| ├── TemplateKit<https://github.com/vapor/template-kit.git@1.0.1>
| | ├── Core<https://github.com/vapor/core.git@3.1.6>
| | | └── swift-nio<https://github.com/apple/swift-nio.git@1.6.1>
| | | └── swift-nio-zlib-support<https://github.com/apple/swift-nio-zlib-support.git@1.0.0>
| | └── Service<https://github.com/vapor/service.git@1.0.0>
| | └── Core<https://github.com/vapor/core.git@3.1.6>
| | └── swift-nio<https://github.com/apple/swift-nio.git@1.6.1>
| | └── swift-nio-zlib-support<https://github.com/apple/swift-nio-zlib-support.git@1.0.0>
| ├── URLEncodedForm<https://github.com/vapor/url-encoded-form.git@1.0.2>
| | └── Core<https://github.com/vapor/core.git@3.1.6>
| | └── swift-nio<https://github.com/apple/swift-nio.git@1.6.1>
| | └── swift-nio-zlib-support<https://github.com/apple/swift-nio-zlib-support.git@1.0.0>
| ├── Validation<https://github.com/vapor/validation.git@2.0.0>
| | └── Core<https://github.com/vapor/core.git@3.1.6>
| | └── swift-nio<https://github.com/apple/swift-nio.git@1.6.1>
| | └── swift-nio-zlib-support<https://github.com/apple/swift-nio-zlib-support.git@1.0.0>
| └── WebSocket<https://github.com/vapor/websocket.git@1.0.0>
| ├── Core<https://github.com/vapor/core.git@3.1.6>
| | └── swift-nio<https://github.com/apple/swift-nio.git@1.6.1>
| | └── swift-nio-zlib-support<https://github.com/apple/swift-nio-zlib-support.git@1.0.0>
| ├── HTTP<https://github.com/vapor/http.git@3.0.4>
| | ├── Core<https://github.com/vapor/core.git@3.1.6>
| | | └── swift-nio<https://github.com/apple/swift-nio.git@1.6.1>
| | | └── swift-nio-zlib-support<https://github.com/apple/swift-nio-zlib-support.git@1.0.0>
| | ├── swift-nio<https://github.com/apple/swift-nio.git@1.6.1>
```

```
| | | └── swift-nio-zlib-support<https://github.com/apple/swift-nio-zlib-support.git@1.0.0>
| | └── swift-nio-ssl<https://github.com/apple/swift-nio-ssl.git@1.1.0>
| | ├── swift-nio<https://github.com/apple/swift-nio.git@1.6.1>
| | | └── swift-nio-zlib-support<https://github.com/apple/swift-nio-zlib-support.git@1.0.0>
| | └── swift-nio-ssl-support<https://github.com/apple/swift-nio-ssl-support.git@1.0.0>
| ├── swift-nio<https://github.com/apple/swift-nio.git@1.6.1>
| | └── swift-nio-zlib-support<https://github.com/apple/swift-nio-zlib-support.git@1.0.0>
| └── swift-nio-ssl<https://github.com/apple/swift-nio-ssl.git@1.1.0>
├── swift-nio<https://github.com/apple/swift-nio.git@1.6.1>
| └── swift-nio-zlib-support<https://github.com/apple/swift-nio-zlib-support.git@1.0.0>
└── swift-nio-ssl-support<https://github.com/apple/swift-nio-ssl-support.git@1.0.0>
└── FluentSQLite<https://github.com/vapor/fluent-sqlite.git@3.0.0-rc.2.2>
├── Core<https://github.com/vapor/core.git@3.1.6>
| └── swift-nio<https://github.com/apple/swift-nio.git@1.6.1>
| └── swift-nio-zlib-support<https://github.com/apple/swift-nio-zlib-support.git@1.0.0>
├── Fluent<https://github.com/vapor/fluent.git@3.0.0-rc.2.4.1>
| ├── Core<https://github.com/vapor/core.git@3.1.6>
| | └── swift-nio<https://github.com/apple/swift-nio.git@1.6.1>
| | └── swift-nio-zlib-support<https://github.com/apple/swift-nio-zlib-support.git@1.0.0>
| ├── Console<https://github.com/vapor/console.git@3.0.2>
| | ├── Core<https://github.com/vapor/core.git@3.1.6>
| | | └── swift-nio<https://github.com/apple/swift-nio.git@1.6.1>
| | | └── swift-nio-zlib-support<https://github.com/apple/swift-nio-zlib-support.git@1.0.0>
| | └── Service<https://github.com/vapor/service.git@1.0.0>
| | └── Core<https://github.com/vapor/core.git@3.1.6>
| | └── swift-nio<https://github.com/apple/swift-nio.git@1.6.1>
| | └── swift-nio-zlib-support<https://github.com/apple/swift-nio-zlib-support.git@1.0.0>
| ├── DatabaseKit<https://github.com/vapor/database-kit.git@1.0.1>
| | ├── Core<https://github.com/vapor/core.git@3.1.6>
| | | └── swift-nio<https://github.com/apple/swift-nio.git@1.6.1>
| | | └── swift-nio-zlib-support<https://github.com/apple/swift-nio-zlib-support.git@1.0.0>
| | └── Service<https://github.com/vapor/service.git@1.0.0>
| | └── Core<https://github.com/vapor/core.git@3.1.6>
| | └── swift-nio<https://github.com/apple/swift-nio.git@1.6.1>
| | └── swift-nio-zlib-support<https://github.com/apple/swift-nio-zlib-support.git@1.0.0>
| ├── Service<https://github.com/vapor/service.git@1.0.0>
| | └── Core<https://github.com/vapor/core.git@3.1.6>
| | └── swift-nio<https://github.com/apple/swift-nio.git@1.6.1>
| | └── swift-nio-zlib-support<https://github.com/apple/swift-nio-zlib-support.git@1.0.0>
| └── SQL<https://github.com/vapor/sql.git@1.0.0>
├── Service<https://github.com/vapor/service.git@1.0.0>
| └── Core<https://github.com/vapor/core.git@3.1.6>
```

```
|     └──── swift-nio<https://github.com/apple/swift-nio.git@1.6.1>
|     └──── swift-nio-zlib-support<https://github.com/apple/swift-nio-zlib-support.git@1.0.0>
└──── SQLite<https://github.com/vapor/sqlite.git@3.0.0-rc.2.3>
├──── Core<https://github.com/vapor/core.git@3.1.6>
|     └──── swift-nio<https://github.com/apple/swift-nio.git@1.6.1>
|     └──── swift-nio-zlib-support<https://github.com/apple/swift-nio-zlib-support.git@1.0.0>
├──── DatabaseKit<https://github.com/vapor/database-kit.git@1.0.1>
|     ├──── Core<https://github.com/vapor/core.git@3.1.6>
|     |     └──── swift-nio<https://github.com/apple/swift-nio.git@1.6.1>
|     |     └──── swift-nio-zlib-support<https://github.com/apple/swift-nio-zlib-support.git@1.0.0>
|     └──── Service<https://github.com/vapor/service.git@1.0.0>
|     └──── Core<https://github.com/vapor/core.git@3.1.6>
|     └──── swift-nio<https://github.com/apple/swift-nio.git@1.6.1>
|     └──── swift-nio-zlib-support<https://github.com/apple/swift-nio-zlib-support.git@1.0.0>
└──── SQL<https://github.com/vapor/sql.git@1.0.0>
```

You can see that Vapor heavily depends on Swift NIO framework by Apple for asynchronous and non-blocking I/O processing.

Build targets

In the default template, Vapor creates three build targets for you. Each target declares which modules it depends on. For example, the App target depends on Fluent SQLite and Vapor. One target can also depend on another target. For example, the Run target depends on the App target.

Vapor separates the App module from the `helloWorld` executable module. By doing so, the App module can be included in the `AppTest` module for testing.

The Swift package describe command lists the three modules in the boilerplate:

```
# List of modules in a Vapor boilerplate project
Name: helloWorld
Path: /Users/fyeung1/Downloads/Packt/ch3/vapor/helloWorld
Modules:
    Name: App
    C99name: App
    Type: library
    Module type: SwiftTarget
    Path: /Users/Packt/ch3/vapor/helloWorld/Sources/App
    Sources: Controllers/TodoController.swift, Models/Todo.swift,
app.swift, boot.swift, configure.swift, routes.swift
    Name: AppTests
    C99name: AppTests
```

```
Type: test
Module type: SwiftTarget
Path: /Users/Packt/ch3/vapor/helloWorld/Tests/AppTests
Sources: AppTests.swift
Name: Run
C99name: Run
Type: executable
Module type: SwiftTarget
Path: /Users/Packt/ch3/vapor/helloWorld/Sources/Run
Sources: main.swift
```

Starting with an entry point

`main.swift` is always contained in an executable target and cannot be imported by other modules:

```
// File: /Sources/Run/main.swift
import App // [1]

try app(.detect()).run() // [2]
```

The preceding code does two things:

1. The `main.swift` file imports the App module
2. It gets an `app` instance from the `app()` constructor and calls the `run()` function of `app` to launch the server

Vapor uses an `Application` instance, `app`, in every project to run a server and create other services. The instance is obtained from the `app()` function implemented in `app.swift`. Vapor avoids statically accessing the `Application` instance using this approach. It has no need to implement any locking mechanism for thread-safety that is required for static access to variables.

Instantiating an application object

As mentioned earlier, the `app` object used in `main.swift` is actually created in the constructor function declared in `app.swift`:

```
// File: /Sources/App/app.swift
import Vapor

/// Creates an instance of Application. This is called from main.swift in
```

```
the run target.
public func app(_ env: Environment) throws -> Application { // [1]
var config = Config.default() // [2]
var env = env
var services = Services.default() // [3]
try configure(&config, &env, &services) // [4]
let app = try Application(config: config, environment: env, services:
services) // [5]
try boot(app) // [6]
return app
}
```

The preceding code sets up the sequence of calling several functions:

1. The `app()` constructor takes in the environment as a passing-in parameter
2. The `config` variable is assigned to the default configuration
3. The `services` variable is assigned to the default services
4. The `configure()` function is called before an `Application` instance is created
5. A new `Application` instance is created and assigned to `app`
6. The `boot()` function is called after an `Application` instance is created

The `app()->Application` function instantiates an `Application` object with passing in parameters of default configuration, run environment, and default services. The `configure()` function will be called before the instantiation of `Application`, and the `boot()` function will be called after that.

Configuring before instantiating application

The `configure()` function is declared in `configure.swift`. Services are set up in `configure()` before your application initializes:

```
// File: /Sources/App/configure.swift
import FluentSQLite
import Vapor

/// Called before your application initializes.
public func configure(_ config: inout Config, _ env: inout Environment, _
services: inout Services) throws {
/// Register providers first
try services.register(FluentSQLiteProvider()) // [1]

/// Register routes to the router
let router = EngineRouter.default()
```

```
try routes(router)
services.register(router, as: Router.self) // [2]

/// Register middleware
var middlewares = MiddlewareConfig() // Create _empty_ middleware config
/// middlewares.use(FileMiddleware.self) // Serves files from `Public/`
directory
middlewares.use(ErrorMiddleware.self) // Catches errors and converts to
HTTP response
services.register(middlewares) // [3]

// Configure a SQLite database
let sqlite = try SQLiteDatabase(storage: .memory)

/// Register the configured SQLite database to the database config.
var databases = DatabasesConfig()
databases.add(database: sqlite, as: .sqlite)
services.register(databases) // [4]

/// Configure migrations
var migrations = MigrationConfig()
migrations.add(model: Todo.self, database: .sqlite)
services.register(migrations) // [5]


}
```

A number of services are registered, in the following order:

1. The Fluent SQLite provider is registered
2. Routes are registered to the router engine
3. Error middleware is registered
4. The SQLite database is registered
5. Migration is configured and registered

Fluent is a Swift **Object Relational Mapping** (**ORM**) abstraction layer for building database integration. Vapor's Fluent framework works like a facade that hides away the complexities of database and presents a uniform and consistent front for working with different databases. A Fluent SQLite provider is registered in the application by default.

Each route matches a client request to an endpoint in the server. A web service endpoint is an entity to which web services requests can be addressed. In Vapor, an endpoint is often implemented as a Controller based on the MVC architecture. The routes supported by your application are declared in the routes.swift file. In the preceding code, a new service is registered with Vapor's router engine and the routes.

Middleware is application logic that modifies requests and responses as they pass between the client and your server. The implementation in `configure()` creates an error middleware that catches errors and converts them to HTTP response.

After the Fluent SQLite provider is registered, the SQLite database itself is created and configured. The database is then registered as one of the database services that your application supports. Note that Vapor allows you to support more than one type of database in a server.

Migration makes it easy for you to make changes to your database's structure. You use Vapor's migration to prepare a database schema for your models and make queries to the database. You can see how migration works with both your model, `Todo`, and your database provider, SQLite, in the preceding code.

Adding initialization code after application instantiation

The `boot()` function in `boot.swift` is called after the application is created and initialized. You can conveniently add your own initialization code to this function.

For any services that need to be set up before the application is created, you need to put their initialization code in the `configure()` function instead:

```
// File: /Sources/App/boot.swift
import Vapor

/// Called after your application has initialized.
public func boot(_ app: Application) throws {
// your code here
}
```

At this moment, the `boot()` function doesn't do too much—it simply provides a placeholder for you to add initialization code later.

Registering the application's routes

The routes used in `configure()` to register routing service are declared in the `routes()` function in `routes.swift`. You're expected to put all of your routes in this centralized place:

```
// File: /Sources/App/routes.swift
import Vapor

/// Register your application's routes here.
public func routes(_ router:
// Basic "Hello, world!" example
router.get("hello") { req in // [1]
return "Hello, world!"
}

// Example of configuring a controller
let todoController = TodoController() // [2]
router.get("todos", use: todoController.index) // [3]
router.post("todos", use: todoController.create) // [4]
router.delete("todos", Todo.parameter, use: todoController.delete) // [5]
}
```

The preceding sample code shows different ways of handling routes:

1. A basic endpoint is provided
2. `TodoController` is instantiated
3. The controller's `index()` function is used as an endpoint
4. The controller's `create()` function is used as an endpoint
5. The controller's `delete()` function is used as an endpoint

The basic endpoint is simply a closure that prints out `"Hello, world!"` You can add more endpoints to the `routes.swift` file or you can route some requests to the controller.

A controller is recommended if you want to group several related endpoints together or have other functions to handle more complicated endpoints. The `TodoController` class is one such example. After an instance of `TodoController` is created, the HTTP GET, POST, and DELETE requests are routed to the `TodoController` instance's corresponding functions.

Implementing endpoint logic in controllers

The `TodoController` class introduced previously is declared in `TodoController.swift`:

```
// File: /Sources/App/Controllers/TodoController.swift
import Vapor

/// Controlers basic CRUD operations on `Todo`s.
final class TodoController { // [1]
/// Returns a list of all `Todo`s.
func index(_ req: Request) throws -> Future<[Todo]> { // [2]
return Todo.query(on: req).all()
}

/// Saves a decoded `Todo` to the database.
func create(_ req: Request) throws -> Future<Todo> {
return try req.content.decode(Todo.self).flatMap { todo in // [3]
return todo.save(on: req)
}
}

/// Deletes a parameterized `Todo`.
func delete(_ req: Request) throws -> Future<HTTPStatus> {
return try req.parameters.next(Todo.self).flatMap { todo in // [4]
return todo.delete(on: req)
}.transform(to: .ok) // [5]
}
}
```

Some interesting techniques are noted in the preceding implementation:

1. The final `TodoController` class is defined
2. The `index(_:)` function returns a `Future`
3. The content of the request is decoded and applied with `flatMap(_:)`
4. The parameter of the request is applied with `flatMap(_:)`
5. If the delete operation is successful, use `transform(to:)` to return the OK status

The final modifier before the class keyword prohibits any subclasses of `TodoController`. Any attempt to subclass `TodoController` will cause a compile-time error.

The `index(_:)` function returns the `Future` type. *Futures* and *Promises* are the computing concepts that decouple a value (a Future) from how it was computed (a Promise), so that the computation can be done in parallel. Vapor uses Future to present a read-only placeholder view of a variable. You'll revisit this concept when you are introduced to asynchronous processing.

`flatMap(_:)` is a useful method in the `Swift` library. When working with arrays of optional types, `flatMap(_:)` flattens the arrays and converts any optional types to non-optionals. All the nil values resulted from unwrapping optionals will be removed by `flatMap(_:)`. It is very convenient to use `flatMap(_:)` to parse the content of requests in endpoints. You're going to see the usage of `flatMap(_:)` a lot when working with Vapor applications.

Instead of returning the results of a `Future`, sometimes you simply want to return a success status code. In the preceding implementation, the `transform(to:)` function is chained to `flatMap(_:)` to return the `.ok` status.

Using a data model

The data model used in the SQLite database is implemented in `/Models/Todo.swift`:

```swift
// File: /Sources/App/Models/Todo.swift
import FluentSQLite
import Vapor

/// A single entry of a Todo list.
final class Todo: SQLiteModel { // [1]
/// The unique identifier for this `Todo`.
var id: Int? // [2]

/// A title describing what this `Todo` entails.
var title: String // [3]

/// Creates a new `Todo`.
init(id: Int? = nil, title: String) { // [4]
self.id = id
self.title = title
}
}

/// Allows `Todo` to be used as a dynamic migration.
extension Todo: Migration { } // [5]
```

```
/// Allows `Todo` to be encoded to and decoded from HTTP messages.
extension Todo: Content { } // [6]

/// Allows `Todo` to be used as a dynamic parameter in route definitions.
extension Todo: Parameter { } // [7]
```

The data model is implemented as follows:

1. The final `ToDo` class is subclassing from the `SQLiteModel` class
2. The `id` variable is declared as the unique identifier for this model
3. The `title` variable is used to describe what `Todo` entails
4. An initializer is defined
5. The `Todo` class is extended as a dynamic migration
6. The `Todo` class is extended as `Content`
7. The `Todo` class is extended as a dynamic parameter

Models represent tables in the SQLite database. You'll use model as the primary object of interacting with your data. By conforming to `SQLiteModel`, it requires `Todo` to supply an optional variable, `id`, which is of the `Int` type. If you do not supply an `id` for the title, you'll get an `id` assigned after saving the data to the database.

The `Todo` model also conforms to `Migration`, `Content`, and `Parameter`.

Conforming to `Migration` allows Fluent to use `Codable` when creating the database table scheme, and `configure()` to set up and register the `Migration` service before the application is created.

The conformance of `Content` allows the `Todo` model to be encoded to and decoded from JSON in HTTP messages using `Codable`. This happens automatically so you never have to parse or save your model in JSON.

Conforming to `Parameter` allows you to handle segments of the URL path easily when working with routes. You can take advantage of Vapor's type safe and intuitive method for accessing route parameters using Swift's closures.

Kitura Boilerplate Project

Let's now get a clear understanding the boilerplate code in Kitura. Here is a recap of how you can create the `helloWorld` boilerplate project using Kitura's basic template:

```
$ mkdir helloWorld
$ cd helloWorld
$ kitura init
$ open ./helloWorld.xcodeproj
```

Then you can use *command* + *R* to run your project in Xcode and direct your web browser to `http://localhost:8080`.

The following sections will provide you with a better idea regarding the same:

- Reviewing Kitura-generated files
- Understanding generated sourcecode in Kitura

Reviewing Kitura-generated files

After using `kitura init` to create a Kitura boilerplate `helloWorld` project, use the `ls -a` command in the `helloWorld` project directory to list all files and subdirectories:

```
# List all files and directories, including the hidden ones
ls -a
```

The output lists the files and directories in this project, as follows:

.	.dockerignore	Dockerfile	README.md	iterative-dev.sh
..	.gitignore	Dockerfile-tools	Sources	manifest.yml
.bluemix	.swift-version	Jenkinsfile	Tests	spec.json
.build	.swiftservergenerator-project	LICENSE	chart
.cfignore	.yo-rc.json	Package.swift	cli-config.yml

There are a number of hidden files and directories in the project. They are hidden because Kitura doesn't expect you to modify them very often:

File/directory	Usage
`.gitignore`	List of files to be excluded from git versioning control
`.swift-version`	The Swift version for your project
`.swiftservergenerator-project`	File used by Swift Server Generator
`.yo-rc.json`	JSON file for Yeoman generator configuration
`.bluemix/`	Directory for IBM Cloud pipelines and toolchains
`.cfignore`	List of files to be excluded from cloud deployment

Reviewing a Kitura project's file structure

You can use the `Tree` command to display the file structure of your project. If you haven't installed `Tree` on your system, you can refer to the previous section for the installation instruction.

See the following for the list of files displayed by the `Tree` command. The list is expected to grow longer after `kitura init` fetches dependencies and builds out everything:

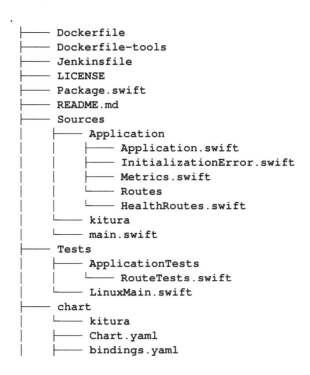

```
.
├── Dockerfile
├── Dockerfile-tools
├── Jenkinsfile
├── LICENSE
├── Package.swift
├── README.md
├── Sources
│   ├── Application
│   │   ├── Application.swift
│   │   ├── InitializationError.swift
│   │   ├── Metrics.swift
│   │   ├── Routes
│   │   └── HealthRoutes.swift
│   ├── kitura
│   └── main.swift
├── Tests
│   ├── ApplicationTests
│   │   └── RouteTests.swift
│   └── LinuxMain.swift
├── chart
│   └── kitura
│   ├── Chart.yaml
│   ├── bindings.yaml
```

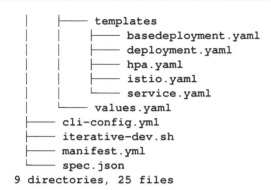

```
|       ├──── templates
|       |     ├──── basedeployment.yaml
|       |     ├──── deployment.yaml
|       |     ├──── hpa.yaml
|       |     ├──── istio.yaml
|       |     └──── service.yaml
|       └──── values.yaml
├──── cli-config.yml
├──── iterative-dev.sh
├──── manifest.yml
└──── spec.json
9 directories, 25 files
```

Don't worry, you don't have to know all of these files before you can start working on a Kitura project. You don't need to modify most of them in a typical project. At this moment, you just need to get familiar with the main function of some of the files.

The following table gives you an overview of the high-level file structure:

File/directory	Usage
Dockerfile	Docker container image spec for running the app
Dockerfile-tools	Docker container image spec for building the app
Jenkinsfile	Definition of Jenkins Pipeline for continuous integration
LICENSE	MIT license for the generated project
Package.swift	Configuration for SPM (Swift Package Manager)
README.md	Readme file in Markdown format
Sources	Directory for source files
Tests	Directory for all tests
chart	Directory used by the Helm package manager for Kubernetes
cli-config.yml	Configuration for IBM Cloud Dev Tool CLI
iterative-dev.sh	Script for relaunching server after updates in Swift files
manifest.yml	Configuration for CloudFoundry deployment
spec.json	Generator spec file for the project

Most of these are configuration files related to the technologies involved in the typical workflow of a Kitura project, such as Swift **Package Manager** (Package.swift) for dependency management, Jenkins (Jenkinsfile) for continuous integration, Docker (Dockerfile, Dockerfile-tools) for building environments in the container, and CloudFoundry (manifest.yml) for deploying your project to the cloud.

Understanding the file structure in a Kitura project

At the start of a development project, your attention is most likely on the skeleton source code that you will leverage to build up to a full application. As shown in the following table, those files with the skeleton source code are in the two subdirectories under Sources: `/Application` and `/helloWorld`:

File/directory	Usage
`/Application`	Module for application logic
`/Application/Application.swift`	Class for application logic
`/Application/InitializationError.swift`	Structure for initialization error handling
`/Application/Metrics.swift`	Structure for gathering application and system metrics
`/Application/Routes/HealthRoutes.swift`	Route function for monitoring server health
`/helloWorld`	Module for your application's executable
`/helloWorld/main.swift`	Code for the entry point of your application

The `App` class in `Application.swift` contains application logic to allow you to receive the flow of control from the framework so you can make modifications on several occasions: during initialization, after the application being initialized, and when the application is running.

The *struct* in `InitializationError.swift` allows you to add additional error handlers using Swift's extension mechanism. You'll be adding error handlers as you write new functions.

Kitura uses the `SwiftMetrics` library to gather monitoring data. The initialization function in `Metrics.swift` routes the monitoring modules to the endpoints in your project. The environment, CPU, memory, latency, and HTTP metrics information data is collected programmatically in Kitura.

Right now, there is one route function implemented in `HealthRoutes.swift` in `/Application/Routes`. As you add more functions to handle requests from client, you can expect to add more routes corresponding to each handler in the same directory.

You can also see how an `app` instance is set up in a do-catch statement in `/helloWorld/main.swift`. The file serves as an entry point for your application. In the same code, the logger framework that is used to post error messages is also initialized and integrated in the do-catch statement.

Understanding generated sourcecode in Kitura

A detailed review of each generated source code file in a Kitura boilerplate project is given in the next section.

Configuring using Swift Package Manager (SPM)

The `Package.swift` manifest file lists the application name, dependencies of other packages, and build target for the project generated using the `kitura init` command:

```
// File: Package.swift
// swift-tools-version:4.0
import PackageDescription

let package = Package(
name: "helloWorld", // [1]
dependencies: [ // [2]
.package(url: "https://github.com/IBM-Swift/Kitura.git",
.upToNextMinor(from: "2.3.0")),
.package(url: "https://github.com/IBM-Swift/HeliumLogger.git",
.upToNextMinor(from: "1.7.1")),
.package(url: "https://github.com/IBM-Swift/CloudEnvironment.git", from:
"7.1.0"),
.package(url: "https://github.com/RuntimeTools/SwiftMetrics.git", from:
"2.0.0"),
.package(url: "https://github.com/IBM-Swift/Health.git", from: "1.0.0"),
],
targets: [ // [3]
.target(name: "helloWorld", dependencies: [ .target(name: "Application"),
"Kitura" , "HeliumLogger"]),
.target(name: "Application", dependencies: [ "Kitura",
"CloudEnvironment","SwiftMetrics","Health", ]),

.testTarget(name: "ApplicationTests" , dependencies: [.target(name:
"Application"), "Kitura","HeliumLogger" ])
]
)
```

The project's package is configured as follows:

1. `helloWorld` is used as the application name
2. The dependencies array includes Kitura, Helium Logger, Cloud Environment, Swift Metrics, and Health packages
3. The build targets are `helloWorld`, `Application`, and `ApplicationTests`

The basic Kitura boilerplate project already includes many useful packages, such as logging, cloud environment tools, server metrics monitoring, and infrastructure health-checking services.

Use the swift package show-dependencies command to list the following required packages in the Kitura project:

```
# List of package dependencies in a Kitura boilerplate project:
.
├── Kitura<https://github.com/IBM-Swift/Kitura.git@2.3.2>
│   ├── Kitura-net<https://github.com/IBM-Swift/Kitura-net.git@2.1.0>
│   │   ├── LoggerAPI<https://github.com/IBM-Swift/LoggerAPI.git@1.7.3>
│   │   ├── Socket<https://github.com/IBM-Swift/BlueSocket.git@1.0.6>
│   │   ├── CCurl<https://github.com/IBM-Swift/CCurl.git@1.0.0>
│   │   └── SSLService<https://github.com/IBM-
Swift/BlueSSLService.git@1.0.6>
│   │       └── Socket<https://github.com/IBM-Swift/BlueSocket.git@1.0.6>
│   ├── Kitura-TemplateEngine<https://github.com/IBM-Swift/Kitura-
TemplateEngine.git@1.7.4>
│   └── KituraContracts<https://github.com/IBM-
Swift/KituraContracts.git@0.0.24>
│       └── LoggerAPI<https://github.com/IBM-Swift/LoggerAPI.git@1.7.3>
├── HeliumLogger<https://github.com/IBM-Swift/HeliumLogger.git@1.7.1>
│   └── LoggerAPI<https://github.com/IBM-Swift/LoggerAPI.git@1.7.3>
├── CloudEnvironment<https://github.com/IBM-
Swift/CloudEnvironment.git@7.1.0>
│   └── CloudFoundryEnv<https://github.com/IBM-Swift/Swift-cfenv.git@6.0.2>
│   └── Configuration<https://github.com/IBM-Swift/Configuration.git@3.0.1>
│   └── FileKit<https://github.com/IBM-Swift/FileKit.git@0.0.1>
│   └── LoggerAPI<https://github.com/IBM-Swift/LoggerAPI.git@1.7.3>
├── SwiftMetrics<https://github.com/RuntimeTools/SwiftMetrics.git@2.3.0>
│   ├── Kitura<https://github.com/IBM-Swift/Kitura.git@2.3.2>
│   │   ├── Kitura-net<https://github.com/IBM-Swift/Kitura-net.git@2.1.0>
│   │   │   ├── LoggerAPI<https://github.com/IBM-Swift/LoggerAPI.git@1.7.3>
│   │   │   ├── Socket<https://github.com/IBM-Swift/BlueSocket.git@1.0.6>
│   │   │   ├── CCurl<https://github.com/IBM-Swift/CCurl.git@1.0.0>
│   │   │   └── SSLService<https://github.com/IBM-
Swift/BlueSSLService.git@1.0.6>
│   │   │       └── Socket<https://github.com/IBM-Swift/BlueSocket.git@1.0.6>
```

```
|   |   |----- Kitura-TemplateEngine<https://github.com/IBM-Swift/Kitura-
TemplateEngine.git@1.7.4>
|   |   '----- KituraContracts<https://github.com/IBM-
Swift/KituraContracts.git@0.0.24>
|   |   '----- LoggerAPI<https://github.com/IBM-Swift/LoggerAPI.git@1.7.3>
|   |----- Kitura-WebSocket<https://github.com/IBM-Swift/Kitura-
WebSocket.git@2.0.0>
|   |   |----- Kitura-net<https://github.com/IBM-Swift/Kitura-net.git@2.1.0>
|   |   |   |----- LoggerAPI<https://github.com/IBM-Swift/LoggerAPI.git@1.7.3>
|   |   |   |----- Socket<https://github.com/IBM-Swift/BlueSocket.git@1.0.6>
|   |   |   |----- CCurl<https://github.com/IBM-Swift/CCurl.git@1.0.0>
|   |   |   '----- SSLService<https://github.com/IBM-
Swift/BlueSSLService.git@1.0.6>
|   |   |       '----- Socket<https://github.com/IBM-Swift/BlueSocket.git@1.0.6>
|   |   |----- Cryptor<https://github.com/IBM-Swift/BlueCryptor.git@1.0.2>
|   |   '----- CommonCrypto<https://github.com/IBM-
Swift/CommonCrypto.git@1.0.0>
|   |----- SwiftyRequest<https://github.com/IBM-Swift/SwiftyRequest.git@1.1.2>
|   |   |----- CircuitBreaker<https://github.com/IBM-
Swift/CircuitBreaker.git@5.0.1>
|   |   |   '----- LoggerAPI<https://github.com/IBM-Swift/LoggerAPI.git@1.7.3>
|   |   '----- LoggerAPI<https://github.com/IBM-Swift/LoggerAPI.git@1.7.3>
|   |----- CloudFoundryEnv<https://github.com/IBM-Swift/Swift-cfenv.git@6.0.2>
|   |   '----- Configuration<https://github.com/IBM-
Swift/Configuration.git@3.0.1>
|   |       '----- FileKit<https://github.com/IBM-Swift/FileKit.git@0.0.1>
|   |       '----- LoggerAPI<https://github.com/IBM-Swift/LoggerAPI.git@1.7.3>
|   |----- SwiftyJSON<https://github.com/IBM-Swift/SwiftyJSON.git@17.0.1>
|   '----- omr-agentcore<https://github.com/RuntimeTools/omr-agentcore@3.2.4-
swift4>
'----- Health<https://github.com/IBM-Swift/Health.git@1.0.1>
'----- LoggerAPI<https://github.com/IBM-Swift/LoggerAPI.git@1.7.3>
```

Similar to Vapor's `Package.swift` for a basic web template, the basic Kitura template also uses three build targets: `helloWorld`, `ApplicationTests`, and `Application`. Use the Swift package describe command to list these three modules in the `helloWorld` boilerplate application:

```
# List of modules in a Kitura boilerplate project
Name: helloWorld
Path: /Users/fyeung1/Downloads/Packt/ch3/kitura/helloWorld
Modules:

Name: helloWorld
    C99name: helloWorld
    Type: executable
    Module type: SwiftTarget
    Path:
```

```
/Users/fyeung1/Downloads/Packt/ch3/kitura/helloWorld/Sources/helloWorld
    Sources: main.swift

Name: ApplicationTests
    C99name: ApplicationTests
    Type: test
    Module type: SwiftTarget
    Path:
/Users/fyeung1/Downloads/Packt/ch3/kitura/helloWorld/Tests/ApplicationTests
    Sources: RouteTests.swift

Name: Application
    C99name: Application
    Type: library
    Module type: SwiftTarget
    Path:
/Users/fyeung1/Downloads/Packt/ch3/kitura/helloWorld/Sources/Application
    Sources: Application.swift, InitializationError.swift, Metrics.swift,
Routes/HealthRoutes.swift
```

The `Application` target is shared by the `helloWorld` executable target and the `ApplicationTests` executable target.

Starting with the entry point

The `main.swift` file contains the entry point for `helloWorld` executable target:

```
// File: /helloWorld/main.swift
import Foundation
import Kitura
import LoggerAPI
import HeliumLogger
import Application

do {

    HeliumLogger.use(LoggerMessageType.info) // [1]

    let app = try App() // [2]
    try app.run() // [3]

} catch let error {
    Log.error(error.localizedDescription) // [4]
}
```

The `do-catch` loop in `main.swift` performs several operations:

1. Initializes Helium logger
2. Creates an application instance
3. Invokes the application instance's `run()` function
4. Catches any runtime errors

Kitura's runtime executes the `App` instance and its `run()` function to boot the server. Any errors encountered by the server will be caught in the `do-catch` loop and localized error descriptions will be logged.

Declaring application classes

`App` is the top class for the `App` module, and it handles the main life cycle functions for the application:

```swift
// File: /Application/Application.swift
import Foundation
import Kitura
import LoggerAPI
import Configuration
import CloudEnvironment
import KituraContracts
import Health

public let projectPath = ConfigurationManager.BasePath.project.path
public let health = Health()

public class App {
    let router = Router()
    let cloudEnv = CloudEnv()

    public init() throws { // [1]
        // Run the metrics initializer
        initializeMetrics(router: router)
    }

    func postInit() throws {
        // Endpoints
        initializeHealthRoutes(app: self)
    }

    public func run() throws {
        try postInit() // [2]
```

```
        Kitura.addHTTPServer(onPort: cloudEnv.port, with: router) // [3]
        Kitura.run() // [4]
    }
}
```

The `App` class runs a couple of initialization and configuration steps before booting up the Kitura server:

1. The class's initializer sets up the metrics monitoring service for this project
2. After an `App` instance is created, post-initialization will be called
3. An HTTP server with a specified cloud environment and router will be created
4. The HTTP server will be booted up

The `init()` initializer function is a good place for you to add any initialization code before `App` is created. In this project, the metrics initialization call, `initializeMetrics(router:)`, is added to `init()`. This makes sure that the metrics monitoring service is properly initialized before `App` is created.

Any initialization code that should take place after the instantiation of `App` should go to the `postInit()` function. `postInit()` is called when the `App` instance's `run()` is invoked but before the Kitura server is started. In the preceding code, the initialization of the health route, `initializeHealthRoutes(app:)`, is added to `postInit()`.

After post-instantiation initialization, an HTTP server with a specified port and router will be added to Kitura's context and then the server will be running. The IP port for a web server is usually 8080. However, if this port is occupied by another network service on your development machine, you need to assign another port number to it.

Handling errors

Kitura provides you with a struct to handle initialization errors in
`InitializationError.swift`:

```
// File: /Application/InitializationError.swift
import Foundation

public struct InitializationError: Error { // [1]
    let message: String
    init(_ msg: String) {
        message = msg
    }
}

extension InitializationError: LocalizedError { // [2]
    public var errorDescription: String? {
        return message
    }
}
```

The following features are implemented:

1. The `InitializationError()` struct is inherited from the `Error()` struct
2. The `InitializationError()` struct is extended from `LocalizedError`

The `InitializationError()` struct does no more than offer you a chance to modify the
error message. You can, for example, replace an error message with a localized version of
the error message.

Setting up monitoring metrics

Kitura offers very good metrics-monitoring and diagnostic services. These services are
created and initialized in the `initializeMetrics(router:)` function in
`Metrics.swift`:

```
// File: /Application/Metrics.swift
import Kitura
import SwiftMetrics
import SwiftMetricsDash
import SwiftMetricsPrometheus
import LoggerAPI

var swiftMetrics: SwiftMetrics?
```

```
var swiftMetricsDash: SwiftMetricsDash?
var swiftMetricsPrometheus: SwiftMetricsPrometheus?

func initializeMetrics(router: Router) {
    do {
        let metrics = try SwiftMetrics() // [1]
        let dashboard = try SwiftMetricsDash(swiftMetricsInstance: metrics,
endpoint: router) // [2]
        let prometheus = try SwiftMetricsPrometheus(swiftMetricsInstance:
metrics, endpoint: router) // [3]

        swiftMetrics = metrics
        swiftMetricsDash = dashboard
        swiftMetricsPrometheus = prometheus
      Log.info("Initialized metrics.")
    } catch {
      Log.warning("Failed to initialize metrics: \(error)")
    }
}
```

`initializeMetrics(router:)` creates the following three metrics frameworks:

1. The variable metrics is assigned to an instance of the `SwiftMetrics()` framework
2. The `SwiftMetricsDash()` object is created with metrics and a router as parameters
3. The `SwiftMetricsPrometheus()` object is also created with metrics and a router as parameters

`SwiftMetrics` is an `open source runtime tool` maintained by the open source community. It instruments Swift runtime to provide your application with the runtime's performance. An extensive amount of data is collected in a Kitura project using SwiftMetrics: system and runtime environment information, CPU and memory usages, dispatch queue latency, and HTTP metric information. The data collected is programmatically fetched by other services, such as `SwiftMetricsDash` and Prometheus.

`SwiftMetricsDash` is a tool used to present the collected data in `SwiftMetrics`. `SwiftMetricsDash` will start its own Kitura server and serve in a dashboard web page. You can try it yourself by directing your web browser to `http://localhost:8080/swiftmetrics-dash/` when your `helloWorld` app server is running:

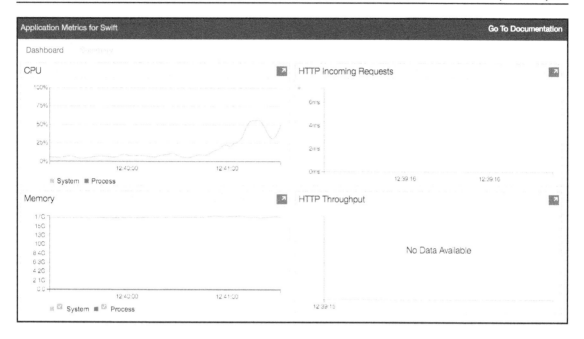

Prometheus is a popular open source monitoring and alerting solution(https://prometheus.io/docs/introduction/overview/) that is integrated into Kitura to monitor application clusters. In
SwiftMetricsPrometheus(swiftMetricsInstance:,endpoint:),SwiftMetrics is configured to export your application's performance data into Prometheus, and a Prometheus metrics endpoint is added the router. The configuration for exporting data from SwiftMetrics to Prometheus is specified in prometheus.yml, which was automatically generated using the kitura init command.

Setting up health check endpoints

All the implementations of endpoints are stored in the /Routes directory. In Kitura's basic template, a health check endpoint (/Routes/HealthRoutes.swift) is created as an example:

```
// File: /Routes/HealthRoutes.swift
import LoggerAPI
import Health
import KituraContracts

func initializeHealthRoutes(app: App) {
```

```
    app.router.get("/health") { (respondWith: (Status?, RequestError?) ->
Void) -> Void in
        if health.status.state == .UP {
            respondWith(health.status, nil) // [1]
        } else {
            respondWith(nil, RequestError(.serviceUnavailable, body:
health.status)) // [2]
        }
    }
}
```

The *Health* endpoint exposes the health of the application. It responds to the health check request with a closure that returns a *health.status* structure:

1. If the health status is "*UP*", it responds with `health.status`
2. If the health status is NOT "*UP*", it responds with an error as well as `*health.status`

Health is `an application health library` in Swift that checks an application's overall health status. The Kitura basic template provides you with a health endpoint to perform a health check on your `helloWorld` app server when a client sends an HTTP GET `/health` request. Health then responds with the Status struct that conforms to the Codable protocol. The content of the status could be a dictionary. The value for the "status" dictionary key is either "UP" or "DOWN", indicating whether your server is running. This is useful for cloud environments, such as Kubernetes, in monitoring and managing your application instance.

Other Books You May Enjoy

If you enjoyed this book, you may be interested in these other books by Packt:

Hands-On Full-Stack Development with Swift
Ankur Patel

ISBN: 9781788625241

- Get accustomed to server-side programming as well as the Vapor framework
- Learn how to build a RESTful API
- Make network requests from your app and handle error states when a network request fails
- Deploy your app to Heroku using the CLI command
- Write a test for the Vapor backend
- Create a tvOS version of your shopping list app and explore code-sharing with an iOS platform
- Add registration and authentication so that users can have their own shopping lists

Learn Swift by Building Applications
Emil Atanasov

ISBN: 9781786463920

- Become a pro at iOS development by creating simple-to-complex iOS mobile applications
- Master Playgrounds, a unique and intuitive approach to teaching Xcode
- Tackle the basics, including variables, if clauses, functions, loops and structures, classes, and inheritance
- Model real-world objects in Swift and have an in-depth understanding of the data structures used, along with OOP concepts and protocols
- Use CocoaPods, an open source Swift package manager to ease your everyday developer requirements
- Develop a wide range of apps, from a simple weather app to an Instagram-like social app
- Get ahead in the industry by learning how to use third-party libraries efficiently in your apps

Leave a review - let other readers know what you think

Please share your thoughts on this book with others by leaving a review on the site that you bought it from. If you purchased the book from Amazon, please leave us an honest review on this book's Amazon page. This is vital so that other potential readers can see and use your unbiased opinion to make purchasing decisions, we can understand what our customers think about our products, and our authors can see your feedback on the title that they have worked with Packt to create. It will only take a few minutes of your time, but is valuable to other potential customers, our authors, and Packt. Thank you!

Index

www.ingramcontent.com/pod-product-compliance
Lightning Source LLC
Chambersburg PA
CBHW080606060326
40690CB00021B/4609